D0069862

AMERICAN DEFENSE AND
FOREIGN POLICY INSTITUTIONS

AMERICAN DEFENSE AND FOREIGN POLICY INSTITUTIONS
Toward a Sound Foundation

Duncan L. Clarke

1817

Harper & Row, Publishers, New York

BALLINGER DIVISION

Grand Rapids, Philadelphia, St. Louis, San Francisco
London, Singapore, Sydney, Tokyo

Copyright © 1989 by Duncan L. Clarke. All rights reserved. No part of this publication may be reproduced, stored in a retrieval system, or transmitted in any form or by any means, electronic, mechanical, photocopy, recording, or otherwise, without the prior written consent of the author.

International Standard Book Number: 0–88730–292–0
0–88730–296–3 (pbk.)

Library of Congress Catalog Card Number: 89-6459

Printed in the United States of America

Library of Congress Cataloging-in-Publication Data

Clarke, Duncan L.
   American defense and foreign policy institutions : toward a sound foundation / Duncan L. Clarke.
      p.   cm.
   Includes index.
   ISBN 0-88730-292-0. — ISBN 0-88730-296-3 (pbk.)
   1. United States—National Security.   I. Title.
UA23.C559   1989
353.0089—dc19   89-6459
                                                                          CIP

89 90 91 92 HC 9 8 7 6 5 4 3 2 1

For the Phillips family:
Harriet, Harvey, Danny, and Rick

Contents

Glossary of Abbreviations

BOB	Bureau of the Budget
C³	Command, Control, and Communication
CBO	Congressional Budget Office
CIA	Central Intelligence Agency
CINC	Commander-in-Chief
CJCS	Chairman of the Joint Chiefs of Staff
DCI	Director of Central Intelligence
DDI	Directorate of Intelligence
DDO	Directorate of Operations
DDP	Directorate of Plans
DG	Defense Guidance
DIA	Defense Intelligence Agency
DNI	Director of National Intelligence
DOD	Department of Defense
DPRC	Defense Program Review Committee
DRB	Defense Resources Board
DSARC	Defense Systems Acquisition Review Council
FAR	Federal Acquisition Regulation
FBI	Federal Bureau of Investigation
FSO	Foreign Service Officer
GAO	General Accounting Office
GDIP	General Defense Intelligence Program
GSA	General Services Administration
IAC	Intelligence Advisory Committee
IC Staff	Intelligence Community Staff
IIM	Interagency Intelligence Memorandum
JCS	Joint Chiefs of Staff

KIQ	Key Intelligence Question
NASA	National Aeronautics and Space Administration
NFIB	National Foreign Intelligence Board
NFIC	National Foreign Intelligence Council
NFIP	National Foreign Intelligence Program
NIC	National Intelligence Council
NIC/AG	National Intelligence Council's Analytic Group
NIE	National Intelligence Estimate
NIO	National Intelligence Officer
NITC	National Intelligence Tasking Center
NSA	National Security Assistant
NSAM	National Security Action Memorandum
NSC	National Security Council
NSCID	National Security Council Intelligence Directive
NSPG	National Security Planning Group
NSSD	National Security Study Directive
NSSM	National Security Study Memorandum
NUWEP	Nuclear Weapons Employment Plan
OCB	Operations Coordinating Board
OES	Bureau of Oceans and International Environmental and Scientific Affairs
OFPP	Office of Federal Procurement Policy
OMB	Office of Management and Budget
ONE	Office of National Estimates
OSD	Office of the Secretary of Defense
OSS	Office of Strategic Services
PDM	Program Decision Memorandum
PFIAB	President's Foreign Intelligence Advisory Board
PGCP	Planning Guidance for Contingency Planning
PM	Bureau of Politico-Military Affairs
POM	Program Objective Memorandum
PPBS	Planning, Programming, and Budgeting System
PRC	Policy Review Committee
PRM	Policy Review Memorandum
SIG/I	Senior Interagency Group for Intelligence
SIGINT	Signals Intelligence
SIOP	Single Integrated Operational Plan
SNIE	Special National Intelligence Estimate
SWNCC	State, War, Navy Coordinating Committee

TIARA	Tactical Intelligence and Related Activities
TOA	Total Obligational Authority
USIB	U.S. Intelligence Board
ZBB	Zero-Based Budgeting

Introduction

The American government's Madisonian system of checks and balances is an effective guardian against abuses of authority, but it also provides a foundation for the existence of vigorous "subgovernments" within the federal system. These autonomous or semiautonomous subgovernments both fragment and confuse policy processes. Congress is a primary locus for the politics of subgovernment, while the executive branch is a collection of often haphazardly coordinated, feuding bureaucractic fiefdoms. The closest the United States government comes to having a central authority is the president, yet Richard Rose states correctly that "the strongest phrase in Washington—the president wants this— is usually voiced as an aspiration."[1]

Consequently, presidential power is only infrequently the power to command. Rather, in Richard Neustadt's elegant phrase, "Presidential power is the power to persuade."[2] An effective president is one who can and will employ his considerable leverage to persuade or bargain with a powerful senator or cabinet officer. But presidential effectiveness requires more than this. It requires, among other things, structure, sensible organization, and an appreciation for sound management. Organization (or reorganization) and management are not panaceas, nor is there a universally "correct" way to structure and direct the U.S. defense and foreign policy system. Each president has his own style, approach, and limitations. Nevertheless, solid organization and the use of appropriate management practices within the government can lead to a number of fundamental benefits:[3]

- *Bolster an elemental assumption of democracy.* Democratic theory assumes that after a president is elected thousands of federal employees in the executive bureaucracy will comply with the chief executive's policy preferences and the law of the land. In other words, the people's will must not be thwarted by bureaucrats who work for the popularly elected leader. Every president tries or should try to "control" his bureaucracy and make it responsive to his directives. Without adequate high-level policy control and guidance over subordinates, anarchy reigns and a critical tenet of democracy is undercut. Sustained and effective presidential control of the bureaucracy is unlikely if the policymaking process and structure, especially at senior levels, are excessively disjointed. Nor will a poorly organized and managed process properly support those policy implementation and monitoring (policing) functions so essential to the realization and enforcement of presidential policies. Although the president and Congress dominate decisionmaking, it is the bureaucracy that implements policy decisions. Breakdowns in the monitoring of national security policy implementation did not begin with the Reagan administration's Iran-Contra affair— they have been a prominent feature of most post-World War II administrations.
- *Maximize the policymaker's access to expertise, information, and advice.* The national security bureaucracy is the primary repository of specialized expertise and information on defense, foreign affairs, and intelligence matters. Usually, decisionmakers are adequately informed only if they tap this resource (which is not to imply that they always do). A well-organized and well-directed national security system will, among other things, see that agencies and departments with unique expertise can contribute to interagency studies in a full and timely manner; that senior policy advisers with diverse views— such as the secretary of state, secretary of defense, and the president's national security assistant—have access to the president; and that intelligence reports are routed to appropriately cleared officials. None of this occurs automatically— conscious political, organizational, and procedural decisions must first be made.
- *Help integrate the many strands of defense, foreign, and interna-*

tional economic policy. International issues interrelate with one another and with a spectrum of domestic considerations. A policy process that fails to integrate distinct yet related issues and weave them into the fabric of policy may be disturbingly, even dangerously, distant from both global and domestic realities. Such integration does not just happen. Systematic attention to issue integration is required.

- *Promote more efficient use of resources.* The weapons acquisition process is a glaring example of an area where greater concern for effective organization and management could contribute to more efficient resource utilization. This applies not simply to the military services but especially to the Office of the Secretary of Defense and, in specified and selective ways, to the White House. Weapons and weapons-related programs compose almost 50 percent of the defense budget, yet the Office of Management and Budget (OMB) in the Reagan administration scrutinized domestic programs, while it was directed not to review defense programs. Obviously, OMB can exercise its management and programmatic expertise in the national security area only if the president so desires. Management and organizational developments are often political acts that follow from political decisions.
- *Contribute to a more coherent defense and foreign policy.* Conflict and some degree of disorder are intrinsic to American national security policymaking. Ambiguity is the norm. A strong dose of "ad hocracy" is always present. Still, an administration that understands and cares about effective organization and management can curb at least some of the forces that pull policy in divergent and often contradictory directions. An administration can, for instance, establish experienced, well-staffed congressional liaison units in the White House, in the departments, and in the agencies; it can enter office with a National Security Council (NSC) system whose principal initial structures, participants, and formal processes have been substantially predetermined by the incoming president (subsequently, of course, they may well change); it can provide regular, authoritative civilian policy guidance to the chairman of the Joint Chiefs of Staff concerning contingency planning for the use of force (as stipulated in the Goldwater-Nichols Defense Reorganization Act of 1986); and it can work

to maintain the integrity of executive branch units, such as the Intelligence Oversight Board and the NSC, that are responsible respectively for overseeing and monitoring ongoing covert operations.

• *Minimize the possibility of surprise, costly policy reversals, or political embarrassment.* President Reagan's evident lack of interest in organizational and managerial matters and of attention to his own NSC system contributed significantly to the Iran-Contra debacle.

This book is about how major United States national security institutions should be organized, managed, directed, and coordinated to achieve a more purposive defense and foreign policy. My treatment is prescriptive. Many measures can be and have been instituted to mitigate persistent problems. Some of my recommendations are made boldly, others are suggested cautiously. None are immune from criticism. Indeed, readers should adopt a questioning, critical attitude toward what follows.

I gave considerable thought to approach and format, wanting above all an uncluttered, focused, condensed treatment of specific elements and practices of selected government institutions. The emphasis on relative brevity invariably requires trade-offs: some institutions and practices cannot be addressed or are examined only briefly. Because of the centrality of the White House, the first two chapters examine two key units of the Executive Office of the President: the NSC and OMB. Chapters 3 and 4 treat the most prominent departmental actors in national security affairs: the State and Defense Departments. Chapter 5 deals with the intelligence community, whose reports inform policy choices. The concluding chapter addresses executive-legislative relations. Few significant policy or organizational developments are beyond the purview of Congress. The focus here is on executive-legislative consultative processes and mechanisms. Foreign policies are unlikely to succeed over the long run without some acceptable degree of consensus between the two branches, and timely and meaningful consultation is thus generally essential.

This book is intended for a diverse readership. Specialists will find a reworking and consolidation of issues that, while sometimes familiar, require reexamination. They will find something else. Despite an outpouring of material on American defense and foreign policy processes, important subject areas have escaped coverage almost entirely. Much of Chapter 2, for instance, falls into this category. Graduate and advanced undergraduate students are another potential audience. The book exposes those students willing to go beyond an elementary understanding of the policy process to important, specific, persistent, nuts-and-bolts issues. I identify with Graham Allison's remark: "The fact that almost as much time has been spent lamenting the lack of theory, and theorizing about theory in international relations, as has been invested in producing substantive work suggests that the 'discipline' is retarded."[4] Finally, anyone who wants to dig rather deeply into various recurrent problem areas of United States defense policy, foreign policy, and intelligence processes should find the book useful.

Those who read and commented on the draft chapters know their respective subject areas well. I asked for criticism, usually got it, and the end product is much the better for it. What each contributed was well put by Mark Twain: "War talk by men who have been in a war is always interesting; whereas moon talk by a poet who has not been on the moon is likely to be dull."

Specifically, I would like to thank Robert E. Hunter and Philip A. Odeen (Chapter 1, "The National Security Council"); W. Bowman Cutter, Elmer Staats, Richard A. Stubbing, Peter L. Szanton and Leonard Zuza (Chapter 2, "The Office of Management and Budget"); William I. Bacchus and I.M. Destler (Chapter 3, "The State Department"); Archie D. Barrett, John G. Kester, Lawrence J. Korb and Walter Ochinko (Chapter 4, "The Department of Defense"); Richard K. Betts, John Elliff, Allan E. Goodman, Jeffrey T. Richelson, George E. Thibault, and some Central Intelligence Agency officials (Chapter 5, "The Intelligence Community"); George Berdes, Philip J. Brenner, Stanley J. Heginbotham, Robert Lockwood, Gale Mattox, and Bruce F. Norton (Chapter 6, "Executive-Legislative Consultation"). Of course, I bear sole responsiblity for errors of commission and omission and for my occasional stubborn resistance to the advice of learned commentators.

Finally, this book is in substantial part both for and by students. Two former graduate students, Elizabeth Johnson Barber and Chris J. Brantley, each coauthored a chapter with me. Uma Balakrishnan, an undergraduate, typed much of the manuscript.

Notes

1. Richard Rose provides an excellent overview of these fundamental considerations in "Government Against Sub-governments: A European Perspective on Washington," in Richard Rose and Ezra N. Suleiman, eds., *Presidents and Prime Ministers* (Washington, D.C.: American Enterprise Institute, 1980), pp. 284–347.
2. Richard E. Neustadt, *Presidential Power: The Politics of Leadership* (New York: John Wiley & Sons, 1960), p. 10.
3. See Duncan L. Clarke, "National Security Policy Coordination and Integration: The Problem and Why It Matters," in Duncan L. Clarke, ed., *Public Policy and Political Institutions: United States Defense and Foreign Policy Coordination and Integration* (Greenwich, Ct.: JAI Press, 1985), pp. 3–18; and Duncan L. Clarke, "Integrating Arms Control, Defense, and Foreign Policy in the Executive Branch of the U.S. Government," in Hans Guenter Brauch and Duncan L. Clarke, eds., *Decisionmaking for Arms Limitation: Assessments and Prospects* (Cambridge, Mass.: Ballinger, 1983), especially pp. 22–26.
4. Graham T. Allison, *Essence of Decision: Explaining the Cuban Missile Crisis* (Boston: Little, Brown, 1971), p. 273.

Many people have come to believe there is something wrong with the way this country makes foreign policy. They probably don't know how wrong.

—Robert C. McFarlane, May 1987

Among the most frequently heard contentions in the field of government management is the allegation that if good people can be placed in an agency, the organization will make little difference. This is nonsense.

—Alan L. Dean, 1981

There is a great need for improvement in the way we think through and tie together our security objectives. . . . Today, there is no rational system whereby the Executive Branch and the Congress reach coherent and enduring agreement on national military strategy, the forces to carry it out, and the funding that should be provided—in light of the overall economy and competing claims on national resources.

—Packard Commission Report, June 1986

CHAPTER 1

The National Security Council: Process and Management Do Matter

Few subjects have been more exhaustively studied and restudied than the National Security Council (NSC) and various NSC systems. However, an important aspect of this topic has received insufficient attention—the NSC staff's institutional functions: managing interagency analytical processes, ensuring policy coordination, monitoring implementation of policy decisions, and so forth. I.M. Destler, Alexander George, the Tower Commission (1987), and others have touched upon some of these functions, but since the Murphy Commission Report (1975), only Philip Odeen and Robert Hunter have treated them systematically.[1]

These functions are this chapter's principal focus. But it also addresses the general importance of process, structure, and management at the NSC and presidential levels, as well as various factors affecting the National Security Assistant (NSA)[2] and the NSC staff. Finally, the chapter examines aspects of the NSC's role in defense and international economic issues. Throughout, the tone is unabashedly prescriptive.

The President's System

Brief Historical Backdrop[3]

The president himself, or a handful of executive agents in the cabinet, provided virtually the sole vehicle for coordinating defense and foreign policy until well into the twentieth century. This coordinative base was generally sufficient, given the small size of the armed forces, limited overseas involvements, the absence of immediate threats, and the relative geopolitical isolation of the United States. This changed, albeit temporarily, when the complex military effort required in World War I imposed demands that the president alone could not meet. The Army Appropriation Act of 1916 established the Council of National Defense (which excluded the secretary of state from membership) for the limited purpose of economic mobilization. The council was disbanded after the war, and the president was once again the sole national security coordinator.[4]

As World War II approached, President Franklin Roosevelt in 1938, introduced the first significant step toward interdepartmental liaison and coordination in the national security sector—the Standing Liaison Committee. It was composed of the under secretary of state, the Army chief of staff, and the chief of naval operations. Although the committee was complemented in 1940 by informal meetings of the secretaries of state, war, and Navy, its utility was limited since it concentrated largely on Latin American issues and met irregularly.[5] During the war the committee was succeeded by an unsatisfactory piecemeal system of multiple interdepartmental bodies. Roosevelt directed the war effort principally through the then de facto Joint Chiefs of Staff (JCS), key advisers, and his personal relationship with Winston Churchill.

But a growing awareness of the need for better coordination was reflected in the 1945 decision to establish the State, War, Navy Coordinating Committee (SWNCC) at the assistant secretary level for the purpose of supporting the heads of these three departments in various political-military matters and coordinating departmental views on foreign policy. The SWNCC had its own secretariat, several regional and functional subcommittees, and interacted well with the evolving JCS system; it was a substantial improvement in civilian-military coordination. Still the SWNCC had its limitations. It did not function at a level high enough to influence policymaking, and, because it dealt only with issues referred by one of the departments, the committee did not address some important questions within its purview. These limitations provided part of the rationale for replacing the SWNCC with the National Security Council.[6]

The NSC, created by the National Security Act of 1947 (P.L. 80–253), was just one element of a complete restructuring of the national security apparatus. It was also probably the least controversial of the major postwar organizational changes. In substantial part, the NSC reflected the views and recommendations of a report prepared by Ferdinand Eberstadt at the request of Secretary of the Navy James Forrestal. The Eberstadt Report found serious weaknesses in overall coordination during the war and concluded: "These ills cannot be cured by one single administrative change. . . . They require integration of the whole organizational structure of the Government in the service of national security."[7]

The National Security Act of 1947, in creating the NSC, brought together with the president and vice president the senior foreign policy, defense policy, and intelligence officials for purposes of policy coordination, integration, and advice:

The function of the Council shall be to advise the President with respect to the integration of domestic, foreign, and military policies relating to the national security so as to enable the military services and the other departments and agencies of the Government to cooperate more effectively in matters involving the national security.[8]

The act gives the president maximum flexibility to use (or not use) the NSC as he sees fit. Indeed, an outstanding feature of the NSC in retrospect has been its reflection of and responsiveness to the personal styles and preferences of successive presidents.[9]

No System Is Ideal, But Structure Is Important

Close observers of the NSC process agree that there is no "ideal" system. No system is acceptable unless it conforms to the president's style and needs. These personal factors will largely determine not only the NSC's institutional and staff functions but also, in substantial part, the quality of advice the president receives. Few assertions are more frequently and appropriately cited than Dean Rusk's wise observation that "the real organization of government at higher echelons [is] how confidence flows down from the President."[10] Moreover, any system must adjust to the specific issues being addressed and the personalities, experience, and standing of other senior officials.

But whether a president opts for a formal, highly structured process or a more informal one, *some* structure is essential. Without structure, the president is unlikely to receive the information and advice he needs, and the NSC's crucial coordination and policy implementation functions are likely to suffer. Experienced, able, and dedicated White House staff and cabinet officials are critical, but structure cannot be neglected. As Robert Hunter says:

Setting policies and priorities in foreign policy is critical, but so too are the mechanisms and the process that the president establishes to help him create and carry out a foreign policy. A president who neglects that engine—in either its design or its operation—is sure to have mammoth difficulties, probably in times of quiet, and surely in times of crisis.[11]

The absence of an explicit, written, presidentially sanctioned NSC structure contributed importantly to the confused process of the Reagan administration's first year. Excessive informality also took its toll in the first year of the Kennedy administration, in Lyndon Johnson's Tuesday Lunch Group, and in President Carter's partial reliance upon informal meetings among principals. Informal or ad hoc meetings have utility. Issues can often be more fully and frankly addressed in an informal setting—especially when they are limited in scope or have already been examined and refined at lower levels—and the omnipresent potential for unauthorized leaks is minimized. Yet there are hazards. For example, in the Carter administration's Thursday luncheons with Secretary of State Cyrus Vance (later Edmund Muskie), Secretary of Defense Harold Brown, and NSA Zbigniew Brzezinski and Friday breakfasts of these principals with the President, Vice President, and one or two senior White House political aides, there was no formal agenda, the principals' staff aides were excluded, and written notes were rarely taken. This obscured agreement on what had actually transpired, hindered follow-through by the respective staffs, and contributed to the frequent gaps between policy decision and execution.[12]

Except for President Eisenhower and, to a degree, President Reagan, presidents have not relied heavily on plenary meetings of the NSC. Their organizational and procedural requirements for coordination and decisionmaking have been met instead by other bodies and mechanisms, as well as by the various institutional functions of the NSC staff and NSA. Although there is no universally correct way to structure an NSC system, experience suggests certain guidelines. For instance:[13]

- Although a president's subsequent behavior will speak much louder than formal directives, a written directive should be issued in the first week of his administration, setting forth his NSC system and delineating the specific functions of the NSA, secretary of state, and other key officials. Much discontent might be avoided or mitigated if clear lines of authority were established at the outset.

- There should be a formal method for preparing national security policy studies and issuing presidential decisions to facilitate White House policy direction. National Security Study Directives (NSSDs—Reagan), Policy Review Memorandums (PRMs—Carter), and National Security Study Memorandums (NSSMs—Nixon, Ford) brought analyses and options to the president. They also created a common pattern of management to which the entire bureaucracy can relate. Similarly, the national security decision directives, presidential directives, and national security decision memorandums of the respective administrations set forth presidential policies and enhance White House authority.
- Senior interagency coordinating committees chaired by the NSC should have clear areas of responsibility and be supported by interagency working groups or secretariats that develop option papers and oversee the policy analysis effort. The support function should generally not be assigned to a single agency, as that agency's viewpoint would then dominate.

The President Is Not a Manager, But. . . . Even presidents who might prefer to deal with domestic matters (Johnson, Reagan) must address substantive arms control, defense, and foreign policy issues. But how deeply should a president be involved personally in the workings of his national security policy *process*?

The president is the nation's chief executive and chief political officer. He is not, and cannot be, its chief manager. Although every major study group since the Brownlow Committee, which issued its famous report to President Franklin D. Roosevelt in 1937 on executive management, has recommended augmenting presidential management tools, the managerial conception of the presidency is untenable. The dispersion of power in the executive branch and Congress's check on the president's administrative authority partly explain why no modern president has fully managed the executive branch. Another factor is the president's lack of time and, often, lack of aptitude for management. A president who overinvolves himself in the foreign policy process or a particular substantive matter invariably slights other important issues requiring his attention. Moreover, management questions usually hold little political appeal and sometimes entail substantial political risk.

However, a president must pay some attention to the administration and operation of his policy process. Without a reasonably well-functioning process, his preferences and objectives are unlikely to be translated into sound policies or effectively implemented programs. That is, the president should attend to his process not because he is a manager but because administration and process are vital elements of the system through which his goals become policies and programs.[14]

Reasons for attending to process are easily illustrated. Zbigniew Brzezinski said of President Carter's immersion in certain *substantive* foreign policy issues: "At times I thought he was like a sculptor who did not know when to throw away his chisel."[15] Yet it was not until the last year of his administration, on 9 February 1980—when he approved all but one of the Odeen Report's recommendations (only some of which were fully implemented) —that Carter belatedly sought to correct several severe problems in his NSC *process*.[16] Carter suffered politically from charges, some of which were valid, that his was a confused policy process. So there may be political incentives as well as disincentives for a president to pay some attention to the functioning of his process.

There are other incentives, too. While most senior-level interagency management of the national security system is generally delegated to the NSC and NSC staff (although the State Department has sometimes played a key role), there are times when the president should intervene personally. Examples of such occasions would be the following: when the NSA proves to be ineffective; when policy papers flowing to the president for decision are deficient; when a department or a senior official does not implement faithfully a clear presidential decision; during intense crises when the use of military force is certain or probable; when even an able NSA lacks the clout to force a major, pressing issue—which cannot or will not be handled adequately at lower levels—up to the president for decision; and when senior advisers differ among themselves so repeatedly and so intensely, whether for personal or policy reasons, that the process itself is in jeopardy.

The hazards awaiting a president who distances himself from his own national security policy process were especially evident in the Reagan administration. President Reagan had relatively little interest in foreign affairs, and his ignorance of the subject, compounded by a poor memory, concerned even his most senior policy advisers.[17] Few presidents were more passive in policy formulation. Only under great pressure would Reagan reluctantly intervene in his own process, and although in attendance, he apparently almost never chaired NSC meetings.[18] Whereas Presidents Kennedy and Carter sometimes overinvolved themselves in some substantive foreign policy matters, President Reagan was often underinvolved. Whereas Nixon overcentralized authority in the White House, Reagan delegated authority excessively, in what he called "cabinet government." Former White House Chief of Staff Donald Regan relates that Reagan "laid down no rules. . . . I found myself in an environment in which there seemed to be no center, no structure, no agreed policy."[19] The consequent insufficient degree of White House–centralized discipline contributed to a perhaps unprecedented fragmentation of policy.

This was glaringly evident in the Iran-Contra affair, when some NSC staffers and others engaged in highly improper and sometimes unauthorized activities. President Reagan's own Tower Commission and the Iran-Contra Congressional committees severely faulted the administration's decisionmaking process, the President's personal role in that process, and Reagan's failure of leadership. The Tower Commission concluded that this damaging episode

. . . resulted in large part from the flaws in the manner in which decisions were made. Established procedures for making national security decisions were ignored. Reviews of the initiative by all the NSC principals were too infrequent. The initiatives were not adequately vetted below the cabinet level. Intelligence resources are underutilized. Applicable legal constraints were not adequately addressed. The whole matter was handled too informally, without adequate written records of what had been considered, discussed, and decided.[20]

The majority report of the Iran-Contra committees stated:

. . . clearly there has been a failure in . . . leadership and supervision. . . . [T]he ultimate responsibility . . . must rest with the President. If the President did not know what his National Security Advisers were doing, he should have. . . .

[F]undamental processes of governance were disregarded and the rule of law was subverted. . . . The record of the Iran-Contra Affair . . . shows a seriously flawed policymaking process. There was confusion and disarray at the highest levels of Government.[21]

President Reagan himself, in March 1987, acknowledged publicly the shortcomings of his "management style."[22]

The challenge for a president and his NSA is to determine when and where to intervene in the process and where centralization or decentralization of authority is advisable. Selectivity is essential. Some tension between the president's immediate staff and departmental leadership is to be expected. The departments invariably seek freedom of action and distance from White House control. The White House staff (when encouraged by the president) often presses for tighter control and some involvement in important departmental activities. The resolution or nonresolution of these tensions says much about the quality and character of an administration's national security policy process. And the quality of the process bears fundamentally upon the coherence and persuasiveness of the policy itself.

National Security Assistant: Selection and Function.   Above all, the NSA must have and retain the president's confidence. Richard Allen, President Reagan's first NSA, did not, and he resigned in less than a year. Second, he should have a solid grounding in arms control, foreign policy, and, ideally, defense policy. (William Clark, Allen's successor, possessed none of these qualities, yet enjoyed Reagan's confidence.) Third, the NSA should share the broad worldview of the president, be personally compatible with him, and be open to and disposed toward ensuring that dissenting views get a hearing. Henry Kissinger shared President Nixon's worldview, but was often intolerant of dissent.

The NSA should be a civilian. When President Reagan appointed Vice Admiral John Poindexter as his fourth NSA, Poindexter took the unusual step of remaining on active military duty. Even before the Iran-Contra scandal broke, this invited concern within and without government, whether warranted or not, of undue military influence in a post most commonly held by civilians. The very day the Iran-Contra committees voted to recommend formally that the NSA "not be an active military officer,"

President Reagan named an active duty Army officer, Lieutenant General Colin L. Powell, as his sixth NSA in almost seven years.[23]

Beyond these considerations and qualities, there is a growing consensus that the NSA should have a background and interest in organization and management, that he should be custodian-manager of the NSC process.[24] In this capacity, the NSA, it is hoped, would be seen as a more or less neutral arbiter who would see that key officials were able to attend important meetings and communicate their views to the president. The NSA and his staff would manage the NSC's various institutional and support functions (discussed more fully below). He would be present at significant meetings and would have open access to the president. While being available to brief the media on a background basis and perhaps dealing privately with individual legislators, he would nevertheless maintain a low profile and generally avoid delivering major policy speeches.

The degree to which the NSA should also be a policy adviser to the president must be resolved. A major concern of some governmental and scholarly observers of the NSC is that the NSA cannot be both an influential policy adviser and a neutral arbiter. Moreover, assumption of the former role invites friction with cabinet secretaries, especially the secretary of state. There is also concern that the NSA might so emphasize his advisory role as to neglect his custodial-managerial duties.

NSAs were not policy advisers before 1961. But from the Kennedy through the Carter administrations, with the notable exception of Brent Scowcroft, NSAs (especially Walt Rostow, Kissinger, and Brzezinski) emphasized their advisory roles to the detriment of institutional functions. The Truman period and, especially, the Eisenhower period are therefore sometimes cited as examples of how the NSA should operate. However, this view should not be accepted too quickly. Truman's NSAs, James Lay and Sidney Souers, functioned poorly as managers. In keeping with President Truman's wishes, their ability to coordinate defense and foreign policy was constrained. They had little authority, staff capability, or (often) desire to monitor the bureaucracy's implementation of presidential decisions.[25] The Eisenhower NSC was reasonably well managed, and his three NSAs had greater institutional authority. Still, some of this authority was not acquired until late in the administration. White House aides Sherman Adams and Wilton

("Jerry") Persons urged—with mixed success—even greater expansion of this authority, but some crucial managerial functions continued to be performed by Staff Secretary Andrew Goodpaster instead of the NSA.[26]

To an important degree, the NSA's managerial and institutional effectiveness depends on his *having* an advisory role. This gives him stature and political clout. Without such stature, the NSA would serve at the pleasure of not only the president but also of the departmental secretaries and powerful White House political aides.[27] The problem, as is so often the case, is one of appropriate balance and personal style. Institutional effectiveness, then, requires that the NSA have some advisory role. Indeed, even if he is principally a custodian-manager, which should be the case, many presidents will naturally solicit advice from NSAs with whom they are in daily contact. Yet the NSA must not usurp the rightful roles of the secretary of state (discussed in Chapter 3). And, of course, the Central Intelligence Agency (CIA), not the NSC, should implement properly authorized covert actions.[28]

The NSC Staff. Members of the NSC staff since 1961 have been, and should continue to be, a mix of inside careerists from the departments and agencies and outsiders, especially academics. Government professionals should predominate; they know how to get things done in a bureaucracy. However, there should be more emphasis than there has been in the past on recruiting staff with experience and interest in policy execution. An incoming administration should also retain some of its predecessor's staffers until the new team settles in. Finally, the NSC staff should be large enough that adequate manpower can be allotted to institutional functions. The professional NSC staff never exceeded twelve under McGeorge Bundy (1961–1966), eighteen under Walt Rostow (1966–1969), and about thirty-nine under Brzezinski (1977–1981).[29] In each case, insufficient staff size impeded the NSC's custodial-managerial role.[30] It appears that at least forty-five and perhaps (although some will object to this) up to sixty-five professional staffers may be required for effective performance of advisory, support, and institutional functions.[31]

A case can be made, borrowing from the British practice, for creating a permanent, nonpartisan, career NSC staff with an experienced private secretary to serve both Democratic and Republican administrations.[32] It has worked well in Britain and could improve efficiency of operations, facilitate policy implementation, and provide much needed institutional memory. If efficiency was the supreme criterion, there would probably be a permanent NSC staff. But partisan political considerations and concerns about loyalty have prevailed. Hence the prospects for instituting this idea are dim.

Less "radical" measures designed exclusively or principally to ensure adequate NSC record-keeping and institutional memory may be more acceptable to succeeding presidents. The Tower Commission suggested three possibilities for addressing this essential yet neglected task: a small, permanent executive secretariat; one person—a permanent executive secretary (Bromley Smith served several administrations' NSCs loyally and well in the 1950s and 1960s); or a pattern of limited tenure and overlapping rotation among NSC staffers, especially during transition periods from one administration to another.[33]

The NSC's Institutional/Support Functions

Presidential styles and preferences decisively influence NSC staff activities. Whereas Lyndon Johnson dealt with others on his NSC staff in addition to Bundy and Rostow, Nixon seldom met with any NSC staffers except Kissinger and, later, Alexander Haig. While Kennedy and Carter were "reading" presidents, Reagan preferred oral briefings and videotapes. Carter demanded detailed, often lengthy, information and analysis, but Nixon generally expected three-page decision papers.[34] Yet as important as these stylistic differences are, they do not fundamentally alter what the NSC staff must do to support the president.

The NSC advises the president and carries out vital institutional/support activities. Distinctions between advisory and institutional functions are not and cannot be entirely clear-cut. Both affect policy. They also invariably affect one another. However, with one or two partial exceptions, such as supporting the president's domestic political interests and helping delineate a policy framework, the NSC's institutional functions share a common trait: they are substantially managerial or administrative in character.

Delineating a Policy Framework[35]

An incoming administration must soon set forth policies and priorities to guide the bureaucracy's programs and actions, engage the Congress, and signal its intentions to the international community. The first months of a new administration are normally a time of intense policy debate and decision. Interagency studies, usually coordinated by the NSC staff, serve as a basis for decisions that form the policy framework. President Nixon initiated eighty-five NSSMs in 1969, and President Carter issued thirty-two PRMs in 1977. There was little such activity in President Reagan's first year. This was partly because of Reagan's primary attention to domestic economic issues, but was also attributable to his preference for decentralized authority, which was reflected in a purposefully weak NSA and NSC staff, heavy reliance on inexperienced and overburdened White House political aides, and an unusual degree of latitude afforded Secretary of Defense Caspar Weinberger in setting defense policies. The subsequent criticisms of the administration's policy process and arms control policy, as well as the later erosion of public and congressional support for its defense budget, suggest that this relative inactivity and initial emasculation of the NSC staff was a mistake.

When a president most needs to create a policy framework and process, he is least equipped to do so. It commonly takes several months to a year for a new chief executive and his team to adjust to one another and to the inevitable realization of the limits on their ability to reshape policy direction. This is a time when institutional memory is often absent, when there is a relative dearth of orderly professional input. Yet, this is the time when most major discretionary policy changes—as opposed to changes mandated by events—occur. Indeed, changes probably must be set in motion (although not necessarily completed) in the first few months, when the new executive has the fewest prior commitments to people, policies, or procedures, when he might enjoy a temporary "honeymoon" with Congress, and when it is advisable to send a strong message to the bureaucracy that a new president is in charge and is determined to use his authority.

It is therefore important that, well before inauguration day, senior advisers and cabinet secretaries be de facto selected, an agenda of policy priorities be tentatively drafted (tentatively, because it should be coordinated with the departments and agencies after the president assumes office), and an NSC process and structure—or some well-defined process and structure—be formulated for execution during the first week of the new administration. There will be substantial costs to pay if these things are not done.

Selecting Matters for the President's Attention and Forcing Decisions on Major Issues[36]

Cabinet secretaries and other senior officials will personally bring issues to the president's attention. But it is the NSC staff that regularly informs the president of matters he will sooner or later be compelled to address, thereby ensuring that important issues are raised to the presidential level. On the other hand, if the president already feels strongly about a particular matter, the NSC is the logical instrument to so inform the bureaucracy at an early juncture.

Deciding when the president should be involved is often as important as selecting issues for his attention. In fact, he must always have an opportunity to render a decision on matters that could significantly affect him and his administration. The NSC should see that the bureaucracy does not present the president with a potentially embarrassing fait accompli. Hence, the president must be brought into the decision process in a timely fashion. NSA John Poindexter provided a textbook example of how not to perform this function. Believing that "the buck stops here with me," Poindexter failed to inform President Reagan of crucial decisions and developments during the Iran-Contra episode.[37] While responsibility for this dismal affair is properly Reagan's, Poindexter's behavior only deepened the President's subsequent humiliation.

The NSC staff must also occasionally *force* major issues up for senior-level consideration. The departments are frequently hesitant to permit White House scrutiny of certain issues. The Defense Department (DOD), for instance, is protective of potentially controversial and costly weapons programs and certain force structure and sizing questions. DOD rarely invites White House attention to such matters, even when there is a pressing need for presidential intervention. If the NSC staff, or perhaps the Office of Management and Budget (OMB), does not perform this function—that is, ensuring senior-level scrutiny of whatever needs it—no one will.[38]

Managing the Policy Analytical Process

Government professionals in State, Defense, the CIA, and throughout the bureaucracy are the principal repositories of the specialized knowledge and analysis necessary for policymaking. Even a large NSC staff can only supplement and refine the input of these primary sources of expertise. How effectively they are tapped is, in substantial part, a function of the policy process.[39]

While most analysis and information comes from the bureaucracy, management of the interagency analytical process is best performed, and is usually performed, by the NSC staff. The NSC staff is unencumbered by parochial departmental interests. It is best positioned to press for sound, critical, balanced analyses; to insist upon and then present to decisionmakers a clear spectrum of policy options reflecting the views of all relevant agencies; and to determine the appropriate manner and forum for issue consideration. When the NSC has not played this role, as in the early Reagan administration, a price has generally been paid.

Supporting the President's Domestic Political Interests

The NSA and NSC staff must be sensitive to the president's domestic political standing. In part, this means preparing him for overseas trips and meetings with the media so that he is, or appears to be, well informed. It also means that the NSA must give the White House timely notice of forthcoming issues that have domestic political ramifications. Finally, and importantly, the NSA must establish working relationships with those who are principally concerned with the president's political well-being: White House political aides.

The NSA and White House Political Aides.[40] Even without personality differences, the potential for tension between the NSA and White House political aides is inherent in their sometimes competitive functional responsibilities. What the aides find to be in the president's best political interests may be considered poor national security policy by the NSA. Although they occasionally experience personal or issue-oriented friction, the NSA and White House aides usually enjoy cordial, or at least working, personal relationships. But there are situations that can engender serious and harmful tension.

When boundaries of responsibility between the NSA and domestical political advisers are drawn so tightly that vital information concerning their respective functional areas is not exchanged in a timely manner, friction is probable. The Kennedy and Carter administrations initially excluded political advisers from early decisions that subsequently embarrassed both presidents. Political advisers had no role in President Kennedy's politically costly 1961 Bay of Pigs decision. Similarly, President Carter's October 1977 announcement of a joint U.S.-Soviet Middle East peace initiative, which caused an uproar in the American Jewish community, was made without consulting political advisers. Subsequently, political advisers participated in all important foreign policy deliberations in both administrations.

A second situation is virtually certain to trigger internal friction: when senior political aides are dissatisfied with the NSA's performance. Kissinger resented measures taken by President Ford's political aides to balance and offset his influence. The aides were concerned that Kissinger's pervasive policy influence jeopardized Ford's public stature in the foreign policy area. In 1981, when James Baker, Michael Deaver, and others concluded that Richard Allen was ineffective, his days as Reagan's NSA were numbered. Later, when Donald Regan was Reagan's White House Chief of Staff, animosity between an NSA (Robert McFarlane) and a chief of staff reached a probably unprecedented level. According to the Tower Commission, Regan sought to exert more personal control over the NSA than virtually any of his predecessors. When McFarlane, Reagan's third NSA, resigned, he complained of Regan's "very chaotic management style."[41]

A third situation is more complex. When an NSA assumes the mantle of major foreign policy spokesman and, sometimes simultaneously, that of senior diplomat, he does so at the behest of the president. Much of what tension has existed between White House political aides and the NSA relates directly to the latter's consequent public visibility. If such visibility causes the aides, and perhaps the president, to believe that the NSA has become a popular figure who, in the public's eye, eclipses the president in national security affairs, intra–White House tension is probable. This occurred in the Nixon-Ford period when Kissinger's diplomatic dances and prominent foreign policy spokesmanship attracted unusual media attention. Moreover, a highly visible and diplomatically active NSA runs a distinct risk of clashing with the secretary of state, who will rightly view foreign policy spokesmanship and diplomacy as among his primary functions. As a rule, this problem can be avoided if the NSA either forgoes these roles or—if asked by the president to play them—keeps his activities limited and well coordinated with those of the secretary.

Just as there is no optimal NSC system, so there is no "best" procedure for integrating domestic political considerations with national security concerns. But doing so is essential. Every president, either at the outset of his administration or shortly thereafter, has found it necessary to include domestic political aides in national security deliberations. Except for the Truman years, one or more political advisers regularly attended NSC meetings in all administrations. The political advisers' counsel was also solicited at important informal policy meetings, such as Gordon Gray's and Andrew Goodpaster's ad hoc sessions with President Eisenhower, and President Carter's Friday breakfasts. Moreover, with some exceptions, information flow between NSAs and political aides has usually been excellent. Finally, except for Richard Allen, the NSA's access to the president has almost never been impeded significantly.

Coordination

Every administration should have mechanisms and procedures for coordinating the views and positions of policy officials. Effective coordination taps and draws together the expertise of departments and agencies, prevents any single departmental view from dominating, and lessens the prospects for bitter internal discord by affording officials a fair hearing. But departments and agencies are not naturally inclined to fully and voluntarily coordinate with one another because of their vested parochial interests, concern that coordination consumes too much time, and fear of harmful unauthorized leaks of information.

Coordination takes time. Leaks occur. Reasonable steps to minimize these problems are certainly appropriate. But there must be adequate coordination, and this requires authority. Says Peter Szanton, "In most matters, an agency's inclinations serve its interests; in important matters, they serve its important interests."[42] Neither logic nor pleas to address the "national interest" will change this. Successful coordination depends ultimately upon supervision from above.

Only with strong presidential backing, and even then only in select policy areas, might this supervision be exercised by the State Department. Institutional jealousies are simply too deep and pervasive. Broad-based interagency coordination of defense, arms control, and foreign policy must come from the NSA and the NSC staff. The NSC staff is unencumbered by a departmental mission, and the NSA is far more likely than a cabinet secretary to appear to be relatively neutral on most issues to the departments and agencies. Even when the NSA is an outspoken policy advocate, there is little persuasive evidence to suggest that coordination can be better managed outside of the White House. Indeed, to some important degree (as urged above), the NSA's ability to ensure adequate coordination is increased if he is a policy adviser as well as a custodian-manager. A system that decentralizes authority away from the White House invariably risks undermining effective coordination. It should be the NSC staff that manages formal interagency studies, affords officials a fair hearing, ensures that issues are considered and decisions made at appropriate levels, sees that necessary meetings are convened, and—with White House political aides—reviews important public speeches and congressional testimony before they are delivered.

The Bottom Line: Policy Implementation/Monitoring Compliance

While it is occasionally argued that bureaucratic resistance to authoritative policy decisions might have the salutary effect of tempering unwise decisions,[43] nothing is more injurious to the policy process—or, indeed, to the very essence of the democratic system—than the failure of executive departments and agencies to implement lawful decisions in a faithful and timely manner. When this happens, the people's elected representatives are effectively thwarted. The president loses control over those who by law are his agents. Presidential decisions and the law of the land mean little unless they are carried out. Implementation, then, is the bottom line of the policy process.

Senior officials stress this point, as well as the difficulty of its realization:

- Brent Scowcroft: "Monitoring policy implementation is the most often overlooked essential function of the White House and NSC staff."[44]
- Henry Kissinger: "The outsider believes a Presidential order is consistently followed out. Nonsense. I have to spend considerable time seeing that it is carried out and in the spirit the President intended."[45]
- Richard Cheney, President Ford's White House Chief of Staff: "You spend most of your time trying to overcome obstacles getting what the President wants done."[46]
- Murphy Commission: *"Implementation is about half the problem in most important decisions and actions."*[47]
- Zbigniew Brzezinski: "I had an insufficient appreciation of the extent to which policy making is chaotic . . . [and of how] much of foreign policy is determined by the deliberate bureaucratic distortion of decisions firmly made and how urgently therefore it requires an enormous output of energy in a purely watchdog capacity."[48]

Every modern president has expressed frustration about policy implementation, yet no NSC system has dealt effectively—or sometimes, much at all—with the problem.[49] Some people point to the Eisenhower administration's Operations Coordinating Board (OCB) as an example of the White House/NSC getting a handle on implementation. But many who actually served on the board, or knew it well, disagree.[50] Indeed, throughout Eisenhower's term in office, the OCB was subjected to constant study and revision. From its creation in 1953 through early 1957, the OCB was outside the NSC structure and had no authority to require agencies and departments to implement policies in particular ways. The OCB did not become a component of the NSC until February 1957, and only in his last year in office, on 13 January 1960, did Eisenhower issue a written directive elevating NSA Gordon Gray from Vice

Chairman to Chairman of the OCB. Only then was White House oversight of implementation reasonably effective—testimony to the wisdom of centralizing this function in the White House under an NSA with explicit presidential authority and backing to perform it.[51]

Addressing Obstacles to Policy Implementation. The several obstacles to translating policy decisions into policy practice are themselves suggestive of ways to address the issue. While implementation problems will not disappear, they can sometimes be kept to manageable proportions through constant White House attention and persistence.

Congress and the president dominate decisionmaking, but the bureaucracy dominates implementation. An agency may be disinclined to faithfully execute a policy decision for many reasons: it threatens budgets or programs, it infringes upon traditional agency jurisdiction, it runs counter to an agency's essential mission, and so forth. Even if an agency is disposed to carry out a decision, it may be impeded by various bureaucratic factors, such as the difficulty of coordinating with other organizational units in order to successfully implement the decision.

A central, authoritative locus for monitoring compliance with policy decisions is necessary to avert confusion and disorder. That locus is the White House and the Executive Office of the President. At the outset of his administration, the president should stress, in personal conversations and in clear written directives, that oversight of policy implementation is a high priority. He should also empower specific White House officials—certainly including the NSA—with presidential authority in this area, require a systematic process under NSC direction for monitoring compliance on a regular basis, and increase the quality and number of NSC staffers with experience and interest in policy execution. In select instances, the president must consider personally enforcing his decisions. The image of the president as "enforcer" may not be sufficiently developed. His power and authority will not be wholly credible unless they are occasionally exercised. The bureaucracy must be made to expect that high-level review of implementation will occur.

In addition to intentional bureaucratic resistance, policy decisions may be poorly executed either because those with responsibility for implementation do not know precisely what they are expected to do or because, even if they are clear about this, they lack sufficient resources (staff, information, facilities, expertise, and so on). The NSC must inform itself about an agency's resources before directing it to implement a decision. Moreover, decisions and follow-up responsibilities, as well as the rationale for the decisions, must be clearly communicated. Vague or ambiguous communication of decisions gives implementers the discretion to interpret them in ways that may not conform with the policymakers' intentions.

An official may balk at implementing a decision simply because he disagrees with its policy content. This is particularly common when a senior official is excluded from the process that led to the decision. Therefore, in order to encourage commitment to successful execution, the system generally should strive to involve all key officials. A senior official will be less inclined to resist a decision with which he disagrees—and less likely to go public with his discontent—if he has his day in court.

Finally, NSAs and other White House officials are often so consumed with making decisions that they overlook or neglect the follow-up function. If those inside and outside government who know the importance of monitoring policy implementation cannot convince the White House to attend to this matter, events will sooner or later highlight the substantive and political costs of ignoring it.

Crisis Management and Planning

Management. All administrations have mechanisms for managing crises: the Executive Committee (Kennedy), the Washington Special Action Group (Nixon-Ford), the Special Coordination Committee (Carter), the Special Situation Group (Reagan) and other bodies. Such bodies are properly located in the White House, since serious crises will command presidential attention. Secretaries of State Cyrus Vance and Alexander Haig each argued, unsuccessfully, that they should chair the crisis management group. Whatever the merits of their respective cases, it is clear that the chairman should be a senior official regularly involved in the policy process. This person is often the NSA, although Vice President George Bush performed this role in the Reagan administration.

Planning. Crisis management is a universally accepted institutional function of government. Crisis planning (and long or medium-term policy planning) is another matter. For most seasoned bureaucrats, planning is an unnatural act. The seemingly endless impediments and objections to crisis or policy planning are thoroughly, even morbidly, documented in the literature.[52] Among them is a familiar dilemma: planners who are isolated from operations may have the time and independence to produce analytically sound plans, but they are likely to be ignored by policymakers; planners involved in daily operations can have a policy impact, but they will have little time or independence to plan.

Crisis and policy planning are assigned a low priority in State and throughout much of the rest of the national security bureaucracy.[53] Interagency crisis planning has occasionally been undertaken, but invariably on a short-term or ad hoc basis.[54] And, as will be seen in Chapter 4, contingency planning by the JCS and Commanders-in-Chief (CINCs) for the use of force has been severely and repeatedly criticized.[55]

The difficulties of crisis planning are evident. But so is the need for it. A sustained, systematic, interagency crisis planning effort cannot tell policymakers the "right" thing to do, nor can it usually predict the future. The real value is not in the plan, but in the planning process itself. That process can help challenge and sharpen the assumptions, preferences, and expectations of analysts and policymakers, as well as clarify perceptions of U.S. interests and options and foster working relationships among personnel from various agencies who, in turn, provide analyses and an institutional memory that can be tapped when a crisis breaks.[56] Crisis planning is not an academic exercise (the word "academic" being perjorative throughout much of the national security bureaucracy); rather, it offers a partial and preferable alternative, or supplement, to the usual ad hoc, muddling-through approach. Policymakers should view crisis planning as a regularized procedure for prior examination of major problems and issues that, in some form, at some time, will very likely confront them.

Those who use the plans must encourage and direct the interagency crisis planning effort. If the State Department has the lead, DOD, and perhaps others, will object, thereby jeopardizing the enterprise.[57] The NSC, with the president's support, must therefore have management responsibility for this function. The NSC must see that crisis planning is done and must ensure coordination, present critical policy assumptions to planners, and review the results. The NSA should chair a senior interagency committee for crisis planning, although the actual planning would be coordinated through lower-level interagency groups, probably chaired by assistant secretaries. The senior committee would need to meet only once or twice annually to provide planners with a limited number of significant issues to consider, review ongoing planning efforts, and see that planning retains a high priority.[58]

Defense, International Economics, and the NSC

Hands-off Defense?

The White House has a daily, detailed, and frequently dominant hand in foreign policy. Defense policy is different. Except for setting annual budget ceilings and addressing issues with high public and political visibility—such as the Strategic Defense Initiative (SDI), the MX missile, and the "neutron bomb"—few presidents or NSC staffs get deeply involved in defense matters. No NSA had a longer policy reach than Henry Kissinger, yet he reports that during his tenure, "the White House never achieved the control over defense policy that it did over foreign policy."[59] Unlike most presidents, Jimmy Carter frequently urged his NSA and NSC staff to be more active in defense budgetary, programmatic, and policy issues. But Brzezinski acknowledges that he "never quite succeeded" in doing this.[60]

In addition to multiple pressures on a president's and NSA's time, and various political disincentives to mounting a sustained campaign to increase White House influence over defense matters, there are at least three other reasons for this state of affairs.[61] First, there is usually a dearth of defense expertise in the White House. No modern president, except Dwight Eisenhower, had deep expertise in defense. (Indeed, upon assuming office, some secretaries of defense lacked significant experience or training in defense.)[62] Second, many defense issues are, or appear to the uninitiated to be, more complex and technical than foreign policy. Presidents are more comfortable with large foreign policy questions, which they can relate easily to their political philosophy, such as the overall tone of Soviet-American relations, general human rights issues, and the broad sweep of American policy toward Central America. Finally, the public expects the president to have a high profile in foreign affairs. It is in this arena, not in defense program decisions, that he can best generate positive publicity.

Why, Where, and How Should the NSC Have a Substantial Role? There are persuasive reasons for a greater NSC and presidential role in select defense and defense-related areas.[63] If DOD is to have an authoritative and reasonably well-informed policy framework, it must come from the White House and the NSC. The NSC should also be actively engaged in assessing the long-term costs and affordability of select defense programs. The NSA should urge the president and his senior advisers to address such concerns. President Reagan often asserted that budgetary restraint was necessary for domestic programs, but inappropriate for defense.[64] Yet Congress made it clear by 1985 that, in peacetime, defense was also a budget issue. By then, the Reagan administration's sharp, annual increases in defense appropriations had ceased.

The NSA, perhaps working closely with the OMB director, should sensitize the president to the realization that a sound, stable defense program is inherently tied to a close appraisal of budgetary realities. If the president accedes uncritically to the budget requests of his secretary of defense—as Reagan did during his first term—his defense priorities, as well as the federal deficit, may eventually suffer.[65]

OMB directors are almost always outclassed when they go one-on-one with secretaries of defense. NSC cooperation with OMB has the potential for changing this. But the potential has not been realized. These two units have never cooperated on a sustained basis, partly because presidents have not specifically encouraged it. Moreover, OMB and the NSC sometimes disagree on issues, they recruit personnel with different interests and expertise, and there are jurisdictional jealousies. This pattern of noncooperation is a major reason why presidents seldom have a coordinated or systematic method for determining "how much is enough" for defense. It is certainly advisable for the president to change this practice by directing closer OMB-NSC coordination. Otherwise, vital defense issues will continue to be poorly addressed by the White House.[66]

In addition to crisis management duties and monitoring implementation of White House defense policy decisions, Philip Odeen rightly advises selective NSC involvement in at least three other defense areas.[67] First, the NSC (and, of course, OMB) should be active in the annual budget process that sets DOD's authorization and outlay levels, and it should review the broad allocation of funds by mission and purpose. Second, the NSC should play a role when the president risks public embarrassment and congressional criticism if he does not personally address a particular defense matter—for example, the MX-basing issue in the first Reagan term. The third area for NSC involvement concerns those defense programs and actions that significantly affect the legitimate responsibilities and expertise of non-DOD agencies and departments. Many defense issues bear importantly, sometimes decisively, on arms control, energy, international economic, or foreign policy. Absent NSC intervention, timely and effective interagency coordination in these instances is unlikely.[68]

Odeen also suggests several "keys" to a fruitful interagency and NSC role in defense matters. For instance, address issues early, before DOD's position is firm, and, keep the process at a senior level so as to avoid perceptions of outside "micromanagement" that might tempt the Pentagon to stall or thwart the process.

Another of Odeen's prescriptions partly reflects his personal experience with the interagency Defense Program Review Committee (DPRC) of the Nixon administration.[69] The DPRC was, and remains today, the only instance since 1960 in which a formal interagency group not chaired by Defense reviewed the defense program. The committee, which existed from 1969 to 1975 and was chaired by Kissinger, was initially to review defense budgets and select defense programs in light of changing national and international economic and political conditions. It was to afford the White House, OMB, the State Department, and some other non-DOD units a regular, high-level say in some major defense issues. At first, Kissinger also wanted his NSC staff to participate in the Pentagon's planning and programming documents. But DOD predictably viewed the DPRC as a clear and present danger to its unique degree of budgetary and programmatic autonomy. Secretary of Defense Melvin Laird soon outmaneuvered Kissinger, successfully stripping the committee of its intended mission. Indeed, not only was the DPRC removed from essential phases of the defense budgetary process, but it was used by the services as a court of appeals for weapons proposals that Laird himself had earlier rejected.[70]

Odeen draws an instructive lesson from the DPRC experience: such an interagency committee, which should be chaired by the NSA, should not have, or be seen to have, direct decisionmaking authority over DOD's budget and programs. Otherwise, fierce resistance can be expected. Rather, this kind of committee should be defined as advisory to the secretary of defense. Crucial differences with the secretary should be brought to the president for decision by the NSA or the appropriate agency head, although, ideally, this will be an infrequent occurrence. As long as the secretary of defense is receptive to input from other agencies, the presumption in most instances should be that, except for the president, he is the principal defense decisionmaker.[71]

Hands-off International Economic Policy?

American international economic policies may intersect with security interests or foreign policy considerations in several areas: international trade and monetary relations, international capital transfers, energy and food policy, international economic development programs, international investment patterns, the practices of multinational corporations, and scientific/technical exchanges and transfers. Moreover, presidents have sometimes chosen economic means to advance foreign policy or security objectives: freezing a nation's assets in the United States, imposing sanctions, trade embargoes or restraints, and so forth. However, in most peacetime situations international economic policy should not be derived from national security priorities. Instead, as Stephen D. Cohen argues persuasively, international economic policy occupies a distinctive area between national security policy and economic policy. It is neither the external dimension of domestic economic policy nor the economic branch of foreign policy. It is a continuously changing blend of foreign and domestic policy considerations.[72]

Therefore, senior-level coordinative processes for international economic policy must not be wholly co-opted by either the national security or economic policy sectors of the bureaucracy. No NSA has had or has sought a dominant, sustained, across-the-board role in formulating international economic policy. Such a role would be very time-consuming, and the NSA would soon discover that most economic issues do not raise clear national security concerns deserving of his attention. The Treasury Department would object, with reason, to continuous, high-level NSC intrusion into an area where it has traditionally had the lead. Other departments such as Commerce, Agriculture, and State might also resist such intervention. Moreover, since international economic policy bears much more directly on domestic politics and policies than do most national security issues and, additionally, intersects an area of Congress's specific constitutional authority (commerce), getting involved in it might plunge the NSA more deeply into domestic issues than may be advisable. Finally, in contrast to foreign policy, few NSAs have had the expertise or standing to be accepted by senior economic policy officials as interagency coordinators.

Treasury should generally chair the senior international economic policy coordination committee, although this committee should have NSC and vigorous State Department representation.[73] However, there will be instances when national security considerations are deemed to override economic factors—for example, President Carter's freezing of Iranian assets in the United States, and President Reagan's imposition of economic sanctions against Nicaragua. At those times, the White House and NSC will intercede decisively.

NSAs and NSC staffs have differed substantially in the depth, constancy, and effectiveness of their involvement in international economic policy.[74] Yet, beyond the general requirement that the NSC be involved and represented in this area and that there be a strong in-house NSC economic capability (like Henry Owen's operation in the Carter years), there is no obvious correct way to proceed. Some observers, however, have offered structural and procedural prescriptions that may be appealing to some administrations.[75]

Conclusion

How an NSC process is managed, structured, and operated matters greatly. That process materially affects the quality and viability of national security policy. And it is improper to view the NSC's institutional functions as mere administrative details or secondary considerations. Rather, these functions must be attended to thoughtfully for they are integral elements of any effective policy process.

Incoming administrations, flush with victory at the polls, tend to believe that nothing so needs reforming as the practices and habits of prior administrations. Considerable care is given in the first months to setting forth a new policy agenda. Much less attention is usually paid, both initially and later in the administration, to managing the policy process. This is a mistake. Instead, the management practices and experiences of past administrations should be assessed for the lessons they might hold.

Notes

1. See, for instance, the following: I.M. Destler, *Presidents, Bureaucrats and and Foreign Policy: The Politics of Organizational Reform* (Princeton, N.J.: Princeton University Press, 1972). I.M. Destler, "A Job That Doesn't Work," *Foreign Policy* 39 (Spring 1980): 80–88. Alexander George, *Presidential Decisionmaking in Foreign Policy* (Boulder, Colo.: Westview Press, 1980). *Report of the President's Special Review Board* (hereafter cited as Tower Commission Report) (Washington, D.C.: Government Printing Office, 26 February 1987). David Kent Hall, *Implementing Multiple Advocacy in the National Security Council, 1947–1980*, vols. I–II (Ph.D. dissertation, Stanford University, 1982). Commission on the Organization of Government for the Conduct of Foreign Policy (hereafter cited as Murphy Commission), *Report* (Washington, D.C.: Government Printing Office, 1975). *National Security Policy Integration* (hereafter cited as Odeen Report), President's Reorganization Project (September 1979); the essence of the Odeen Report is found in Philip A. Odeen, "Organizing for National Security," *International Security* 5 (Summer 1980): 111–129. Philip A. Odeen, "The Role of the National Security Council in Coordinating and Integrating U.S. Defense and Foreign Policy," in Duncan L. Clarke, ed., *Public Policy and Political Institutions: United States Defense and Foreign Policy—Policy Coordination and Integration* (Greenwich, Ct.: JAI Press, 1985), pp. 19–41. Robert E. Hunter, *Organizing for National Security* (Washington, D.C.: Center for Strategic and International Studies, 1988). Robert E. Hunter, *Managing National Security: The Reagan/Mondale Challenge* (Washington, D.C.: Center for Strategic and International Studies, 1984). Robert E. Hunter, *Presidential Control of Foreign Policy: Management or Mishap?* (New York: Praeger, 1982).
2. There have been several changes in the official title of the White House official charged with overseeing the operations of the NSC. Since 1969 he has been titled the President's Assistant for National Security Affairs. The term National Security Assistant is used throughout this book.

3. See generally U.S. Congress, Senate, Committee on Government Operations, *Organizing for National Security: Inquiry of the Subcommittee on National Policy Machinery*, 86th–87th Cong., 1961; Mark M. Lowenthal, *The National Security Council: Organizational History* (Washington, D.C.: Congressional Research Service, 27 June 1978), pp. 3–16.

4. Paul Y. Hammond, "The National Security Council as a Device for Interdepartmental Coordination: An Interpretation and Appraisal," *American Political Science Review* 54 (December 1960): 899.

5. Mark Skinner Watson, *Chief of Staff: Prewar Plans and Preparations* (Washington, D.C.: Office of the Chief of Military History, Department of the Army, 1950), pp. 89–91, 93–94.

6. U.S. Department of State, *Foreign Relations of the United States, 1944*, vol. I (Washington, D.C.: Government Printing Office, 1966), pp. 1466–70; John Lewis Gaddis, *The United States and the Origins of Cold War* (New York: Columbia University Press, 1972), p. 126; Ernest R. May, "The Development of Political-Military Consultation in the United States," *Political Science Quarterly* 70 (June 1955): pp. 161–180.

7. U.S. Navy, *Report to the Honorable James Forrestal, Secretary of the Navy, on Unification of the War and Navy Departments and Post-War Organization* (Eberstadt Report) (Washington, D.C., 1945), p. 30; Demetrios Caraley, *The Politics of Military Unification: A Study of Conflict and the Policy Process* (New York: Columbia University Press, 1966), pp. 38–44.

8. National Security Act of 1947, 50 U.S.C. Sec. 402(a).

9. Individual presidential NSC systems since the Truman administration are not treated as such. Among the many studies of this subject are: Keith Clark and Laurence Legere, eds., *The President and the Management of National Security* (New York: Praeger, 1969), pp. 55–98; Murphy Commission, *Making Organizational Change Effective*, vol. 6, Appendix O, pp. 79–99; Joseph G. Bock and Duncan L. Clarke, "The National Security Assistant and the White House Staff: National Security Policy Decisionmaking and Domestic Political Considerations, 1947–1984," *Presidential Studies Quarterly* 16 (Spring 1986): 258–79; William Bundy, "The National Security Process," *International Security* 7 (Winter 1982–83): 94–109; I.M. Destler, "National Security Advice to U.S. Presidents: Some Lessons from Thirty Years," *World Politics* 29 (January 1977): 143–76; Destler, *Presidents, Bureaucrats and Foreign Policy*, pp. 95–153; I.M. Destler, "The Rise of the National Security Assistant, 1961–1981," in Charles W. Kegley, Jr. and Eugene Wittkopf, eds., *Perspectives on American Foreign Policy* (New York: St. Martin's Press, 1983), pp. 260–81; George, *Presidential Decisionmaking in Foreign Policy*; Hall, *Implementing Multiple Advocacy in the National Security Council, 1947–1980*, vols. I–II; Phillip G Henderson, *Managing the Presidency: The Eisenhower Legacy—From Kennedy to Reagan* (Boulder, Colo.: Westview Press, 1988); R. Gordon Hoxie, ed., *The Presidency and National Security Policy* (New York: Center for the Study of the Presidency, 1984); Karl F. Inderfurth and Loch K. Johnson, eds., *Decisions of the Highest Order: Perspectives on the National Security Council* (Pacific Grove, Calif.: Brooks/Cole, 1988), especially pp. 41–188; Lowenthal, *The National Security Council*, pp. 67–84, 93–99; James A. Nathan and James K. Oliver,

Foreign Policy Making and the American Political System, 2d ed. (Boston: Little, Brown, 1987), pp. 33–96; U.S. Congress, Senate, *Organizing for National Security*.

10. Quoted in *Life* (17 January 1969): 62B.

11. Hunter, *Presidential Control of Foreign Policy*, p. 91.

12. Odeen Report, p. 12; Hunter, *Presidential Control of Foreign Policy*, pp. 33–36.

13. See Odeen, "The Role of the National Security Council . . . , p. 38; Hunter, *Managing National Security*, p. 9; Hunter, *Organizing for National Security*; Tower Commission Report, p. V–5.

14. See generally Peri E. Arnold, *Making the Managerial Presidency: Comprehensive Reorganization Planning, 1905–1980* (Princeton, N.J.: Princeton University Press, 1986), pp. 361–63; Stephen Hess, *Organizing the Presidency* (Washington, D.C.: The Brookings Institution, 1976), pp. 146–47; Odeen, "The Role of the National Security Council," pp. 31, 39; Hunter, *Presidential Control of Foreign Policy*, pp. 64–65.

15. Zbigniew Brzezinski, *Power and Principle: Memoirs of the National Security Adviser, 1977–1981* (New York: Farrar, Straus & Giroux, 1983), pp. 522, 526.

16. Duncan L. Clarke, "Integrating Arms Control, Defense and Foreign Policy in the Executive Branch of the U.S. Government," in Hans Guenter Brauch and Duncan L. Clarke, eds., *Decisionmaking for Arms Limitation: Assessments and Prospects* (Cambridge, Mass.: Ballinger, 1983), p. 11.

17. See, for instance, Bob Woodward, *Veil: The Secret Wars of the CIA: 1981–1987* (New York: Simon & Schuster, 1987), p. 254; Lou Cannon, "Baker Shows Light Touch in New Job," *Washington Post*, 3 March 1987, p. A4.

18. Woodward, *Veil*, pp. 336, 403–404; Phil McCombs, "McFarlane and the Web of Rumor," *Washington Post*, 18 April 1986, p. D1; David Hoffman, "President's Aides Seek Harmony," *Washington Post*, 8 December 1985, p. B7; Donald T. Regan, *For the Record: From Wall Street to Washington* (New York: Harcourt Brace Jovanovich, 1988), pp. 228, 290.

19. Regan, *For the Record*, pp. 142–44, 235, 266–68. See Zbigniew Brzezinski, "NSC's Midlife Crisis," *Foreign Policy* 69 (Winter 1987–88): 91–92. Says Brzezinski, "In the field of foreign policy, [Reagan] became largely a ceremonial president" (p. 90).

20. Tower Commission Report, pp. IV–1, 10.

21. U.S. Congress, *Report of the Congressional Committees Investigating the Iran-Contra Affair* (hereafter cited as *Report: Iran-Contra Affair*), H. Rept. 100–433, 100th Cong., 1st sess., 1987, pp. 11–13, 21, 420.

22. "The Crisis of the Reagan Presidency: Text of the President's Speech," *Washington Post*, 5 March 1987, p. A12.

23. Walter Pincus, "Iran-Contra Committees Avoided Casting NSC's Powell in a Critical Light," *Washington Post*, 16 November 1987, p. A1; *Report: Iran-Contra Affair*, p. 426. The Iran-Contra committees also recommended "that there should be a limit placed on the tour of military officers assigned to the staff of the National Security Council" (p. 426).

24. For example, Tower Commission Report, pp. II–3, V–2; Destler, "A Job That Doesn't Work," 80–88; George, *Presidential Decisionmaking*, pp. 162–63, 195–97.

25. Hall, *Implementing Multiple Advocacy*, pp. 243–49; Bock and Clarke, "The National Security Assistant," p. 259.
26. Bock and Clarke, "The National Security Assistant," p. 260. For a very positive assessment of the Eisenhower NSC, see Henderson, *Managing the Presidency*.
27. Testimony of Brent Scowcroft and Richard E. Neustadt, U.S. Congress, Senate, Committee on Foreign Relations, *Hearing: The National Security Adviser: Role and Accountability*, 96th Cong., 2d sess., 1980, pp. 26–27, 29; Tower Commission Report, p. V–3. However, it is probably unwise for a president to make his NSA a cabinet member, as Carter did with Brzezinski. Friction between the NSA and secretary of state is common enough without this added irritant.
28. *Report: Iran-Contra Affair*, pp. 18, 425.
29. Destler, "The Rise of the National Security Assistant," p. 261.
30. See, for instance, the remarks of Brzezinski's deputy, David Aaron, in American Enterprise Institute, *Proceedings of the Symposium on Integrating American National Security Policy* (Washington, D.C.: AEI, 1980), p. 90.
31. There is, of course, no necessary correlation between a large NSC staff and NSC effectiveness. The Reagan NSC, for instance, grew to about seventy. Cf., Brzezinski, "NSC's Midlife Crisis," pp. 91, 97.
32. Lincoln P. Bloomfield, "What's Wrong with Transitions" *Foreign Policy* 55 (Summer 1984): 38; John Lewis Gaddis, "The Rise, Fall and Future of Detente," *Foreign Affairs* 62 (Winter 1983–84): 372.
33. Tower Commission Report, p. V–4.
34. Odeen, "The Role of the National Security Council," p. 23.
35. See ibid., pp. 23–24; Robert R. Bowie, "The President and the Executive Branch," in Joseph S. Nye, Jr., ed., *The Making of America's Soviet Policy* (New Haven, Ct.: Yale University Press, 1984), p. 66; Hunter, *Presidential Control of Foreign Policy*, pp. 15–16; I.M. Destler, "Reorganization: When and How?" in Peter Szanton, ed., *Federal Reorganization: What Have We Learned?* (Chatham, N.J.: Chatham House, 1981), pp. 114–15.
36. Odeen, "The Role of the National Security Council," pp. 22, 24.
37. *Report: Iran-Contra Affair*, pp. 16, 21; "Closing Statement by Rep. Hamilton," *Washington Post*, 22 July 1987, p. A8.
38. Issues that probably should have been "forced up" for decision in the Carter and first Reagan administrations are cited in Odeen, "The Role of the National Security Council," pp. 24–25; Odeen Report, pp. 9–10.
39. Of course, even the soundest analyses grounded in the most reliable information will not guarantee wise decisions. So David Stockman, who admits his own shortcomings in serving President Reagan, laments, "What do you do when your President ignores all the palpable, relevant facts and wanders in circles." (David A. Stockman, *The Triumph of Politics: Why the Reagan Revolution Failed* [New York: Harper & Row, 1986], p. 375).
40. Much of my treatment of this subject is drawn from Bock and Clarke, "The National Security Assistant," especially pp. 271–73, and Joseph G. Bock, *The White House and the National Security Assistant: Friendship and Friction at*

the Water's Edge (Westport, Ct.: Greenwood Press, 1987). See also, Samuel Kernell and Samuel L. Popkin, eds., *Chief of Staff: Twenty-Five Years of Managing the Presidency* (Berkeley: University of California Press, 1986).

41. Tower Commission Report, p. IV–11; McCombs, "McFarlane and the Web of Rumor," p. D1. Cf., Regan, *For the Record*, pp. 322–24, 364.
42. Peter Szanton, "So You Want to Reorganize the Government," in Szanton, *Federal Reorganization*, p. 9.
43. See, for example, Hunter, *Presidential Control of Foreign Policy*, p. 16. Hunter does not condone such behavior.
44. Brent Scowcroft, address at the National War College, Washington, D.C., 22 April 1983.
45. Quoted in Saul Pett, "Henry A. Kissinger: Loyal Retainer or Nixon's Svengali," *Washington Post*, 23 August 1970, p. B3.
46. Quoted in George C. Edwards III, *Implementing Public Policy* (Washington, D.C.: Congressional Quarterly Press, 1980), p. 5.
47. Murphy Commission, *Adequacy of Current Organization: Defense and Arms Control*, vol. 4, Appendix K (Washington, D.C.: Government Printing Office, 1975), p. 6.
48. Quoted in George Urban, "A Long Conversation with Dr. Zbigniew Brzezinski," *Encounter* 56 (May 1981): 29.
49. Murphy Commission, *Adequacy of Current Organization*, p. 45; Edwards, *Implementing Public Policy*, p. 155; Clark and Legere, *The President and the Management of National Security*, p. 28; Odeen, "The Role of the National Security Council," pp. 26–27; Morton H. Halperin, *Bureaucratic Politics and Foreign Policy* (Washington, D.C.: The Brookings Institution, 1974), pp. 279–93; Brzezinski, "NSC's Midlife Crisis," pp. 96–97.
50. Clark and Legere, *The President and the Management of National Security*, p. 29.
51. Henderson, *Managing the Presidency*, pp. 85–90.
52. Philip S. Kronenberg, "Planning and Defense in the Eighties," in Philip S. Kronenberg, ed., *Planning U.S. Security: Defense Policy in the Eighties* (Elmsford, N.Y.: Pergamon Press, 1982), pp. 148, 162–65; Murphy Commission, *Report*, pp. 144–45; Clarke, "Integrating Arms Control, Defense and Foreign Policy," pp. 15–16.
53. Murphy Commission, *Three Introductory Research Guidelines*, vol. 7, Appendix X (Washington, D.C.: Government Printing Office, 1975), p. 332.
54. For examples of past interagency crisis planning efforts, see Odeen, "The Role of the National Security Council," pp. 29–30.
55. Ibid., pp. 28–29; Odeen Report, pp. 33–37.
56. Kronenberg, "Planning and Defense in the Eighties," pp. 102, 107; Odeen, "The Role of the National Security Council," p. 27; Brzezinski, *Power and Principle*, p. 538.
57. For DOD objections, see Walter B. Slocombe and Franklin D. Kramer, "The Secretary of Defense and the National Security Process," in Clarke, *Public Policy and Political Institutions*, pp. 122–23.
58. See, and cf., Odeen, "The Role of the National Security Council," pp. 27,

30. Proposals for creating planning mechanisms among and within departments are also made by Hunter, *Managing National Security*, pp. 15–16, and Murphy Commission, *Report*, pp. 147–48.
59. Henry Kissinger, *White House Years* (Boston: Little, Brown, 1979), p. 396.
60. Brzezinski, *Power and Principle*, p. 46; see also, pp. 12, 45, 70–71, 456, and Brzezinski, "NSC's Midlife Crisis," p. 97.
61. Odeen, "The Role of the National Security Council," pp. 34–35.
62. John M. Collins, *U.S. Defense Planning: A Critique* (Boulder, Colo.: Westview Press, 1982), pp. 232–39.
63. Odeen, "The Role of the National Security Council," p. 35.
64. Stockman, *The Triumph of Politics*, pp. 283, 317.
65. Ibid., pp. 106–109, 278–99.
66. Odeen, "The Role of the National Security Council," pp. 31–33. For specific recommendations for instituting closer OMB-NSC relations, see Odeen Report, pp. 26–31; Murphy Commission, *Budgetary and Foreign Affairs Coordination*, vol. 6, Appendix T (Washington, D.C.: Government Printing Office, 1975), pp. 449–50.
67. Odeen, "The Role of the National Security Council," pp. 36–37.
68. For numerous specific examples of linkages between defense policies/programs and other substantive policy areas, as well as of the negative consequences of poor coordination, see Slocombe and Kramer, "The Secretary of Defense and the National Security Process," pp. 114–17, 124–25; Murphy Commission, *Adequacy of Current Organization*, pp. 21–23, 107–108; Odeen Report, pp. 18–27.
69. Odeen, "The Role of the National Security Council," pp. 37–38.
70. Lawrence J. Korb, *The Fall and Rise of the Pentagon: American Defense Policies in the 1970s* (Westport, Ct.: Greenwood Press, 1979), pp. 92–93; Henry Kissinger, *Years of Upheaval* (Boston: Little, Brown, 1982), p. 266; Clarke, "Integrating Arms Control, Defense and Foreign Policy," pp. 5–6; Richard A. Stubbing, *The Defense Game* (New York: Harper & Row, 1986), pp. 301–302.
71. Odeen, "The Role of the National Security Council," p. 37. Cf., Murphy Commission, *Report*, pp. 77–78.
72. Stephen D. Cohen, "Coordination and Integration of U.S. International Economic Policy," in Clarke, *Public Policy and Political Institutions*, pp. 237–39.
73. In the Ford and early Reagan administrations, the secretary of state boycotted this committee for a period of time. In neither instance did this further State's interests (Cohen, "Coordination and Integration of U.S. International Economic Policy," pp. 241, 253, 255). Treasury is not without problems of its own. Colin Campbell describes Treasury as "an unwieldy conglomerate" that "finds it difficult enough to coordinate its own affairs, let alone take the lead in integrating an administration's economic policy" (Colin Campbell, S.J., *Managing the Presidency: Carter, Reagan, and the Search for Executive Harmony* [Pittsburgh, Pa.: University of Pittsburgh Press, 1986], pp. 264–65).
74. Cohen, "Coordination and Integration of U.S. International Economic Policy," pp. 243–44; Hunter, *Presidential Control of Foreign Policy*, pp. 50–51;

Kissinger, *White House Years*, pp. 950–51; Brzezinski, *Power and Principle*, pp. 60–61.

75. See Murphy Commission, *Report*, pp. 6–7; Hunter, *Managing National Security*, p. 17; Cohen, "Coordination and Integration of U.S. International Economic Policy," pp. 261–66.

CHAPTER 2

The Office of Management and Budget: Review of Defense Budgets and Programs

with Elizabeth Johnson Barber

There is no detailed study of the important relationship between the Office of Management and Budget and the national security bureaucracy.[1] This chapter, which focuses on various relationships between OMB and the Department of Defense, is a "first."[2] Because of the subject's complexity, the chapter is both condensed and selective, yet it raises most of the truly vital issues in this relationship. It also touches upon various problems within DOD (all of which have been exhaustively addressed by others) and examines issues internal to OMB and the Executive Office of the President (many of which have not been adequately addressed).

Budgetary control is a principal vehicle for policy control. Moreover, control of budget formulation (a shared executive-legislative function) and budget execution (an executive function) affords an *opportunity* for better integrating the many strands of national policy. OMB is the president's central, White House–level staff for budgetary matters. Its role or nonrole in the budgetary process bears critically on the federal budget's coherence, fiscal affordability, prospects of passage in Congress, and effective implementation.

The policy control afforded through the budget process was one reason the budgeting and management functions were originally colocated within the old Bureau of the Budget (BOB), and later, within OMB. It was hoped that budget examiners would identify problems that OMB's management experts could address and that the latter's association with the budget process would give them sufficient clout to implement needed changes.[3] It was not unreasonable to expect that, through the budget process and (a critical assumption) with presidential support, OMB might play a major role in better integrating defense budgets and programs with overall presidential policies and objectives. Indeed, such a role was consistent with the responsibility assigned the new OMB when it was created in 1970: to assist the president—who can delegate any of his management responsibilities to OMB—in developing and maintaining effective government by reviewing the organizational structure and management procedures of the executive branch so they will produce the intended results.[4]

However, in the defense area and, to varying degrees, in other national security areas as well, these initial expectations went unrealized. OMB's integrative role has been disappointing, and it has had little impact on DOD management practices.

OMB and Defense Budget Formulation

OMB's National Security Division

OMB is responsible for annually reviewing the defense budget before its submission to Congress and for working with DOD on management initiatives. Since OMB's creation, management and budget functions sometimes have been colocated in the same division and at other times have been located on separate "sides" of the organization. One of OMB's four major units on the budget side is the National Security and International Affairs Division, headed by an associate director who is a political appointee. This division is subdivided into the National Security Division and the International Affairs Division, each headed by deputy associate directors who are senior career civil servants. The former reviews DOD and intelligence community programs and budgets. The latter is responsible for other agencies and programs with international missions: the State Department, economic development, security assistance, and so forth. Since the late 1970s these two divisions have not interacted closely with each other.[5]

The Office of the Secretary of Defense (OSD) allocates DOD resources through the triphased Planning, Programming and Budgeting System (PPBS).[6] Each phase presents problems for effective OMB and/or OSD review.

Planning Phase. A basic document in the planning phase is the Defense Guidance (DG)—formerly the Consolidated Guidance—

which defines the national security threat against which DOD programs are supposedly measured and provides objectives, strategy, and resource guidance. The DG is developed by a steering group composed of major OSD elements, the Joint Chiefs of Staff, and the military services. It is then reviewed by the Defense Resources Board (DRB) and sent to the secretary, who reviews and signs it by late February.[7] OMB's associate director for national security and international affairs became a formal DRB member in the Reagan administration, thereby affording OMB an opportunity to review the DG before the secretary signs it.[8] But the planning phase has at least two major problems that contribute to inadequate linkage between it and subsequent programming and budgeting decisions.

First, OSD does not assume a strong leadership role in developing program priorities *from* national security objectives. Instead, OSD immerses itself in programmatic and budgetary details from which an overall military plan might later be deduced. In short, the cart is placed before the horse. A second problem is that planning reflects the reluctance of the services to question one another's programs and make difficult tradeoffs among these programs. Rather, each service accepts virtually all program proposals of the other services. Hence, the JCS unrealistically assumes the availability of resources for service programs that, in fact, are not and never can be there. Not surprisingly, therefore, these JCS decisions are largely ignored by OSD in the programming and budgeting phases. Actual national military force planning is the product of OSD discussions with individual services. These separate plans, to put it charitably, hardly contribute to coherent, joint, national military planning.[9]

Programming Phase. During the programming phase, the services and Defense agencies develop their Program Objective Memorandums (POMs) projecting the cost and manpower estimates required to implement their assigned DG objectives. The POMs are submitted in May to the DRB for review. The DRB is supposed to ensure POM consistency with the DG and fiscal constraints and guard against duplications, overlaps, and missed opportunities for economies and efficiencies. OMB can nominate any issue it considers to be a problem for DRB review; in practice, these are usually items whose cost exceeds $50 million. Review results are completed by mid-August and forwarded to the secretary, who makes any necessary changes to the POMs through Program Decision Memorandums (PDMs). The POMs, as amended by PDMs, then become the basis for the 15 September budget submissions to the DOD comptroller from all DOD elements.[10]

OMB's effectiveness in this phase is seriously impeded by overly optimistic fiscal guidance from the secretary and by service underestimates of projected costs. The secretary issues fiscal guidance to the services according to how much he *hopes* to get, rather than on the basis of a realistic estimate of what DOD is *likely* to receive. This partly reflects his preparation for and anticipation of congressional budget cuts. But the practice is an expensive one. It means that the secretary often approves more programs than can, in fact, be purchased. Programs must then be cut back or stretched out, thereby driving up long-term costs. Moreover, optimistic initial guidance disrupts planning. POM development and review is a time-consuming, painstaking process undertaken each spring. If planning figures are substantially reduced in December, DOD does not have time to make sound, carefully considered program cuts.[11] While OMB fully understands the importance of realistic early fiscal guidance by the secretary, it lacks the political leverage to change this customary practice.

A second programming problem is the tendency of the services to underestimate the costs of purchasing and operating future programs and to exclude cost estimates of accompanying support programs. Here, OMB scrutiny could be useful and could help ensure that the armed forces have adequate spare parts and repair facilities.

Budgeting Phase. When the final PPBS phase, budgeting, begins in mid-September, OMB goes to the Pentagon for a "joint review" with OSD in which service budgets are examined for cost, feasibility, scheduling, and consistency with established policies. The OMB staff prepares papers for the OMB director on troublesome, budget-related issues. The director and the secretary then try to reach agreement on these issues. Matters that cannot be settled at this level are elevated to the president for decision. In early December, DOD receives changes to its proposed budget resulting from OMB's revised economic assumptions and presidential decisions on fiscal levels and programs.[12]

Several aspects of the budgeting phase bear importantly on OMB's role.

Revisiting Decisions. One consideration is whether decisions made during the programming phase should later be "revisited" in budgeting. When PPBS was instituted in 1961, it was expected that senior DOD officials would evaluate alternative programs in the programming phase, and that these would simply be costed out mechanically in the budgeting phase. But it has not worked that way. In practice, the only issues not subsequently raised again (revisited) during budgeting are those in which the secretary was personally involved in the earlier programming phase. Thus, the services criticize PPBS for allegedly wasting time in revisiting "settled" issues. This trend continues even though OMB was given formal membership on the DRB partly in the hope that its active participation in programming decisions would prevent their being revisited in budgeting.

Yet, a strong case can be made that OMB and the president should view the revisiting tendency as a *strength* of the budgeting phase andact accordingly. Economic conditions do change, with obvious implications for the projected costs of individual programs. Therefore, at least some previous decisions should be reevaluated.[13]

Joint Review. It is doubtful that the strengths of the joint review outweigh its weaknesses. The joint review is unique to DOD; all other agencies and departments submit their budgets to OMB for independent scrutiny.

The case for the joint review is essentially twofold. Many within OSD and OMB assert that the complexity of the defense budget precludes any other realistic alternative. In addition, some OMB analysts argue that the joint review permits OMB to become involved in defense questions before the secretary is committed to certain positions, thereby maximizing OMB's impact. But other experienced observers describe the so-called joint review as essentially an OSD review—one in which OSD does 95 percent of the review while OMB staffers are observers making only minor contributions. OMB's small staff size and relative lack of technical expertise means that its budget examiners are overshadowed and frequently co-opted by OSD. These are weighty criticisms that strongly suggest the advisability of terminating the joint review. OMB would be less prone to co-option if it ceased giving DOD special treatment and conducted an independent review of its budget. If staff size and expertise are problems, they should be augmented.[14]

OMB Acquiescence on Budget Authority. In the Reagan administration, OMB focused principally on DOD's budget outlays (what the Pentagon actually spends in a given year) because of their direct, near-term effect on the economy and federal deficits.[15] However, because OSD requires stable, reliable, longer range funding for programs like weapons systems, *its* major budgetary focus is on Total Obligational Authority (TOA), since budget authority amounts to a deposit in DOD's bank account from which individual programs can withdraw funds in the future. Because of this relative difference in emphasis, OMB/DOD budget disputes are often resolved through OMB consent to increased TOA—called "side payments"—in return for DOD agreement to outlay reductions. But when OMB yields on budget authority it runs a real risk that the administration will thereby not only lose effective control over future defense expenditures but compromise its ability to make future tradeoffs between defense and domestic programs. This is essentially what happened in 1981 when, with President Reagan's backing, DOD agreed to a modest cut in defense outlays in exchange for a TOA figure that was a $4 billion *more* than even the so-called "blue sky" requests of the military departments.[16]

Weapons Acquisition

Weapons systems costing more than $100 million in research and development or more than $500 million in procurement are subject to periodic program review by the Defense Systems Acquisition Review Council (DSARC).* DSARC evaluates each major weapons system using a series of "decision milestones" that begin with the program's initiation and extend through full-scale development. At each milestone, DSARC considers a program's status and readiness to proceed to the next phase in the acquisition process.[17] OMB is neither a member of DSARC nor a major player in acquisition decisions, even though these decisions have a fundamental impact on the size and shape of the defense budget.

Several features of the weapons acquisition process require

---

*The DSARC was supplanted in 1986 by the Joint Requirements and Management Board (possibly to be renamed the Defense Acquisition Board), chaired by a new under secretary for acquisition. For convenience, the acronym DSARC will be employed in this book.

greater attention by the White House-OMB and/or OSD.[18] For instance, OSD's failure to ensure that specific acquisition decisions are clearly related to reasonably defined national security objectives effectively permits (and compels) the services to develop weapons independently according to their own core missions and their own sense of national priorities. Joint requirements are slighted or ignored. Moreover, the services often remain committed to systems that have little relationship to national objectives, perform poorly, or experience excessive cost overruns. Without effective OSD guidance and oversight, there is no assurance that the weapons procured will meet truly *national* defense priorities.

Another problem is that there is often an imperfect linkage between the weapons acquisition process and PPBS. When DSARC approves a program, the acquisition community assumes, or would like to assume, that funds will be available throughout the budget process to finance it. But this assumption is ill founded when a program is identified too late in the PPBS cycle to be included in the service POM. When this occurs, the program may be inadequately funded. Indeed, budget problems frequently arise when large numbers of underfunded systems reach full-scale development and production phases within a short period of time. While low-priority programs *could* be cut back or terminated to provide needed funds, in practice, the absence of timely, committed resources to fund programs has meant that DSARC-approved programs are merely delayed or stretched out, thereby raising costs.

Finally, initial cost estimates for weapons are habitually understated. For example, Congress has been regularly asked to appropriate more funds for weapons programs than had been originally budgeted—by an annual average of 32 percent from 1963 to 1983. Even so, the services were often unable to purchase the quantity of weapons initially planned.

Constraints on and Within OMB

Poor Coordination Between OMB's Two "Sides." OMB has never been clear on how or whether to meld its two functional activities—management and budget. At first, these two functions were assigned to separate sides of the organization. But it was soon evident that they did not communicate systematically with one another and that there was confusion about how to improve management through the budget process and, indeed, about what *management* meant. To address these problems, Budget Director Roy Ash merged the management and budget sides in 1973, thereby establishing management divisions alongside program divisions under each of OMB's associate directors. But this, too, failed to improve internal coordination, partly because many budget officers felt that management people wasted much of their time on unrealistic initiatives, and many management specialists believed they were more effective when they were more independent of the budget function (so they would not be seen by the agencies as "spies" for the budget side).[19]

In the Carter administration, although each of the four major divisions on the budget side retained a management unit, OMB was essentially redivided into two halves, with the traditional budget function on one side and the management and reorganization effort on the other. The management side spent most of its time on reorganization, the utility of which was regarded with some skepticism by OMB's national security budgeting personnel. Once again, there was little constructive exchange between these two groups. Budget Director James McIntyre was aware of this lack of coordination, thought it should be addressed, but had no time to do so.[20]

This organization of OMB remained basically intact during the Reagan administration and continued to be poorly coordinated. A former management adviser to the Reagan OMB said that OMB "has shrunk its staff resources, narrowed the range of its interests and lost relevance with the agencies. Even inside OMB there seems to be no clear pattern of how management and budget problems should be related, nor is there a well-developed sense of how their respective staffs need to work together."[21]

The National Academy of Public Administration, noting that OMB had lost its effectiveness in governmentwide management matters, recommended transferring this function from OMB to a new office of federal management to be located in the Executive Office of the President.[22] But this proposal seems inadvisable. Most presidents devote little sustained attention to management matters. If an already established, integral component of the White House, one with "management" in its very title, cannot arouse presidential interest, it is unlikely that a new and separate office could do so. An office of federal management would still have to work with those with budget responsibility. But coordination between two completely separate organizational entities would surely be more difficult than coordinating within a single unit. Finally, the new office would lack the clout that accompanies (or could accompany) close association with the budget. In short, OMB should probably retain the management function.

Constraints on OMB's Management Function. The management side is the sister not asked to the prom, especially when the ballroom is at the Pentagon.[23] And it is gun-shy. When DOD cries that (to use a commonly heard refrain) OMB "is getting into our knickers," management specialists run for cover even faster than budget examiners because they know from experience that presidents almost invariably side with the secretary. Also, the budget gets first priority within OMB. The press of budget deadlines and the accompanying heavy workload overwhelm management concerns and leave OMB's leadership with little time for, or sometimes, as in the Reagan years, interest in defense management issues. Compounding matters is the low esteem budget examiners have for their inelegant sister. Finally, management matters require OMB to assume an unaccustomed stance. That is, OMB's usual budget posture is negative: "No, you cannot have more money." But management initiatives often call for a more positive, creative stance.[24]

Constraints on OMB's Budgetary Function. The budget side is the fairer sister and is sometimes asked to Pentagon dances, but only to a select few. Yet she, too, is shy, her partners are limited, she has an early curfew, and her father often seems more interested in brass and braid than his daughter's welfare. So OMB's National Security Division is regularly rebuffed by DOD on even those defense *policy* questions with obvious budgetary implications, especially when these implications are not immediately and explicitly budget-related. The Pentagon does not consider OMB a legitimate player on such issues. To raise a "policy" question concerning, for instance, the relative costs of alternative force structures in Europe, OMB officials must usually work behind the scenes with similarly inclined DOD officials or, less frequently, the NSC staff.[25] In practice—certainly in the Reagan administration, but not necessarily in other administrations—DOD, not OMB, determines which policy issues are off-limits for review by OMB.[26] The wisdom of continuing a practice that sustains a unique degree of DOD sovereignty over defense policy matters with budget ramifications seems highly questionable.

One of OMB's priorities in conducting DOD budget reviews is to keep the president out of political trouble. He must not be subjected to charges by political opponents that he is "weak on defense," that national security is being "held hostage" to the budget. Of course, as the Reagan administration illustrates, a president may also be embarrassed politically by runaway deficits fueled by high defense expenditures and gross Pentagon mismanagement. But presidents know that it is politically safer to err on the side of a "strong defense."

Another OMB concern is self-preservation, that is, keeping *itself* out of trouble. It therefore often approaches defense issues cautiously.

DOD generally considers OMB's role legitimate in two areas —total defense spending levels and such personnel matters as salaries and benefits. The president's final decision on the defense budget's size normally reflects some degree of compromise between the competing advice of the secretary of defense and the OMB director (although President Reagan regularly sided with Defense Secretary Caspar Weinberger). Usually, DOD is granted a small increase over the president's initial defense budget target.

OMB's involvement in assessing selected weapons programs and readiness and modernization issues varies from administration to administration, depending on the inclination and support of the president. In the Nixon, Ford, and Carter years, OMB challenged a number of dubious programs. While DOD usually defeated these challenges, OMB's position was occasionally sustained by the President—for example, Carter's 1978 cancellation of the short-range AMST transport plane. In the Reagan administration, however, OMB was directed not to challenge weapons programs. Its role was restricted to merely identifying a system's impact on the federal deficit. Depending on a president's sympathies, as was particularly evident in the Reagan years, OMB must exercise care in raising cost issues and, especially, in questioning the appropriateness of defense programs, lest it be accused of intruding into matters "better left to military judgement."[27]

Caution in clashing with the Pentagon is also advisable because presidents generally side with their defense secretaries on budget and program issues. Said former Defense Secretary Robert McNamara: "I can't remember a single instance in which the Bureau of the Budget and I differed on a recommendation in which the President accepted the Bureau's . . . view."[28] While McNamara's successors have not all pitched perfect games, OMB knows, in the (somewhat exaggerated) words of former OMB official W.Bowman Cutter, that "it can win them all with domestic agencies and is much less likely to win *any* with Defense."[29] Among the reasons presidents tend to side with their secretaries are: perceptions that it is politically advantageous to do so; genuine substantive agreement with DOD's position; dependence on certain information or services that only DOD can provide; concern that overruling the secretary may signal lack of confidence in him; and closer personal relations with the secretary than with the OMB director.

But always saying yes to Defense may jeopardize the prospects for a sound economy, effective civilian control of the military establishment, and an efficient, cost-effective military capability. Sooner or later it may even be a political boomerang. Moreover, while virtually all presidents have attended to defense *totals*, chief executives tend to give relatively less attention to defense *programs*, unless the programs are very large or politically controversial. With presidential backing and an adequate staff, OMB could be far more effective in challenging wasteful defense programs and mismanagement. But both of these preconditions for greater effectiveness are often in short supply.

Heavy Workload, Small Staff. OMB's already substantial responsibilities were increased sharply with the passage of the Congressional Budget Impoundment and Control Act of 1974 (P.L. 93-344). Among other things, the act requires OMB to report periodically to Congress on a variety of budget issues and to present the president's budget to Congress cast in terms of functional categories and its fulfillment of national needs. Moreover, the act's creation of new House and Senate budget committees and the Congressional Budget Office (CBO) augmented Congress's capability and involvement in budget matters. OMB consults actively with Congress both before the presentation of the president's budget and during congressional budget deliberations.[30]

Despite this heavy workload, the number of authorized positions in OMB declined from 682 in 1977 to 594 in 1985, and only 560 slots were actually occupied in 1985. The National Security and International Affairs Division shrank from 84 to 52 people (including administrative personnel) during this period; 31 of these 52 individuals were in the National Security Division. By April 1987 the National Security Division had a mere 25 professionals.[31] In short, during the Reagan administration—which featured huge defense budgets—OMB lacked the staff capability to perform adequately. There was little chance that OMB could have done a credible job reviewing defense budgets and programs even if it had been encouraged to do so, which was emphatically not the case.

Congress and OMB. Congress has generally resisted enlarging the size of OMB's staff. Moreover, because congressional access to and influence with DOD are enhanced by DOD's relative decentralization and pluralism, OMB attempts to improve White House and OSD direction and to streamline Pentagon management practices may encounter opposition in Congress.[32] However, the public and congressional mood shifted noticeably by the second Reagan term, partly because of glaring cost overruns, the defense budget's supposed impact on the escalating federal deficit, $600 toilet seats, and pervasive DOD mismanagement (highlighted in 1986 by President Reagan's own Blue Ribbon Commission on Defense Management—the Packard Commission). Moreover, the Balanced Budget Act (1985), popularly known as Gramm-Rudman-Hollings, mandated automatic defense cuts when federal spending exceeded mandated deficit targets; the House and Senate Armed Services Committees were pushing aggressively for organizational and managerial reform in several defense sectors; and Congress passed major JCS reform legislation in 1986.[33]

Of course, none of this necessarily translates into an upgraded OMB role vis-à-vis Defense. In the Reagan administration it certainly did not. Even if Congress is receptive to such a role, the president must be supportive.

But history indicates that organizational and managerial reforms left wholly to DOD to institute and implement are unlikely to be very effective. DOD's resistance to change is too pervasive. There must be outside monitoring and oversight. This means that

Congress and the president must take an active, continuing interest in the subject. Within the executive branch, the only unit, despite its limitations, with the *potential* capability to keep DOD honest is OMB. Neither DOD's budgetary and programmatic abuses nor its management problems are likely to be addressed satisfactorily if this potential continues to be ignored.

Federal Procurement

OMB'S Office of Federal Procurement Policy

Congress enacted legislation in 1969 to create the Commission on Government Procurement. A well-staffed, twelve-member commission with legislative, executive, and private-sector membership convened that year to systematically review government procurement policies and practices.

Commission Findings and Recommendations. The commission found that a major source of procurement problems was the conflict between two nonconforming statutes with more than thirty inconsistencies between them: the Armed Services Procurement Act of 1947 and the Federal Property and Administrative Services Act of 1949, which, together, provided the foundation for government contracting and regulation issuance. The complexities and inconsistencies of procurement regulations proliferated further when regulations were tailored to meet the unique requirements of individual governmental units. A contracting officer at the U.S. Army's Electronics Command, for instance, was responsible for knowing and applying a five-foot–long maze of procurement regulations. Moreover, in addition to the two basic statutes, over 4000 other provisions of law related to federal procurement.[34] This bewildering profusion of regulations and the absence of an identifiable executive branch focal point for procurement confused government agencies and private contractors, contributed enormously to procurement-related costs (25 percent of the 1972 federal budget went for procurement), and resulted in serious inefficiencies.[35]

The commission's 1972 report concluded that an integrated system for managing and operating the federal procurement process was imperative and that what would be the Office of Federal

Procurement Policy (OFPP) was "urgently needed." It suggested that OFPP reconcile inconsistent procurement policies and make final decisions on irreconcilable executive branch differences on procurement policy and regulatory development. The commission developed 149 other recommendations, including enactment of legislation to consolidate the military and civilian procurement statutes and the establishment of a system of uniform procurement regulations.[36] Although some OFPP supporters opposed locating it in OMB (fearing procurement would receive insufficient attention), the commission favored the OMB location because of OMB's governmentwide policy and management responsibility, its demonstrated ability to promote interagency coordination, and its supposed objectivity in procurement matters.[37]

OFPP's Creation.   Leading defense contractors and trade associations strongly endorsed an OFPP, hoping it would simplify a complex regulatory system that cost them $4.4 billion in 1969 in management systems alone. But the only executive unit that supported the proposal was the General Services Administration (GSA). OMB wanted procurement responsibilities to remain with the operating agencies or, at the very least, to reside outside of OMB. Officially, OMB's opposition rested upon the assertion that it lacked the expertise and manpower. But another concern was unspoken: that an OFPP created by legislation and housed within OMB would make OMB directly answerable to Congress.

The Pentagon was adamantly opposed to an OFPP and started shooting at the idea even before the commission issued its report. DOD asserted that the existing procurement system was working well and that procurement was its responsibility, not an OFPP's. There was concern that an OFPP, no matter where it was located, might threaten DOD's massive procurement bureaucracy, which was responsible for 75 percent of all government procurement.[38]

Despite OMB/DOD opposition, Congress enacted legislation in 1974 establishing the OFPP within OMB. It was authorized to establish a system of coordinated and (where feasible) uniform procurement regulations; establish criteria and procedures for timely solicitation of the viewpoints of interested parties on pending regulations; recommend and promote procurement training programs; monitor, revise, and research procurement policies and procedures; and establish a procurement data system. However,

OFPP's mandate was severely restricted. Its size was limited, reauthorization was required after five years, and it was directed not to interfere in an agency's or department's determination of need for property or services, nor to involve itself in specific procurement decisions.[39]

OFPP, 1974–1979. The seas were predictably turbulent during OFPP's maiden voyage. OFPP's first two administrators resigned after encountering vigorous objections from powerful members of Congress when they challenged excessive costs in defense procurement contracts. During the Carter administration, the office devoted more time to equal employment opportunity and anti-inflation matters than to procurement. When it tried to fulfill its mission, it was thwarted. For instance, when OFPP's third administrator, Karen Williams, sought to organize a federal acquisition regulation council in 1979 (representing the procurement agencies) for the purpose of developing uniform civilian and defense regulations, DOD refused to attend scheduled meetings and succeeded in aborting the effort.[40]

When OFPP came up for reauthorization in 1979, Congress stripped it of regulatory authority, thereby leaving the office with the authority to issue policy directives only with the concurrence of OMB's director. Congress, however, again directed OFPP to focus on developing a proposal for a single, comprehensive, governmentwide, uniform procurement system incorporating all elements and stages of the civilian and military acquisition process.[41]

Uniform Procurement System

DOD persistently attempted to undermine OFPP's efforts to develop a uniform procurement system proposal because this raised the prospect of both OFPP and congressional intervention in Pentagon procurement and management processes. Nevertheless, OFPP submitted a draft uniform procurement proposal to Congress in October 1981 that recommended enactment of either (a) a single consolidated statute for both civilian and military procurement—which, while supported by major defense industry associations and many civilian agencies, was considered by OFPP to be politically infeasible—or (b) dual, but conforming, statutes. DOD initially opposed both alternatives, asserting that the existing two procurement systems should remain in effect and that OFPP should have authority only over civilian procurement. However, when OMB Deputy Director Edwin Harper threatened in late 1981 to go to President Reagan with the matter, Deputy Secretary of Defense Frank Carlucci directed DOD to cooperate with the revision effort, thereby enabling OFPP to submit the final Uniform Federal Procurement System Proposal to Congress in February 1982.[42]

But this final proposal reflected OFPP's complete capitulation to DOD's position. It stipulated that the procurement system should be changed by merely amending existing statutes. Moreover, it vested authority for Federal Acquisition Regulation (FAR)—discussed below—development and promulgation jointly in DOD, GSA, and the National Aeronautics and Space Administration (NASA), with OFPP resolving only those disputes brought to its attention.[43] Congressman Jack Brooks, chairman of the House Government Operations Committee, denounced the proposal as violative of Congress's directive and as an unwarranted accommodation to DOD's insistence on its own separate procurement system.[44]

The proposal died in Congress. In March 1982, President Reagan did sign Executive Order 12352, establishing those elements of the proposed procurement system not requiring legislative action, but it had little real impact on procurement practices.

Federal Acquisition Regulation. The FAR is a cornerstone of the present government procurement system. When the process leading to its development was initiated by OFPP in 1978, the initial objective was to produce a single, governmentwide procurement regulation that would be applicable to all procuring agencies (with supplemental regulations to meet specific agency needs) and would consolidate 64,000 pages of defense and civilian regulations. The FAR was originally to be published in 1980, but bitter DOD opposition and constant DOD/OFPP squabbling postponed its appearance until April 1984.[45]

The FAR has reduced some inconsistencies among agency regulations but, on balance, it has clouded, not clarified, the procurement process. OFPP can assume a "leadership" role only if GSA, NASA, and DOD inform OFPP that they cannot agree on the FAR's content—something they are reluctant to do. Hence,

OFPP cannot investigate charges that, for example, DOD essentially reworked the language in its old regulations and created unnecessary supplemental regulations. OFPP is powerless to insist that supplemental regulations be granted only to meet an agency's truly unique needs. Consequently, the American Bar Association correctly concluded that a single, simplified, governmentwide acquisition regulation has *not* been achieved:

Instead, the FAR system consists of 17 procurement regulations, including a proliferation of voluminous agency acquisition regulations that are not required, and the result is little different from the pre-FAR era. In fact, contracting officers and industry must now cope with a massive bewildering set of new regulations on top of superseded regulations. . . . The FAR supplements presently exceed the FAR itself in sheer magnitude of pages.[46]

The Commission on Government Procurement's 1972 call to curb the "burdensome mass and maze of procurement and procurement-related regulations" remains unfulfilled.[47] Government contracting remains a bewildering and confusing process, and the FAR has actually reduced competition by making it even more difficult for all but the largest private contractors—who commonly employ about 120 contracting specialists—to do business with the government. Small firms with, say, five contracting specialists cannot afford to compete. Finally, the original hope that the FAR would permit more public participation in regulatory development has not been realized. Despite the FAR requirement for public participation, several agencies, including DOD, withhold their supplementary regulations from public comment.[48]

OFPP's 1983 Reauthorization

In 1983 OFPP was up for its second congressional reauthorization. A coalition of industry representatives, procurement professionals, the General Accounting Office (GAO), and several small agencies—all of whom sought cost-saving through procurement reform—urged Congress to create a vigorous OFPP *with regulatory authority*. Senator William Cohen was the leading advocate for this position.[49] DOD, of course, opposed granting OFPP regulatory authority or, indeed, reauthorizing it at all. Secretary of Defense Weinberger wrote Senator John Tower, Chairman of the

Senate Armed Services Committee, that if OFPP was given regulatory authority, Congress could not then "hold the Secretary of Defense accountable for meeting our national security requirements [because this] would put OFPP in a position to dictate how the U.S. should build forces to meet its defense needs."[50] Tower agreed with Weinberger. OMB, too, opposed granting regulatory authority, although it supported OFPP's reauthorization.

Senators Cohen and Tower then negotiated the Senate authorization bill. This version was enacted into law. It gave OFPP only very limited regulatory authority—to be used when DOD, NASA, and GSA were unable to agree on or failed to issue governmentwide regulations, procedures, and forms to be followed by the executive agencies. Furthermore, the OMB director was given authority to rescind procurement regulations, and OFPP was required to submit any major policy or regulation to Congress thirty days before its effective date.[51]

Hurry-up Spending

OFPP has been involved in procurement initiatives other than the Uniform Procurement System Proposal and the FAR project, but with little evident effect. Its efforts toward controlling "hurry-up" spending—the tendency for departments to spend all available funds toward the end of the fiscal year in order to ensure full funding for the next year—is illustrative. OFPP Policy Letter 81–1 (1981), supplemented by an additional letter from OMB Director David Stockman, specified procedures for detecting and preventing end-of-year procurement abuse. While the policy letter seemed initially to have some success, DOD rushed to spend funds before the end of the fiscal year ending 30 September 1983 (among other things, it purchased 57,600 softballs), and the Air Force purchased over $1 billion of spare parts in the last twelve days of 1985 (a tenfold increase over its normal buying pace).[52] It is doubtful that national security or public support for defense spending is furthered by showing the Soviets how fast the U.S. government can spend money.

The OFPP Experience

Perhaps the most telling critique of OFPP's performance was made by President Reagan's Packard Commission, which repeated the recommendation made fifteen years earlier by the Commission on Government Procurement. Stating that it was virtually impossible for operating levels within DOD to assimilate legislative or regulatory refinements promptly or effectively, the Packard Commission suggested that Congress work with the administration to recodify federal laws governing procurement into a single, greatly simplified statute applicable governmentwide.[53] Although President Reagan was receptive to the Packard Commission's report, DOD has long and successfully opposed this and other initiatives to improve the procurement process, and OFPP has always been considered the "black sheep of the OMB family."[54] By the second Reagan term, OFPP—weary from being beaten back repeatedly by DOD and lacking enthusiastic support from OMB— had become resigned. It was essentially folded into OMB's management side and did not even have an administrator from January 1985 to November 1986. OMB itself has not been on the cutting edge of procurement reforms, largely because such efforts are viewed as losing battles.[55]

Procurement reform, and the effectiveness of OFPP and OMB in this area, will continue to be a losing proposition unless there is sustained presidential commitment to work with the secretary of defense toward this end. Such commitment was not forthcoming from Presidents Nixon, Ford, Carter, or Reagan. This is, of course, a policy question, but it is also, fundamentally, a matter of process and management. In procurement reform, as in so many other vital areas, it is essential that a president take at least some personal interest in large management questions and in the functioning of his own policy process. Otherwise, wasteful and inefficient practices are likely to continue largely unabated.

Overview of OMB–White House–DOD Relations from the Nixon through the Reagan Administrations

Nixon Administration

In accordance with presidential preference, OMB had a modest role in most defense matters during the Nixon administration. Neither Nixon nor National Security Assistant Henry Kissinger were very interested in defense budget details, and they rarely challenged major DOD weapons decisions. While the President set the broad parameters of defense strategy and policy, Kissinger's preeminence in foreign policy did not extend to defense policy. Although Nixon spent twenty hours reviewing the 1971 federal budget, by 1974 his personal review lasted only ten hours.[56]

At first it looked as if the White House might play an active role in defense programs and budgets. As discussed in Chapter 1, the NSC's Defense Program Review Committee—chaired by Kissinger, with OMB membership—was initially intended to provide a senior-level forum for considering the defense budget and selected weapons programs and weighing defense needs against other national priorities. But, in practice, the DPRC never achieved its intended purpose.

Also, the incoming Nixon administration expressed dismay over DOD's de facto exemption from budgetary review during the Johnson years. Nixon introduced his first budget chief, Robert Mayo (1969–1970), on television with, "When Bob Mayo says something, I mean it."[57] This was followed by a 1969 presidential directive instructing the Bureau of the Budget to apply restrictive fiscal policies to *all* agencies and departments, which Mayo and James Schlesinger (who was then with BOB) correctly interpreted to include DOD. Indeed, there was more scrutiny of DOD's budget then ever before, although it was still rather scant compared with the scrutiny given to other departments. But Mayo soon learned that White House support for this effort was more apparent than real. Defense Secretary Melvin Laird (1969–1972), a master at bureaucratic politics and executive-legislative relations, skillfully fended off both OMB and the DPRC. Moreover, Nixon and Kissinger generally supported increased expenditures in non-Vietnam defense areas. Mayo had little access to Nixon, senior White House political aides H. R.("Bob") Haldeman and John Ehrlichman considered OMB too liberal, and Erlichman—at the second director's review meeting in 1970—even questioned OMB's loyalty to the President.[58]

George Shultz (1970–1972), Mayo's successor, had such excellent rapport with President Nixon that he was sometimes called an "assistant president." Shultz was regularly summoned to the Oval Office for consultation on matters ranging from budgetary policy to school desegregation. He was even sent on extended presidential missions overseas. Shultz's extra (non-OMB) responsibilities meant that OMB was essentially managed by a triumvirate of Shultz, Caspar Weinberger (Deputy Director for Budget), and Arnold Weber (Associate Director for Management). Because of Shultz's busy schedule, by 1971 Weinberger chaired the director's review meetings.[59]

Shultz and OMB were exceedingly influential on domestic matters, but this influence did not transfer to defense issues. Indeed, one of Shultz's few defeats as OMB director came when he failed in an effort to trim more than $1.5 billion from the Pentagon's 1972 budget request. When Shultz became secretary of the treasury in 1972, he was succeeded by his deputy, Caspar Weinberger, who served as director for only a few months.[60]

Roy Ash replaced Weinberger in late 1972 and served into the first year of the Ford administration. As President Nixon became preoccupied with the mounting Watergate crisis, he essentially disengaged from budget matters. While this afforded OMB greater leeway, Secretary of Defense James Schlesinger (who succeeded Laird) argued vigorously for increases in defense spending. Over Ash's objections, Nixon's final budget (FY 1974) held the line on defense while cutting many other federal programs.[61]

Ford Administration

President Ford's prior service on the House Defense Appropriations Subcommittee gave him an understanding of and interest in defense issues and the budget process. He believed that a president controls his administration through the budget. Ford devoted considerable personal attention to the budget and allotted time in his schedule for cabinet secretaries to bring budget appeals directly to him. He supported ample defense expenditures, but tried to balance this interest against the need for fiscal constraint brought on by an inflationary economy.[62]

James Lynn replaced Ash in 1974 as OMB director, a post that Ford considered particularly important. Lynn had access to the President and enjoyed a reasonably good relationship with him. The personal relationship between Ford and Defense Secretary Schlesinger was cool at the outset and deteriorated rapidly thereafter. Ford at first considered replacing Schlesinger, but kept him on until November 1985, when he was succeeded by the President's trusted friend, White House Chief of Staff Donald Rumsfeld.[63]

In early 1976, Ford initially agreed to Lynn's proposed reduction in FY 1977 defense TOA, but at Rumsfeld's urging, he later restored $3 billion of this amount. He also restored most of the military services' procurement items cut by OMB, but did uphold reductions in military salaries and perquisites. Ford was eyeing the 1976 election and feared that Schlesinger—who, when secretary, publicly advocated large defense increases—had made him appear "soft on defense." The defense numbers were raised partly to deflect criticism from his Republican primary opponent, Ronald Reagan.[64]

Carter Administration

President Carter's penchant for detail extended into the defense area. Unlike most presidents, he spent long hours on the defense budget and personally made many large and small defense decisions. OMB was more involved in defense matters during the Carter administration than at any other time since 1971. This was especially so under Director Thomas Bertram ("Bert") Lance who, because of his time-consuming role as close presidential political adviser, delegated considerable authority to OMB professionals. When Lance was forced to resign in September 1977, he was replaced by his deputy, James McIntyre, who enjoyed a cordial relationship with Defense Secretary Harold Brown.[65]

Development of Carter's first real defense budget (FY 1979) was contentious largely because of the President's own conflicting priorities and commitments. Candidate Carter had promised to eliminate waste in defense spending, balance the federal budget by FY 1981, and reduce the Ford administration's last budget (although Congress later cut that budget by $7 billion). But key Carter advisers opposed curtailing military spending, and the internal debate grew sharper when the President, in 1977, pledged NATO to increase real defense spending by 3 percent.

Presidential Directive 18 (PD-18) left unanswered questions regarding the NATO increases. It suggested a 3 percent increase in defense spending beginning in FY 1979. But it did not specify whether the entire budget or only NATO-related portions would be increased, nor whether the base year for the increase would be the FY 1978 budget submitted by the administration or the final budget as reduced by Congress. Consequently, the military services argued that the 3 percent applied to the administration's FY 1978 budget and requested $135 billion for FY 1979. OSD considered the figure that Congress had approved as the base and asked for $130 billion. OMB sought a $125 billion FY 1979 defense budget. Then, during the review, Carter established a $126 billion ceiling on defense spending for FY 1979.[66]

This matter spilled over into 1978, when Carter announced a deficit reduction program. Whereas McIntyre believed this program could be advanced through a $2 billion cut in DOD's budget, Harold Brown, supported by Secretary of State Cyrus Vance and NSA Zbigniew Brezezinski, wanted a 3 percent increase; White House political aides were divided on the issue. The dispute was never resolved before the matter went to the President. Carter, therefore, was burdened with having to conduct his final defense budget review (For FY 1980) from three separate and conflicting books (DOD's, OMB's, and the NSC's).[67]

Fueled partly by public feuding among some of its senior officials, the Carter administration was faulted for evident inconsistencies in some of its defense and foreign policies. Carter himself contributed to this perception. For example, Carter paid a well-publicized visit to a Navy task force in the Atlantic in March 1978 and there stated that the United States would match Soviet defense expenditures and force levels. However, contrary to the subsequent and understandable expectations of many in Congress, DOD, and elsewhere, he shortly thereafter proceeded to cut the Navy's budget. Again, in 1980, following Congress's addition of $3.7 billion in outlays to Carter's budget request, the President instructed McIntyre to hold a not-for-attribution briefing announcing his opposition to this action. But the next day Carter flew to the U.S.S. *Nimitz* to announce his support for a $700 million increase in military compensation that was *not* included in his budget.[68]

President Carter was interested in defense management and organization, although management remained very much a junior partner within OMB during his administration. Several thorough studies of this subject were prepared by outside consultants and DOD at the request of the President. OMB provided Carter with the rationale for the projects and monitored their preparation. Some of their findings, many of which were actively supported by the chairman of the JCS, General David Jones, laid much of the analytical groundwork for the DOD reorganization legislation enacted by Congress in 1986.

One study, directed by Philip Odeen with active assistance from OMB, dealt with a variety of national security integration and management issues. Odeen, a former OSD and NSC officer, was a partner of Coopers & Lybrand Management Consulting Group in Washington, D.C. He offered specific prescriptions—deserving of serious consideration even (and perhaps especially) today—for, among other things: closer involvement of OMB and other non-DOD actors in the weapons acquisition and defense budgetary processes, OMB-NSC cooperation, crisis planning, and improving the NSC's managerial and coordinative roles. The President approved all but one of Odeen's recommendations in 1980, but some measures were never fully instituted before the presidential election of that November. Those that were implemented died with the incoming Reagan administration.[69]

Reagan Administration

President Reagan was determined to increase defense spending sharply in order to meet what he considered to be an ominous Soviet military threat. Defense Secretary Caspar Weinberger worked incessantly toward this end.

The 1980 Republican Party platform had castigated OMB's "ill-formed, capricious intrusions" into defense budgets, programs, and management systems during the Carter administration.[70] This plank was soon operationalized. While David Stockman, Reagan's first OMB director, initially assumed unprecedented and public prominence in domestic policy matters, DOD was specifically and emphatically exempted from spending reductions and OMB "intrusions."[71] Only in the first few months of the administration did Stockman, who shared the President's desire for a strong defense, attempt to question defense issues. He soon discovered that Reagan would not overrule Weinberger. Thereafter, OMB's defense role was limited strictly to salaries, benefits, and (as best it might) the total defense spending level. When a disillusioned and frustrated Stockman left government in 1985, he was followed at OMB by a low-profile team player—James C. Miller III.[72]

Candidate Reagan had pledged a real growth in the defense budget of between 5 and 9 percent. When Weinberger and Stockman met in January 1981, they agreed on a figure of 7 percent. But Stockman miscalculated the budgetary base for this increase.

He quickly realized that he and Weinberger had, in fact, agreed upon an alarming 12 percent increase that had ominous implications for the federal deficit. In August 1981 Stockman prepared for the President a slower growth alternative that would have given DOD $1.33 trillion over five years instead of the $1.46 trillion that Stockman and Weinberger had agreed upon earlier. But, except for relatively insignificant trimming, Reagan ultimately sided with Weinberger. Throughout this and subsequent defense budget discussions, the President demonstrated scant knowledge of or interest in the subject. What he did know was that he wanted more for defense. Reagan apparently did not understand even such elementary considerations as the difference between constant and current dollars and the distinction between TOA and outlays. Moreover, the personal relationship between Weinberger and Stockman deteriorated into one of the most strained between a defense secretary and an OMB director in recent history.[73]

Weinberger prevailed with the President, but toward the end of the first Reagan term he encountered growing resistance, even antagonism, in Congress. As Congress became increasingly concerned about ballooning deficits, it asked the secretary to suggest areas where reasonable defense reductions could be made. But Weinberger demurred, reasoning that this would only whet Congress's appetite for more cuts. He adamantly maintained that even minor defense reductions posed clear and present dangers to the country. But in trying to defend everything, he lost credibility. His stance contributed importantly to weapons programs being cut back by Congress in a particularly inefficient manner—generally, by stretching them out and slowing production rates.[74] Many in OMB were deeply concerned about DOD's profligacy and Weinberger's approach to Congress, but the administration expected OMB to be a cheerleader for Defense and the President's budget.

Six years into the Reagan administration, the Packard Commission found DOD plagued with virtually all of the problems the administration had initially said it would address. Commission Chairman David Packard noted that poor overall defense planning, management, and budgeting practices wasted tens of billions of dollars. While most of these problems predated the Reagan years, neither Weinberger nor the President made any significant attempt—except belatedly, and under considerable pressure—to address them. In 1986 President Reagan directed DOD to institute the Packard Commission's central recommendations, but it was highly questionable whether they would be implemented effectively. In 1987 and 1988 the Pentagon, which had opposed the creation of the Packard Commission, successfully resisted key elements of the commission's acquisition reform proposals—by now embodied in both presidential directives and legislation. The commission reconvened in 1987 at the president's request to provide a progress report on implementation. That report was not optimistic about acquisition policy changes.[75]

President Reagan never did adjust his approach to defense. His unyielding position on the defense budget reflected his oft-remarked belief: "Defense is not a budget issue. You spend what you need."[76] Thus, he approved annual defense budgets without heeding Stockman's repeated warnings about how these defense decisions clashed directly with other high-priority administration policy objectives. Reagan supported Stockman's determined pursuit of social spending cuts, but DOD was off-limits. The President's unwillingness to touch defense, coupled with his dogged resistance to tax increases, probably helped to ensure that the deficit would loom as a long-range threat to the American economy.

The massive deficit also jeopardized, both politically and economically, the very defense program Reagan and Weinberger so badly wanted. A lower real growth rate—perhaps 3 percent annually—might have helped to avert this outcome. It bears repeating that grave problems are inevitable if a president does not take *some* interest in his own policy process, if he effectively gives DOD a free hand in determining its budget and program, and if he does not make even a minimal effort to educate himself on the most *basic* defense budgetary issues and nomenclature. Reagan's hands-off approach to DOD illustrates the dangers of effectively removing OMB from meaningful review of defense budgets and programs and of consistently acceding to the wishes of the secretary of defense. By 1985 many in the Pentagon must have regretted that the absence of central White House/OMB scrutiny permitted its profligacy to go unchecked.[77]

OMB was battered severely in the Reagan administration. The migration of analysts from its National Security Division came close to eliminating its ability to conduct analyses. But if there is to be a White House–level custodian of the principle that policy competence requires an ability to address the analytic dimension of issues, that custodian is OMB. The essential rationale for having an OMB remains secure, and that rationale is linked intrinsically to responsible leadership. A priority concern of succeeding administrations must be the rebuilding of the OMB.[78]

OMB's Role in Selected Defense Areas

Peter Szanton, former OMB associate director and head of reorganization studies in the Carter administration, offers several recommendations, here examined in some detail, for a president who is interested in augmenting OMB's role in defense and defense-related areas:[79]

- OMB should be active in overseeing changes in such areas as cost overruns, uncoordinated service programs, and threat inflation.
- OMB should pay more attention to possible "trade-offs" between defense and nondefense, security-related programs.
- The NSC and OMB should work more closely on select defense issues.

Cost Overruns

The Defense Department regularly underestimates the costs of proposed weapons systems. The consequent cost overruns have serious fiscal and other ramifications. There are numerous, often interrelated, causes of cost overruns, only some of which are briefly discussed here.[80]

Inflation Estimates. Prior to 1982 DOD was required to use OMB's inflation estimate in projecting program costs. Since this estimate was almost always lower than the actual inflation rate turned out to be, it contributed substantially to cost overruns, through no fault of the Pentagon. To meet this problem and to allow for the frequently greater inflation in various defense commodities than in the economy as a whole, DOD requested, and in 1982 received, a special inflation index (called a "deflator") unique to DOD. David Stockman had resisted this special index, arguing that it would *invite* defense industries to raise labor rates and overhead costs to the high inflation rate anticipated by the index, whether or not the actual inflation rate rose to the anticipated level. DOD, in fact, reaped a windfall when inflation turned out to be *lower* than predicted between 1982 and 1986. Before the index/deflator was discontinued in FY 1987, it provided DOD a bonanza of at least $37 billion![81]

Optimistic Initial Estimates. Contractors often consciously underestimate program costs in order to "buy into" new weapons programs (the so-called foot-in-the-door tactic). Their expectation is that subsequently, through frequent contract change orders, actual cost can *later* be recovered through various engineering and design changes. Among the reasons DOD tolerated this practice are the following:

- The services traditionally view cost factors as secondary to other considerations such as performance, keeping production lines open, and early delivery.
- The services' program managers have been rewarded less for keeping a weapons system's costs down than for their skill in convincing superiors to fund their program instead of someone else's, in ensuring the system's technical performance, in keeping the program "out of trouble" with Congress, and in adherence to delivery schedule.
- Low early cost estimates help the services obtain initial congressional funding for weapons programs.[82]

Qualitative Improvements/Goldplating. The weapons acquisition community tends to focus heavily on maintaining qualitative supremacy over an enemy that is thought to enjoy quantitative advantages. The services define their requirements in terms of technology that is "better," not just "good enough." Engineers tend to overdesign a system, expecting to overcome subsequent problems in the development phase. Contractors know they are more likely to obtain a contract by promising to advance the state of the art. This tendency ("goldplating") is expensive partly because complex weapons require costly engineering and support changes during development. In addition, pushing the state of the art results in the "last 5 percent syndrome"—the tendency for the last 5 percent improvement in performance to result in a

30 to 50 percent increase in costs.[83] Said the Packard Commission: "All too often, requirements for new weapons systems have been overstated. This had led to . . . higher cost equipment. Such so-called goldplating has become deeply embedded in our system."[84]

Program Stretchouts. Program stretchouts occur when production rates for a system must be slowed. Stretchouts contribute to cost overruns. As explained above, they often result from an inadequate linkage between the acquisition process and PPBS.

OMB Impact on Cost Overruns. Szanton suggests that OMB could impose "pricing realism" on DOD because it is skilled in cost analysis, familiar with cost increases, and largely free of the pressures that affect contractors and the services to underestimate costs.[85] Prior to 1981, at which time it was compelled to ignore the subject, OMB often recommended discontinuing weapons programs because of gross cost overruns. But this was never a high-priority function. When OMB succeeded in curbing cost overruns, it was generally because it allied with OSD units like the Office of Program Analysis and Evaluation or the Office of the Comptroller. Moreover, some, like Franklin Spinney, a senior OSD systems analyst, argue that OMB may be unable to substantially expand its role in this area because it generally lacks the requisite depth in defense expertise and is ever vulnerable to the charge that its analysts are mere "bean counters" treading on issues better left to military judgment. Indeed, even if the president directed OMB to enforce pricing realism on DOD, the Pentagon would likely mobilize its forces to fight the initiative in Congress. This might defeat the effort and perhaps embarrass the president politically.[86]

Service Autonomy

Despite an unbroken trend in legislation since 1947—and particularly since 1958—toward centralizing de jure Pentagon authority in the secretary of defense, the de facto independence of the four military services, certainly in the weapons acquisition sector, remains a pervasive reality. This leads to mission and program duplication in some areas; neglect of critical missions when such missions fall outside the services' traditional roles; development of systems that are not interoperable among the services; seriously inadequate coordination and information exchange within the weapons acquisition community; and the development of weapons according to the services' own sense of priorities, even when these systems bear little systematic relationship to *national* objectives, perform poorly, or experience excessive cost overruns. This inefficient autonomy sharply increases the cost of national defense and often impairs overall combat effectiveness. The secretary of defense has the legal authority to substantially rectify this situation. But successive secretaries have lacked the will, interest, or requisite political support to do so.[87]

Szanton, and Admiral Alfred Thayer Mahan before him, rightly asserts that no military service is going to reform itself from within. Indeed, few secretaries have seriously challenged the services' relative sovereignty in the weapons acquisition area. This is why the new position of under secretary of defense for acquisition, created in 1986 by the Goldwater-Nichols Department of Defense Reorganization Act, is unlikely to resolve this core problem. If service programs and budgets are to be better integrated with one another, determined and prolonged White House pressure will be necessary. Szanton therefore recommends that a supportive president direct OMB to oversee such integrative efforts by the secretary and the services. He further recommends that OMB compare force levels with readiness expenditures, assess the compatibility of service programs, and weigh the consistency of budget implementation with budget requests.[88]

Lack of service integration is clearly a major problem. It is also one of the most intractable. Even with presidential backing, OMB questioning of military requirements will be adamantly resisted by the services (and probably by the secretary of defense) since requirements determinations are core service activities. While OMB has important roles to play here, fundamental change can only be authorized and pushed by the president who, in turn, must work most closely not with the OMB director but with a supportive secretary of defense. That military requirements are core service functions makes change exceedingly difficult. But continued, unquestioning deference to the services on requirements gives away the store.

As long as this problem remains unaddressed, national (as opposed to service) interests will suffer. The need for change is clear. Said the Packard Commission in the first substantive sentence of its report to President Reagan: "The Commission finds that there is a great need for improvement in the way we think through and tie together our security objectives, what we spend to achieve them, and what we decide to buy."[89] It would be tragic if only a prolonged economic depression, a series of global political-military setbacks, or a massive scandal of unprecedented scale could provide sufficient political stimulus for reform. But the persistent absence of political will to alter the status quo suggests that this may, indeed, be what has to happen.

Threat Inflation

The proclivity of the Defense Intelligence Agency (DIA) and service intelligence units to inflate the Soviet threat is widely acknowledged, sometimes even by senior Defense intelligence officials. Overestimating the threat exerts a formidable push toward large service budgets since the estimates are employed by OSD and the services to justify increased funding from Congress and the president.[90]

Szanton suggests that OMB play a role in challenging exaggerated threat estimates.[91] Prior to the Reagan administration, OMB did occasionally bring such matters to the president's attention, but usually without much effect. Some presidents *want* inflated threat estimates in order to build support for the defense budget in Congress and with the public.[92] Moreover, the secretary of defense, the military services, the DIA—and possibly other members of the intelligence community—would object vigorously to OMB's active entry into this area.

OMB has—or, with additional staff and funds, could have—expertise in defense budgetary, programmatic, and management matters. But it is not and should not be viewed as a member of the intelligence community. A president concerned about DOD "threat inflation" is best advised to turn to the Director of Central Intelligence (DCI), the Central Intelligence Agency, the President's Foreign Intelligence Advisory Board, or some other intelligence entity for an alternative perspective. Within the intelligence community, unanimity on threat estimates or on most other intelligence products is a rarity. Such diversity of opinion affords choices for policymakers (intelligence consumers) in search of "the truth."

National Security Trade-offs

Szanton calls for OMB to become involved in recommending conceivable "trade-offs" between defense and other security-related government activities and programs.[93] There are many possibilities. For example, $1 billion might be shifted from DOD's budget (about one-third of one percent of military spending) to the Agency for International Development for economic assistance to impoverished nations in Central America. There was virtually no coordination, or trade-offs anywhere in government, between foreign assistance and defense budgets and programs during the Reagan administration.[94] And Richard Stubbing, who supports Szanton's proposal, relates that in his twenty years with OMB, he never witnessed an explicit budgetary trade-off between DOD and other national security agencies. Says Stubbing:

Budgets were decided on an individual-agency basis with the relative balance among the agencies an after-the-fact accident. The OMB staff posed the possibility of cross-agency budgetary tradeoffs in national security to several administrations, but in each instance this approach was dismissed as a basis for decision. Even in the halcyon days of budgetary tradeoffs from 1977 to 1980 when zero-based budgeting was in favor, defense was deliberately *excluded* from priority ranking in the overall budget for the federal government. Thus the President is never presented with a comprehensive set of possible budgetary actions affecting national security.[95]

There should be some more-or-less systematic procedure for considering such trade-offs. Perhaps a senior interagency group roughly analogous to the Nixon administration's DPRC, chaired by the NSA or OMB director with an explicit presidential mandate to weigh trade-offs among security programs, could play a useful role if it had active White House support. But, as the Carter administration's experience with Zero-Based Budgeting (ZBB) illustrates, OMB's role would have to be limited.

The Carter administration attempted to make interagency program trade-offs through ZBB. Each agency was required to evaluate its programs, identifying those that should be discontinued or continued at reduced or increased funding levels. Agencies developed "decision packages": several alternative budgets presenting various methods of executing programs at different funding levels—for example, a program might be funded at 75, 100, or 125 percent of its current level. OMB then attempted to make interagency trade-offs by comparing and assessing these agency decision packages.

But ZBB did not settle any *important* trade-offs issues. Absent clear-cut cases (a rarity), trade-offs were generally made in an informal, ad hoc fashion during the spring budget preview. And many participants felt that ZBB changed actual budget figures so little that it was not worth the effort.[96]

A key problem with the attempts to make informed inter-agency trade-offs is the inherent absence of objective analytic criteria. It is impossible to demonstrate scientifically, for instance, that money is "better" spent on economic assistance than on the F-15 fighter. These trade-offs are quintessentially *political* choices. The president and Congress, not OMB analysts, will continue to make such decisions. However, trade-off decisions might well be better informed if OMB presented policymakers with several options to consider.

OMB/NSC Coordination

Except occasionally for some defense programs with high public and political salience, neither the NSA nor his NSC staff get deeply involved in defense budgets or programs. Moreover, the NSC and OMB have never worked closely together on a sustained basis. But the president can, of course, change this. Some informed observers, as well as the Packard Commission, have urged him to do just that. As discussed in Chapter 1, there are persuasive reasons for closer OMB-NSC relations and for a larger NSC (and presidential) role in select defense and defense-related areas.[97]

Of Szanton's several proposals for OMB examined here, only one seems both desirable and *relatively* easy to institute: better OMB-NSC coordination. Another proposal is inappropriate and virtually impossible for OMB to implement: curbing DOD's propensity for threat inflation. A third—considering trade-offs among various national security–related programs—is conceptually appealing and substantively advisable. Such trade-offs defy "objective" analysis, but not analysis per se. OMB would have to act closely with the president and perhaps with Congress on a case-by-case basis. Szanton's remaining two recommendations—curbing cost overruns and moderating the several problem areas in the weapons acquisition process that stem in substantial part from the relatively autonomous status of the armed services—are directly germane to roles that probably should be assumed, in some degree, by OMB. Both proposals will encounter vigorous resistance from the military services, and possibly from other quarters as well.

For these latter two proposals to be realized, it will be necessary *at a minimum* to have a determined presidential commitment to change and a strong secretary of defense who is himself fully committed to ensuring that OMB plays the role that the president desires. There must be a de facto alliance between OSD and the White House since the specific prescriptions for reform must come from the president himself. If necessary—and it probably will be—the secretary and the president must be prepared to put flag rank officers on notice that the White House and OSD will assume the role of "enforcers." That is, sanctions will be imposed upon those who attempt to thwart this effort.

OMB and Congress

Aspects of OMB's relationship with Congress have been discussed throughout the chapter. It is a subject deserving far greater treatment than is possible in this study. But some additional remarks are in order.

When President Nixon became increasingly preoccupied with the Watergate crisis in 1973–1974, much of the responsibility for day-to-day governmental operations was delegated to OMB. Many congressmen believed such responsibility properly belonged to cabinet officers. Moreover, the Nixon OMB served as the President's vehicle for regularly impounding lawfully appropriated funds. In 1974, a frustrated Congress decided to get a handle on this situation by enacting legislation requiring Senate confirmation for the OMB director and his deputy.[98]

That same year the Congressional Budget and Impoundment Control Act of 1974 effectively forced OMB to develop closer contacts with Congress. The size of OMB's legislative affairs staff gradually increased from two people in the mid-1970s to five under Carter, and to seven in the Reagan administration. The closeness, even intimacy, of OMB's contacts with Congress was amply illustrated by David Stockman's discussion of his efforts in behalf of President Reagan's domestic agenda. The Reagan administration also introduced a congressional tracking system to provide the director with current CBO estimates, as well as timely appropriations and authorization committee actions.[99]

The Carter administrations's major defense budgetary concern, particularly before 1979, was budgetary restraint. Much of OMB's energy focused on countering DOD's skillful and persistent backdoor lobbying to persuade Congress to fund pet projects that the administration opposed. The services and retired military officers lobbied aggressively for such projects by, among other things, delivering congressional testimony and providing committee members with questions designed to elicit responses supportive of these programs. The Reagan OMB, on the other hand, concentrated on seeing that Congress funded the defense budget at the high levels requested by the President. Of course, in all administrations, a central OMB objective is to defend and promote the president's budget request, whatever it may be.[100]

Prescriptions

In defense and other areas, OMB can be a vital tool for executive budget review, management, and presidential leadership. Its effectiveness may be constrained for any of several reasons, but the most important constraint has generally been the president's disinclination to tap its full potential. Yet since its creation in 1970, no president more thoroughly crippled OMB's authority and capability for reviewing DOD budgets and programs than did Ronald Reagan. In so doing, President Reagan ultimately paid a high price in soaring federal deficits, unchecked Pentagon inefficiencies, and growing public and congressional opposition to much of his national security agenda. Of course, many other factors besides a weak OMB contributed to these developments, not the least of which were the President's values and style, his inability or reluctance to inform himself about some of the most rudimentary elements of defense, arms control, and foreign policy, and his inattention to the workings of his own executive branch policy process. A president who neglects, ignores, or misuses units of his executive office like OMB and the NSC (the Iran/Contra affair), whose central purpose is to serve him, runs a high risk of jeopardizing his administration's policy agenda.

On the assumption that future presidents may, in varying

degrees, wish to tap OMB's capabilities or potential capabilities in defense matters, this chapter has suggested various measures that might be considered. The rationale for these prescriptions— as well as, in some instances, their difficulty of implementation —has been discussed. The following are some of the more important recommendations:

- The size of OMB's National Security Division should be increased substantially—to *at least* fifty professionals. Indeed, a strong case can be made for enlarging this figure. Virtually all past and present OMB analysts agree that the division was seriously understaffed in the Reagan years, but they differ as to its appropriate size.
- The management component of OMB should be reinvigorated, and the White House–level unit responsible for governmentwide management matters should continue to reside within OMB, not in a separate executive management office.
- The joint OMB/OSD review of the defense budget should be modified or eliminated so as to enhance OMB's impact.
- If the government is to retain more effective control over future defense expenditures, OMB, the president, and Congress must pay much more attention to restraining DOD's TOA.
- OMB membership in the DSARC (Defense Acquisition Board) might be a useful, if modest, step toward better integrating DSARC and PPBS decisions.[101]
- OMB should work more closely with the NSC on select defense programs.
- The president should encourage OMB to examine possible trade-offs between defense and other security-related programs.
- In cooperation with the secretary of defense, the president might consider selectively enhancing OMB's role in troublesome weapons acquisition areas.

Notes

1. But see Peter Szanton, "OMB's Defense Cop-out," *Foreign Policy* 58 (Spring 1985): 99–114. This article evolved from and is virtually identical to Peter Szanton, "Coordinating National Security Policy: The Role of the Office of

Management and Budget," in Duncan L. Clarke, ed., *Public Policy and Political Institutions: United States Defense and Foreign Policy—Policy Coordination and Integration* (Greenwich, Ct.: JAI Press, 1985), pp. 43–59.

2. The chapter evolved from Elizabeth Johnson Barber, "The Office of Management and Budget/Department of Defense Relations" (Ph.D. dissertation, The American University, Washington, D.C., May 1987). I suggested the topic to Elizabeth Barber and chaired her dissertation committee. We coauthored a condensed, revised draft of the dissertation—"The Office of Management and Budget: Watchdog of or Lap Dog for Defense Budgets and Programs?" (Paper prepared for the International Studies Association Convention, Washington, D.C., 15–18 April 1987). This chapter, prepared by myself, revises the above works substantially. All but one of the interviews prior to 1987 were conducted by Dr. Barber. I conducted subsequent interviews and written communications with past and present government officials. Requests for confidentiality were honored.

3. National Academy of Public Administration, *Panel on Executive Organization and Management* (Washington, D.C., 1985), p. 6.

4. Reorganization Plan 2 of 1970, 84 *Statutes at Large* Sec. 2085 (1970).

5. Interviews, Philip DaSault, OMB Deputy Associate Director/International Affairs, 26 July 1985; Harry Shaw, former OMB Deputy Associate Director/International Affairs, 17 January 1986; David Sitrin, OMB Deputy Associate Director/National Security, 12 June 1985.

6. For more detailed description and assessment of PPBS, see U.S. Congress, Senate, Committee on Armed Services (hereafter cited as SASC), *Staff Report: Defense Organization—The Need for Change*, 99th Cong., 1st sess., 1985, pp. 483–528.

7. See SASC, *Hearings: Organization, Structure and Decisionmaking Procedures of the Defense Department*, 98th Cong., 1st sess., 1983, Part 1, pp. 53, 55, 57, and Part 9, pp. 366–67, 393, 398. The Reagan administration discontinued the practice of annually writing the DG from scratch.

8. In the Carter administration, OMB attended DRB meetings as a nonmember.

9. Archie Barrett, *Reappraising Defense Organization: An Analysis based on the Defense Organization Study of 1977–1980* (Washington, D.C.: National Defense University Press, 1983), pp. 3–4, 61; "Report of the Working Group on Defense Planning and Resource Allocation," in Barry M. Blechman and William I. Lynn, eds., *Toward a More Effective Defense: Report of the Defense Organization Project* (Cambridge, Mass.: Ballinger, 1985), pp. 69, 72–73. These and other PPBS-related problems might be mitigated through implementation of the Goldwater-Nichols Department of Defense Reorganization Act of 1986, P.L. 99–433 (discussed in Chapter 4), but it is too early to make judgments about this.

10. SASC, *Organization, Structure and Decisionmaking*, Part 9, p. 368; Sitrin, interview 12 June 1985.

11. Commission on the Organization of Government for the Conduct of Foreign Policy (hereafter cited as Murphy Commission), *Report* (Washington, D.C.: Government Printing Office, 1975), p.77; Herschel Kanter, "The Politics of the Defense Budget," in Michael J. Boskins and Aaron Wildavsky, eds.,

The Federal Budget: Economics and Politics (San Francisco: Transaction Books, 1982), p. 284; confidential interview, 7 October 1985.

12. SASC, *Organization, Structure and Decisionmaking*, Part 9, pp. 368–69, 391.

13. "Report of the Working Group on Defense Planning," p. 79; "OMB and the Pentagon: Adversaries or Collaborators?" *Defense Monitor* 11 (1982): 5; Jack Quetsch, Principal Assistant Secretary of Defense/Comptroller, interview 7 October 1985.

14. Murphy Commission, *Report*, p. 76; "OMB and the Pentagon," p. 5; interviews, Sitrin, 12 June 1985; James Tozzi, former OMB Deputy Administrator for Information and Regulatory Affairs, 18 June 1985; David Hessler, DOD Deputy Comptroller, 8 October 1985.

15. However, this was much less the case during the 1970–1980 period. Prior to 1981, budget outlays constituted only one area of OMB interest (Richard Stubbing, former OMB/BOB analyst and Deputy Chief of the National Security Division from 1974 to 1981, interview, 8 May 1987).

16. Side payments are sometimes justified on the frequently erroneous assumption that expanding federal revenues and low inflation rates will permit future dollars to buy currently authorized programs. See David Mowery and Mark Kamlet, "Games Presidents Do and Do Not Play: Presidential Circumvention of Executive Branch Budget Process," *Policy Sciences* 16 (March 1984): 303–27; Murphy Commission, *Report*, p. 78; Samuel P. Huntington, "The Defense Policy of the Reagan Administration, 1981–1982," in Fred I. Greenstein, ed., *The Reagan Presidency: An Early Assessment* (Baltimore, Md.: Johns Hopkins University Press, 1983), p. 106.

17. U.S. Congress, House of Representatives, Committee on Armed Services (hereafter cited as HASC), Special Panel on Defense Procurement, *Report: Weapons Acquisition Policy and Procedures: Curbing Cost Growth*, 97th Cong., 1st sess., 1982, pp. 6, 19.

18. "Report of the Working Group on Defense Planning," p. 72; "Report of the Working Group on Weapons Acquisition," in Blechman and Lynn, *Toward a More Effective Defense*, pp. 87–101; HASC, *Weapons Acquisition Policy*, pp. 4–5, 19, 25; "Defense Spending: The Source of the Problem," *International Currency Review* 16 (February 1985): 19; U.S. General Accounting Office (hereafter cited as GAO), *DOD Needs to Provide More Credible Weapon Systems Cost Estimates to the Congress*, GAO/NSIAD–84–70 (Washington, D.C.: Government Printing Office, 1984).

19. Interviews, Dwight Ink, former OMB Associate Director for Management, 30 August 1985, and Dale McComber, former OMB Assistant Director for Budget Review, 8 October 1985; Joel Havemann, "Executive Report/OMB's New Faces Retain Power, Structure Under Ford," *National Journal* 7 (July 1975): 1074; Larry Berman, *The Office of Management and Budget and the Presidency, 1921–1979* (Princeton, N.J.: Princeton University Press, 1979), pp. 113–15.

20. Interviews, James McIntyre, Carter administration OMB Director, 9 July 1985; Al Burman, budget analyst/National Security Division, 19 June 1985; DaSault, 26 July 1985.

21. Charles F. Bingman, "The President as Manager of the Federal Govern-

ment," in C. Lowell Harriss, ed., *Control of Federal Spending* (New York: Academy of Political Science, 1985), p. 158.

22. National Academy of Public Administration, "Revitalizing Federal Managers and Their Overburdened Systems," in Harriss, *Control of Federal Spending*, pp. 165, 167. The Grace Commission agreed with NAPA (J. Peter Grace, *War on Waste: President's Private Sector Survey on Cost Control* (New York: Macmillan, 1984), pp. ix, 451–52). See also, Gary Bombardier, "The Managerial Function of OMB," *Public Policy* 23 (Summer 1975): 345–47, 360.

23. The Pentagon's reluctance is hardly unique. No agency is likely to invite OMB's management team to review *its* management.

24. Bombardier, "The Managerial Function of OMB," pp. 345–47, 360; W. Bowman Cutter, former OMB Executive Director/Budget, interview 5 August 1985. But in a letter to Duncan L. Clarke 27 July 1987), Cutter said: "With the advantage of my life after government, I have to say that neither OMB nor the academy have any idea of what a management consulting task is or how it might be done."

25. Cutter, interview, 5 August 1985; "OMB and the Pentagon," p. 4.

26. The president's support of OMB is, of course, the key to its influence. With that support, OMB killed the Manned Orbiting Lab in the Nixon years and went after both the Division Air Defense (DIVAD) and Bradley fighting vehicle in the Carter years. Carter cancelled the Bradley, but funds for the program were later restored by Congress.

27. Interviews, Cutter, 5 August 1985, and Sitrin, 12 June 1985; "OMB and the Pentagon," p. 4; Richard Stubbing, *The Defense Game* (New York: Harper & Row, 1986), pp. 83–84.

28. U.S. Congress, House of Representatives, Committee on Government Operations (hereafter cited as HCGO), *Hearings: Government Procurement and Contracting*, 91st Cong., 1st sess., 1969, p. 427. Former BOB Deputy Director and, later, GAO Comptroller General Elmer Staats, disagrees with McNamara's comment. Staats relates that he "sat in on meetings both with McNamara and the President during the period from 1961 to 1966 and, while the President did not accept all of our recommendations vis-à-vis McNamara, he did in a substantial number of cases. . . . During this same period, the Office of Science and Technology played an important role, participating in every phase of the budget review, including meetings with the Secretary of Defense and the President" (Elmer Staats, letter to Duncan L. Clarke, 31 July 1987).

29. Cutter, interview 5 August 1985.

30. Bruce E. Johnson, "From Analyst to Negotiator: The OMB's New Role," *Journal of Policy Analysis and Management* 3 (1984):503–504, 509.

31. U.S. Congress, House of Representatives, Committee on Treasury, Postal Service and General Government, *Hearings: Treasury, Postal and General Government Appropriations for 1985*, 98th Cong., 2d sess., 1984, Part 3, p. 171; interviews: Daryl Johnson, OMB/Office of Administration, 18 April 1986, and Barbara Clay, OMB/Office of Public Affairs, 29 January 1986; Leonard Zuza, OMB analyst, written communication to Duncan L. Clarke, 8 April 1987.

32. Robert J. Art, "Congress and the Defense Budget: Enhancing Policy Oversight," *Political Science Quarterly* 100 (Summer 1985): 244–45; Charles Bingman, former OMB Deputy Associate Director for Government Organization, interview 1 October 1985.

33. President's Blue Ribbon Commission on Defense Management (hereafter cited as Packard Commission), *A Formula for Action: Report to the President on Defense Acquisition* (Washington, D.C.: Government Printing Office, 1986); Paul Taylor, "Most Americans Oppose Reagan Budget Priorities," *Washington Post*, 14 February 1986, p. A4.

34. Commission on Government Procurement (hereafter cited as COGP), *Report* (Washington, D.C.: Government Printing Office, 1972), pp. 3, 12, 15 –16, 33. The Armed Services Procurement Act of 1947, 10 U.S.C. Secs. 2301–2314, established procurement policy for the military departments and the National Aeronautics and Space Administration. The Federal Property and Administrative Services Act of 1949, 41 U.S.C. Secs. 242(a), 251– 260, set policies for civilian agencies.

35. COGP, *Report*, pp. 3, 12, 15–16.

36. Ibid., pp. viii, 12–13, 185–86.

37. Ibid., pp. 9, 13.

38. U.S. Congress, Senate, Committee on Government Operations (hereafter cited as SCGO), *Hearings: Establishing Office of Federal Procurement Policy*, 93d Cong., 1st sess., 1973, pp. 100–125, 143; SCGO, *Hearings: Establish a Commission on Government Procurement*, 91st Cong., 1st sess., 1969, pp. 28 –29; U.S. Congress, Senate, Committee on Governmental Affairs (hereafter cited as SCGA), *Report: Reauthorization of the Office of Federal Procurement Policy*, 98th Cong., 1st sess., 1983, pp. 13–14; James G. Phillips, "Economic Report: Fight Looms in Senate over Procurement Office," *National Journal* 5 (February 1974):181; interviews, Hugh Witt, first Administrator of the Office of Federal Procurement Policy, 17 June 1985; Staats, 14 August 1985.

39. Office of Federal Procurement Policy Act, 41 U.S.C. Secs. 401 et seq. See also, Phillips, "Fight Looms in Senate," p. 182.

40. Karen Williams, former OFPP Administrator, interview 15 August 1985; HCGO, *Report: Office of Federal Procurement Policy Act Amendments of 1979*, 98th Cong., 1st sess., 1979, p. 6; Richard Stubbing, written communication to Duncan L. Clarke, 28 April 1987.

41. Office of Federal Procurement Policy Act Amendments of 1979, 41 U.S.C. Secs. 401 et. seq.

42. Interviews, Harvey Gordon, former OSD Assistant Deputy Under Secretary for Acquisition, 13 June 1985, and Burt Hall, GAO Group Director/OFPP Task Force member, 2 April 1985; Office of Federal Procurement Policy (hereafter cited as OFPP), *Draft Proposal for a Uniform Federal Procurement System* (Washington, D.C.: October 1981), p. 69; OFPP, *Proposal for a Uniform Federal Procurement System* (Washington, D.C.: Government Printing Office, February 1982), p. 49; Deputy Secretary of Defense Frank Carlucci, letter to OFPP Administrator Donald Sowle on draft proposal for a Uniform Federal Procurement System, 9 December 1981 (mimeo).

43. OFPP, *Draft Proposal for a Uniform Federal Procurement System*, p. 15; OFPP, *Proposal for a Uniform Federal Procurement System*, pp. vii, 13.

44. HCGO, *Activities Report*, 97th Cong., 2d sess., 1982, p. 48.
45. Interviews, Gordon, 13 June 1985, and Williams, 15 August 1985; SCGA, *Reauthorization of the Office of Federal Procurement Policy*, pp. 7–8.
46. American Bar Association (hereafter cited as ABA), Public Contracts Section, *Public Comments on the Federal Acquisition Regulation*, Policy Letter 80–5, 6 July 1984; Williams, interview, 15 August 1985.
47. COGP, *Report*, p. 12.
48. ABA, *Public Comments on the Federal Acquisition Regulation*; Williams, interview 15 August 1985.
49. Bureau of National Affairs, *Federal Contracts Report* 41 (30 January 1984), p. 172; SASC, *Hearings: Impact of Proposed Regulatory Authority of the Office of Federal Procurement Policy on National Defense and Related Government Activities*, 98th Cong., 1st sess., 1983, p. 5.
50. SASC, *Impact of Proposed Regulatory Authority of the Office of Federal Procurement Policy*, p. 8. Weinberger's assertion was rebutted convincingly by GAO (see p. 28).
51. Office of Federal Procurement Policy Act Amendments of 1983, 41 U.S.C. Secs. 403, 405, 407.
52. SCGA, *Reauthorization of the Office of Federal Procurement Policy*, pp. 11–12; Fred Hiatt, "12-Day Air Force Spree Nets $1 Billion in Parts," *Washington Post*, 9 April 1986, p. A21; Murray L. Weidenbaum, "The Budget Dilemma and Its Solution," in Harriss, *Control of Federal Spending*, pp. 49–50.
53. Packard Commission, *A Formula for Action*, p. 18.
54. Confidential interview, 7 June 1985.
55. Ibid.; interviews, Pat Szervo, former OFPP Associate Administrator for Procurement Law and Legislation, 14 June 1985; Staats, 14 August 1985.
56. Henry Kissinger, *White House Years* (Boston: Little, Brown, 1979), p. 397; Frederick Malek, *Washington's Hidden Tragedy* (New York: Free Press, 1978), p. 25; Murphy Commission, *Adequacy of Current Organization: Defense and Arms Control*, vol. 4, Appendix K (Washington, D.C.: Government Printing Office, 1975), p. 89.
57. Quoted in John Pierson, "Holding the Line: Budget Director Mayo Wages Unending Battle to Curb U.S. Spending," *Wall Street Journal*, 13 November 1969, p. 1.
58. Ibid., p. 1; interviews, Bingman, 1 October 1985, Ink, 30 August 1985, and McComber, 8 October 1985; "New Pentagon Budget Policy Takes Shape Under Laird," *National Journal* 1 (1 November 1969): 9–15; Murphy Commission, *Adequacy of Current Organizations*, p. 89; Dom Bonafede, "Budget Plan: Nixon Set Tone for 1971 Proposals," *National Journal* 2 (7 February 1970): 271; Kissinger, *White House Years*, pp. 395–97.
59. "Budget Director Shultz: The President's Man," *National Journal* 3 (23 January 1971): 156; "White House Report: Making of the President's Budget," *National Journal* 3 (23 January 1971): 151, 154; John Osborne, *The Second Year of the Nixon Watch* (New York: Liveright, 1971), p. 149.
60. Bingman, interview 1 October 1985; James Naughton, "Shultz Quietly Builds Up Power in Domestic Field," *New York Times*, 31 May 1971, p. 7.
61. John Gerners, "Since Watergate, Major Shifts in Power Have Given Presidency Gains and Losses," *New York Times*, 28 January 1974, p. 14; Philip

Sharecoff, "Budget Office Withstands Moves to Cut Its Powers," *New York Times*, 11 November 1974, p. 16; John Herbers, "The Other Presidency," *New York Times*, 3 March 1974, p. 1; Stubbing, *The Defense Game*, pp. 313–14.

62. Gerald Ford, *A Time to Heal* (New York: Harper & Row, 1979), p. 65.

63. On Schlesinger's dismissal, see ibid., pp. 320; Robert Hartmann, *Palace Politics: An Inside Account of the Ford Years* (New York: McGraw-Hill, 1980), pp. 109, 365; Douglas Kinnard, *The Secretary of Defense* (Lexington: University Press of Kentucky, 1980), pp. 185–86; Stubbing, *The Defense Game*, pp. 334–35.

64. Kinnard, *The Secretary of Defense*, pp. 185–86; "*NJ* Checklist: Ford Proposes Tax, Spending Cuts, Consolidation of Federal Programs," *National Journal* 7 (24 January 1976): 117.

65. Jimmy Carter, *Keeping Faith: Memoirs of a President* (New York: Bantam Books, 1982), pp. 39, 55, 128; interviews, Burman, 19 June 1985; Sitrin, 12 June 1985; Robert Howard, OMB officer, 12 June 1985; Edward R. (Randy) Jayne II, "Office of Management and Budget and National Security Policy in the Carter Administration," in David C. Kozak and James M. Keagle, Eds. *Bureaucratic Politics and National Security: Theory and Practice* (Boulder, Colo.: Lynne Rienner, 1988), pp. 158–173.

66. Lawrence Korb, "National Security Organization and Process in the Carter Administration," in Sam Sarkesian, ed., *Defense Policy and the Presidency: Carter's First Years* (Boulder, Colo.: Westview Press, 1979), pp. 121, 124, 131–32; Leslie Gelb, "Budget Office Seeks Cuts from the Pentagon," *New York Times*, 1 December 1977, p. B5.

67. *National Security Policy Integration* (hereafter cited as Odeen Report), President's Reorganization Project, (September 1979), p. 11; McIntyre, interview 9 July 1985; Bernard Weintraub, "Key Advisors to President Support Efforts to Increase Defense Outlays," *New York Times*, 4 December 1978, p. 1.

68. George Wilson, "Navy Told to Fix Shipbuilding Problems Before Expecting New Money for New Fleet," *Washington Post*, 29 March 1978, p. A3; Timothy Clark, "Budget Focus: A Forum for Debate," *National Journal* 12 (7 June 1980): 943.

69. Odeen Report. For an account of the process leading to the Odeen Report and an assessment of it, see Duncan L. Clarke, "Integrating Arms Control, Defense and Foreign Policy in the Executive Branch of the U.S. Government," in Hans Guenter Brauch and Duncan L. Clarke, eds., *Decisionmaking for Arms Limitation: Assessments and Prospects* (Cambridge, Mass.: Ballinger, 1983), pp. 6–16. The principal Carter administration Defense reorganization/management studies are analyzed in Barrett, *Reappraising Defense Organization*.

70. *National Party Platforms of 1980* (Urbana: University of Illinois Press, 1982), p. 210.

71. See Frederick C. Mosher, *A Tale of Two Agencies: A Comparative Analysis of the General Accounting Office and the Office of Management and Budget* (Baton Rouge: Louisiana State University Press, 1984), pp. 182–85, 187. The scope of DOD's exemption from OMB's purview was vast. For instance, virtually

all federal agencies except Defense were subject to Reagan's January 1985 executive order permitting OMB to screen agencies' regulatory proposals before they were drafted formally or announced publicly (see Mary Thornton, "New Reagan Order Grants OMB Expanded Authority," *Washington Post*, 5 January 1985, p. A2).

72. Interviews, Howard, 12 June 1985, Burman, 19 June 1985, and Sitrin, 12 June 1985; Stubbing, *The Defense Game*, pp. 374–79; Judith Havemann, "Miller, No Schemer, Learns on Job at OMB," *Washington Post*, 20 August 1986, p. A1.

73. David Stockman, *The Triumph of Politics: Why the Reagan Revolution Failed* (New York: Harper & Row, 1986), pp. 105–109, 125–31, 277–300; interviews, Howard, 12 June 1985; Sitrin, 12 June 1985.

74. Michael Gordon, "For the Pentagon's 'Minimal' Budget, It's Not Whether to Cut But How Much," *National Journal* 14 (27 March 1982): 544–49; George Wilson, "Defense Budget 'Disaster' Ahead, Weinberger Told," *Washington Post*, 22 April 1986, p. A6; Michael Gordon, "Business As Usual," *National Journal* 16 (12 May 1984): 938; Russell Murray, former Assistant Secretary of Defense for Program, Analysis and Evaluation in the Carter administration, interview 11 October 1985; George Wilson, "House Plan Would Force Weapon Cuts," *Washington Post*, 20 May 1986, p. A6; Lou Cannon, "Changing the Course," *Washington Post*, 7 April 1986, p. A2.

75. Packard Commission, *A Quest for Excellence: Final Report to the President* (Washington, D.C.: Government Printing Office, June 1986); Thomas L. McNaugher, "Weapons Procurement: The Futility of Reform," *International Security* 12 (Fall 1987): 100; *U.S. Defense Acquisition: A Process in Trouble* Washington, D.C.: Center for Strategic and International Studies, Georgetown University, 1987), p. 8. A crucial new position created by this directive and the Department of Defense Reorganization Act of 1986, on the recommendation of the Packard Commission, was that of Under Secretary of Defense for Acquisition. Richard Goodwin, the first to occupy the post, resigned after a year when he encountered insurmountable internal Pentagon resistance (R. Jeffrey Smith and Molly Moore, "Pentagon's Purchasing Chief to Quit," *Washington Post*, 14 September 1987, p. A1); James Locher, "Organization and Management," in Joseph Kruzel, ed., *1988–1989 American Defense Annual* (Lexington, Mass.: Lexington Books, 1988), pp. 175, 180–82.

76. Quoted in Stockman, *The Triumph of Politics*, pp. 283, 317.

77. At the outset of the Reagan administration, many defense experts inside and outside the Pentagon expressed concern about increasing the defense budget too sharply. In early 1981 two members of the JCS expressed misgivings about this, both because of the inability of the defense industrial base to handle such an influx of funds efficiently and because they believed it invited a future political backlash. Each officer expressed his preference for a stable 3 percent real annual growth rate (confidential sessions, Washington, D.C., spring 1981).

78. See Colin Campbell, S.J., *Managing the Presidency: Carter, Reagan, and the Search for Executive Harmony* (Pittsburgh, Pa.: University of Pittsburgh Press,

1986), pp. 175, 187, 197–98, 266–67; Felicity Barringer, "OMB Defense Analysts Migrating," *Washington Post*, 9 March 1983.

79. Szanton, "OMB's Defense Cop-out," pp. 99–114. Szanton fully appreciates that these are long-range goals that would be difficult to achieve.

80. Many of the more serious problems are summarized in Packard Commission, *A Quest for Excellence*, pp. 44–48.

81. The actual dividend is estimated to range from $37 to $46 billion. Reportedly, when some Reagan administration DOD and OMB analysts initially tried to raise the issue, senior Defense officials told them not to purse it (GAO, *Budget Issues: Potential for Excess Funds in DOD—March 1986 Update*, GAO/NSIAD 86–76 [Washington, D.C.: Government Printing Office, March 1986]; GAO, *Potential for Excess Funds in DOD*, GAO/NSIAD 85–145 [Washington, D.C.: Government Printing Office, 3 September 1985]; "OMB and the Pentagon," p. 7; confidential interview, 28 October 1986).

82. David Lockwood, *Cost Overruns in Major Weapons Systems: Current Dimensions of a Longstanding Problem* (Washington, D.C.: Congressional Research Service, 1983), p. 21.

83. Ibid., pp. 8, 29; HASC, *Weapons Acquisition Policy and Procedures*, p. 27.

84. Packard Commission, *A Quest for Excellence*, p. xxiii.

85. Szanton, "OMB's Defense Cop-out," p. 111.

86. Interviews, Franklin Spinney, senior analyst, OSD, Office of Program Analysis and Evaluation, 8 August 1986 and 28 October 1986; Burman, 19 June 1985.

87. See Packard Commission, *A Quest for Excellence*, p. xxiii; Robert C. Moot, "Accounting and Budgeting Systems in the Department of Defense," in Blechman and Lynn, *Toward a More Effective Defense*, pp. 204–205; "Report of the Working Group on Weapons Acquisition," pp. 87–101.

88. Szanton, "OMB's Defense Cop-out," p. 112.

89. Packard Commission, *A Quest for Excellence*, p. xvii.

90. Major General Daniel O. Graham, "Estimating the Threat: A Soldier's Job," *Army* (April 1973): 14–16; Patrick J. McGarvey, *The CIA: The Myth and the Madness* (Baltimore, Md.: Penguin Books, 1972), pp. 154–56; Stansfield Turner, *Secretary and Democracy: The CIA in Transition* (Boston: Houghton Mifflin, 1985), p. 245; U.S. Congress, Senate, Select Committee to Study Governmental Operations with Respect to Intelligence Activities (Church Committee), *Foreign and Military Intelligence*, 94th Cong., 2d sess., 1976, Book I, p. 350.

91. Szanton, "OMB's Defense Cop-out," pp. 105–106.

92. Confidential interview, 13 June 1985.

93. Szanton, "OMB's Defense Cop-out," pp. 100–101.

94. Zuza, written communication to Duncan L. Clarke, 8 April 1987.

95. Stubbing, *The Defense Game*, p. 67.

96. Interviews, Cutter, 5 August 1985; Howard 12 June 1985; McIntyre, 9 July 1985; McComber, 8 October 1985; Bingman, 1 October 1985. See also, Peter Phyrr, "The Zero Base Approach to Budgeting," *Public Administration Review* 37 (January/February 1977): 438–39; Aaron Wildavsky, *The Politics of the Budgetary Process*, 4th ed. (Boston: Little, Brown, 1984), pp. 128, 202–21.

97. Philip Odeen, "The Role of the National Security Council in Coordinating and Integrating U.S. Defense and Foreign Policy," in Clarke, *Public Policy and Political Institutions*, pp. 31–33, 35; Packard Commission, *A Quest for Excellence*, pp. xix, 13; interviews: Brent Scowcroft, former Assistant to the President for National Security Affairs in the Ford administration, 16 October 1985; Edward Sanders, former OMB Deputy Associate Director/International Affairs, 20 June 1985.

98. 88 *Statutes at Large* Sec. 11 (1974); Berman, *The Office of Management and Budget*, pp. 121–25. Congress also authorizes OMB's budget.

99. Stockman, *The Triumph of Politics*, pp. 159–238; Shelley Lynne Tomkin, "Playing Politics in OMB: Civil Servants Join the Game," *Presidential Studies Quarterly* 15 (Winter 1985): 167.

100. Interviews, Herbert Harris, Chairman of OMB's Budgetary Task Force in the Carter administration, 2 September 1986; Gordon Wheeler, Special Assistant to the OMB Director, 3 September 1986; Paul Heileg, staff, Senate Budget Committee, 27 August 1986. Heileg said Stockman surreptitiously suggested some defense cuts to the Senate Budget Committee.

101. However, Elmer Staats maintains a contrary viewpoint: "I do not believe it appropriate for OMB to be a member of any [DOD] boards or committees. It can always sit in as observers and have access to information developed there. The reality and perception of independence of the OMB in the eyes of Congress and the public should always be preserved" (Staats, letter to Duncan L. Clarke, 31 July 1987).

CHAPTER 3

The State Department and Foreign Policy Leadership

One of the most recurrent proposals for the American foreign policy process is that the Department of State assume overall direction of U.S. foreign policy. This chapter argues that it is an idea that will not work.[1]

Since 1947, with a few exceptions, the secretary of state has been a significant foreign policy adviser to the president. Often he has been the leading adviser. Moreover, after the president, he usually has been the nation's chief foreign policy spokesman and diplomat. That the secretary should be a policy adviser, spokesman, and diplomat is widely acknowledged.

But it is also often asserted that the *Department* of State should have the central, or at least leading, role in making and coordinating foreign policy. This view is incorrect. In fact, there is a growing perception among informed observers that the State Department is ill equipped to assume such a position of prominence. A State Department–centered system is simply not in the cards.

Failing at Coordination—For Good Reason

Contributors to the 1975 Murphy Commission study concluded, "Establishing the [State] Department as the . . . centerpiece of foreign policymaking by constructing coordinating mechanisms around it simply will not do."[2] Neither formal delegations of presidential authority nor powerful secretaries have enabled the department in the past to coordinate important activities of other departments and agencies.

There is a powerful bureaucratic reason for this persistent failure. State encounters vehement resistance from other departments when the policy issues it tries to control affect their areas of jurisdictional responsibility and interest. Neither the Department of Defense nor the Treasury Department will accept State's lead in their respective areas. Indeed, relatively few secretaries of state and defense have enjoyed close working partnerships. More often their relationships have been variously characterized as "peaceful coexistence," "discreet disagreement," and "open warfare."[3] Tensions in a State-centered system would burden the president with a disproportionate number of interagency disputes to resolve.

It is true that the National Security Council has not been notably successful in integrating defense and international economic policy into overall national security policy.[4] But there is no indication that State can perform these functions more effectively. And the NSC has one key advantage over State: only the NSC has the *potential* to be a neutral broker. If the problem is ever to be mitigated, therefore, it is to the NSC and the White House, not State, that an administration must look. If, by some miracle, State were offered the role of neutral broker, it probably should reject it. For State, like any other department, must be an advocate and spokesman within interagency councils for its own essential missions. A stance of neutrality would ensure inadequate representation of State Department positions.

When State has been assigned central coordinative responsibility, it has performed poorly. Although President Eisenhower's Operations Coordinating Board served some useful purposes, it was, at best, only a moderately effective coordinating mechanism from 1953 to January 1960, during which period it was chaired by the under secretary of state. The department, whose role on the board was challenged by other agencies, saw the OCB not as an opportunity for leadership but as a time-consuming and disturbing departure from routine. Consequently, State often sent low-ranking officials to various OCB committees. Performance improved slightly in 1957 when NSA Robert Cutler was made vice chairman of the OCB, and it improved again, this time more substantially, in Eisenhower's last year when the board's chairmanship passed to NSA Gordon Gray. Former Foreign Service Officer (FSO) Smith Simpson observes, "State's reaction to the Eisenhower process made it evident that the Department was . . . not constituted or prepared . . . to play effectively the role it claimed. . . . Its negative reactions . . . condemned . . . the system of coordination the President had handed it."[5]

The same story was repeated in 1966 when Lyndon Johnson issued National Security Action Memorandum (NSAM) 341, which declared that the President had "directed the Secretary of State, as his agent to assume responsibility to the full extent permitted by law for the overall direction, coordination and supervision of interdepartmental activities of the United States Government overseas (less exempted military activities)."[6] The NSAM 341 system was a failure. Some of the reasons for this had nothing to do with State. But contributing to its demise was the predictable opposition of other departments, their conviction that the system was an instrument of the State Department rather than of the entire national security bureaucracy, and the inability or unwillingness of Secretary of State Dean Rusk to play a dominant policy role.[7] There is little reason to suppose that future grants of major coordinative authority to State, even if it is headed by an assertive and influential secretary, will have a substantially different outcome. Not surprisingly, State has not received a similarly broad delegation of authority since 1966.

Disappointing Presidential Expectations

Most modern presidents either before or shortly after their inauguration have indicated a desire for the secretary and the Department of State to play a leading role in formulating and directing foreign policy. Some secretaries do, indeed, assume such a role. The department rarely does. A major reason for this is the gap between what presidents want and expect and what they come to believe State can or will give them. Among other things, they expect loyalty, responsiveness to their needs and directives, an opportunity to exercise foreign policy leadership, and sensitivity to their domestic political requirements. No recent president has found the department able or willing to perform as expected.

Suspect Loyalty. Upon assuming office, President Nixon reportedly told his staff that foreign policy was to be handled by the White House, "not by the striped pants faggots in Foggy Bottom."[8] The offensive language apart, such uneasiness about the State Department appears to be the rule rather than the exception. Recent presidents seem to have quickly concluded that, except for the secretary and a handful of others, people in State are not to be trusted. Many New Deal, Kennedy, and Carter Democrats believed State to be hidebound and resistant to progressive policies; many Eisenhower, Nixon, and Reagan Republicans were convinced it was infested with suspect left-wingers and liberals.[9] Regardless of party, presidents often are disposed to blame State for unauthorized leaks of sensitive information.[10] Some of the more telling reasons for presidential suspicions relate to various traits and attitudes of the Foreign Service "subculture" (discussed below).

Since his initial study, no one has been a more articulate and supportive advocate of a prominent State Department role than I.M. Destler. He has variously urged a State-centered foreign policy system facilitated by the president, "building lines of confidence" down to at least the assistant secretary level (1972), abolition of the post of NSA (1980), and "alliance" between State and the NSC (1985).[11] But even in his early and most ambitious vision of State's role, Destler acknowledged that the department was "strikingly un-Presidential," and that the Foreign Service subculture constituted "a formidable problem for those who would make State *the* central foreign affairs agency."[12]

In any administration, the president's confidence is gained through demonstrated loyalty and competence, which normally come only through daily interaction with the president. Usually only the president's White House advisers, including the NSA, and cabinet officials like the secretary of state can meet this condition. A sprawling bureaucracy cannot. Consequently, no postwar president has sought to build lines of confidence down through the State Department bureaucracy.

Unresponsiveness. The inclination to center foreign policymaking in the White House is further strengthened by a sense that State is insufficiently responsive to presidential requirements and directives. The NSA and NSC staff are more immediately dependent on the president than is the State Department and, therefore, are usually more responsive to him.[13] The secretary knows, of course, that he too must be responsive to the president if he is to retain his confidence. But he confronts a dilemma. As Destler puts it:

[P]ostwar history suggests how difficult it is for both relationships (the presidential-secretarial and the secretarial-departmental) to flourish simultaneously; they really have not, it seems, since the presidency of Harry S. Truman. . . . It is hard for the secretary to be responsive to the President and his perspective while responding to his department because the department's prime focus, relations with foreign countries, is only one of the president's major international concerns.[14]

Phrased somewhat differently—the secretary can either distance himself from his own department, thereby setting it adrift, or he can become State's advocate at the risk of being suspect himself. Either way, State suffers.[15] Former Secretary of State Cyrus Vance was reasonably successful for a while in balancing these two roles. Vance was later eclipsed in the competition for the president's ear by NSA Zbigniew Brzezinski, in large part because President Carter increasingly preferred the latter's substantive advice. But it is also noteworthy that Carter referred frequently to State's "inertia," and he found that "Cy Vance mirrored the character of the organization he led. He was . . . extremely loyal to his subordinates, and protective of the State Department and its status."[16]

The notion of responsiveness does not imply that departments and presidential advisers must refrain from giving the president unpleasant advice; nor does it imply that State's advice is invariably wrong. Rather, the perception of State Department unresponsiveness has several components (including, for instance, the quality of its work, discussed below). One element often mentioned by presidents and NSAs is State's supposed reluctance to faithfully and promptly implement White House directives. So Jimmy Carter was disturbed by "the apparent reluctance in the State Department to carry out my directives fully and with enthusiasm";[17] Brzezinski was "amazed at how skillful the State Department was in delaying the execution of decisions which it had not in the first place favored";[18] and Henry Kissinger remarked that FSOs "will carry out clear-cut instructions with great loyalty, but the typical Foreign Service officer is not easily persuaded that an instruction with which he disagrees is really clear-cut."[19] Nor is State's case aided by pointing out that implementation problems are far greater and more pervasive at the Pentagon. No one has seriously proposed a DOD-centered national security policy system.

Presidential Leadership in Foreign Policy. Presidents searching for areas in which to demonstrate international leadership always found foreign policy much easier to dominate than defense policy. When the White House decides to move boldly into a foreign policy area, the State Department, and sometimes even the secretary, is often shunted aside.

State's Insensitivity to Domestic Politics. There is some truth to the observation that NSAs "have not tended to be particularly shrewd in U.S. national politics."[20] But NSAs are located where they come in daily contact with those who are: White House political aides and, of course, the president. Most NSAs have enjoyed better relations with these aides than have secretaries of state, and the NSAs' relationships with presidents since 1961, while varied, generally have been at least as close as those of the secretaries.[21] Moreover, while some individual secretaries have demonstrated a regard for the president's domestic political agenda, the same cannot be said of the department.

With some exceptions, State devotes little attention to framing its proposals in terms that will draw domestic political support. Presidents soon come to know that they and their staffs can frame decisions in a more politically acceptable manner. When the White House becomes convinced that State is out of touch with politics, the White House staff is well on its way to dominating policymaking.

Another factor inexorably pulls policymaking into the White House. Growing global interdependence in international economic and security affairs in an era of instant worldwide communications blurs distinctions between the foreign and the domestic. Pressures at home affect trade and diplomatic relations, while events in Central America, South Africa, and the Middle East influence domestic politics. The requirements for policy integration and responsiveness to public opinion can best be met by the White House, not by State Department foreign policy professionals. It is no accident that British, French, and West German leaders also have felt compelled to establish their *own* foreign policy staffs, distinct from their foreign ministries, at 10 Downing Street, in the Elysée, and in the chancellor's office.[22]

Expertise and Quality of Analysis

How much specialized expertise State requires depends on its role. If its activities are restricted to the traditional diplomatic arena, relatively little deep functional expertise would be necessary since it could draw on other departments. However, if State was the central foreign policy actor it would need substantial depth and breadth of expertise.

The department is clearly ill equipped for the latter role. One of the harshest assessments of the department and the Foreign Service is a 1970 State Department study, informally known as the Macomber Report. It stated that State's lack of specialized "skills and knowledge . . . has eroded the confidence of other Federal agencies in the Department's ability to exercise leadership in the conduct of foreign affairs."[23] Five years later, the Murphy Commission found that State lacked the expertise to "manage and contain" officials from other departments in the international economic, defense, and intelligence areas.[24] William Bacchus knows the department as well or better than anyone. In 1983, when he was Special Assistant to the Under Secretary for Management, he wrote that "State does not have the functional competence . . . to play anything resembling an integrative, policy development role. . . . And there is little current indication that significant improvement is likely."[25]

Since the mid-1970s, some effort has been made to address this issue, particularly in the international economic and political-military fields. Yet the Foreign Service continues to be predominantly generalist in background and orientation, and it resists recruitment of specialists. This resistance has been rooted partly in a long-standing contempt for "lateral entry" specialists from outside government. They were thought incapable of comprehending the "real stuff" of foreign affairs. But the Foreign Service is also concerned that hiring more specialists may harm FSO assignment and promotion opportunities. Unless this pattern of resistance is broken, the Foreign Service's relative inconsequentiality to Washington-based policymaking will increase.[26]

During the Carter and Reagan administrations, the State Department's Bureau of Politico-Military Affairs (PM) hired several excellent people from outside the department. Some FSOs in the bureau also acquired political-military skills on their own. But most of PM's FSOs had insufficient knowledge of the defense community and systems analysis.[27]

State also has been recurrently faulted for its continued relative weakness in international economics, a policy area in which it has steadily lost ground to other departments and governmental units. Hence, it was not surprising that President Carter in 1980 implemented a reorganization plan that stripped State of a major role in commercial representation and trade development.[28] There is also broad agreement that the science and technology area is seriously understaffed, and that State's Bureau of Oceans and International Environmental and Scientific Affairs (OES) cannot meet its present responsibilities.[29]

Perhaps most distressing, the Foreign Service exhibits deficiencies in what should be its core strengths—foreign area expertise and language facility. Despite considerable effort and expense, it appears that the competence of the FSO corps as a whole has not improved sufficiently in these two vital areas. There has been improvement in overall language competence. In 1972 only 55 percent of all language-designated positions at overseas posts were occupied by officers with the acceptable level of competence in the *appropriate* language. By 1980 that figure was 70 percent. But a 1986 State Department study concluded that State was "doing badly in developing real professional proficiency" in Arabic, Chinese, Japanese, and Russian.[30]

Several provisions of the Foreign Service Act of 1980 (P.L. 96–465) afforded an opportunity for, but did not compel enhancement of, FSO skills and expertise.[31] Thus far, the opportunity has not been seized. Bacchus doubts that "the lesson of utility being superior to natural right as the basis of influence has been fully learned" by the Foreign Service.[32]

A problem distinct from, but related to, inadequate expertise is the quality of State Department analysis and reporting. The analytical caliber of State's papers and reports has been criticized roundly by many inside and outside the building. Common complaints include the following:[33]

- The emphasis is on producing numerous descriptive reports and papers, not sound analysis.

- The department is slow to respond to NSC requests for policy studies.
- Based heavily on intuition, and almost never conceptual, many of the analyses are unaccompanied by reliable sources and information, or reflect the FSO's lack of adequate training and expertise.
- Papers are so cautious and vague as to be of little use to policymakers, who long ago concluded that such "waffling" constitutes the quintessential character of the Fudge Factory at Foggy Bottom.

Clientism

Clientism—or "clientitis/localitis," if an allusion to disease is preferred—refers to a perception held widely outside the State Department that FSOs tend to fall in love, blindly in love, with the country to which they are posted or the region of their particular interest.[34] That is, the need to maintain "good relations" with a country or region predisposes FSOs to identify excessively with that country's interests, at the expense of American interests. Many FSOs will confide privately that clientism is a risk to be guarded against, though one that is starkly overdrawn by those whose norms, policy preferences, or bureaucratic interests put them in frequent conflict with the State Department. Other FSOs react heatedly to allegations of clientism, which they see as impugning their patriotism.[35]

But whether there is or is not truth to the charge matters much less than the fact that it is widely believed by officials in other departments, in Congress, and in the White House. FSOs may, with sound reason, argue that long-term U.S. interests are at times best advanced by accommodating legitimate concerns of other countries. However, presidents often view such "accommodationist" advice as soft and out of touch with more pressing American interests. Their inclination, once again, is to discount State's advice.

The notion that "the striped pants types" are selling out to foreigners probably is held even more firmly in Congress. The department's usual relationship with Congress is at best uncomfortable,[36] and State alone among executive departments lacks a significant public constituency. This factor, too, disinclines presidents from considering a State-centered system. Why exacerbate the already endemic constitutional tension between the two branches?

The "country advocate" role, of course, *is* critical. Most foreign policy decisions, and not a few domestic ones, are unlikely to be well informed if taken without an understanding of the thinking and concerns of foreign governments and peoples. Few officials have better insight into such matters than career diplomats who immerse themselves in the culture, politics, society, and language of another country. It surely does not follow that an FSO who has lived in Brazil, knows the country, and speaks Portuguese cannot be a vigorous defender of American interests. The able FSO country specialist, like the responsible intelligence analyst, often bears bad news that decisionmakers must hear. But there are few rewards for the messenger.

Foreign Service Subculture and Attitudes

Other aspects and attitudes of the Foreign Service collectively diminish the prospect that the State Department will assume a central place in the direction and formulation of foreign policy.

Elitism. Except for many junior officers who are too new to government service to have adapted fully to prevailing norms, FSOs see themselves as members of an elite corps of talented, nonpartisan, rather close-knit, and unjustly beleaguered professionals. Many Americans and their elected representatives also view the Foreign Service as an elite—one that is an ingrown, exclusive club enjoying undeserved perguisites.[37] Although the public, or sectors of it, might admire or acknowledge certain elites—the Boston Celtics, the U.S. Marine Corps, or Nobel laureates—most Americans seem to distrust self-perceived elites, especially when they are thought unworthy of such status. And although the image of the Foreign Service has improved somewhat as terrorist incidents have taken their toll among the dedicated diplomats who serve the United States overseas, perceived FSO elitism remains a political liability for the department.

Elitism has other costs. It increases pressures for conformity within a system that already stifles individual initiative and creativity. It contributes to a certain "laager mentality," an "us-against-them" attitude frequently exhibited by FSOs toward many outside of State, and even toward some political appointees and those with specialized expertise within the department. This can only distance the Foreign Service from the political leadership and larger governmental foreign affairs community with which it must interact.[38]

Essence of the Foreign Service.[39] The traditional primary mission of the Foreign Service is *foreign* service. FSOs are thought of (and think of themselves) as diplomats whose principal duty is to execute, not make, policy. The FSO's "essence" is to represent his country overseas, send reports back to Washington, and negotiate with foreign governments. Successful performance of these functions requires a certain compromising, accommodating, and unabrasive style.

The predominant generalist orientation of FSOs and their usual educational background in the liberal arts seems well suited to the duties of the diplomat. However, the very qualities that serve FSOs well in their diplomatic capacity impede their performance in the Washington policymaking environment. American foreign policy, of course, is made in Washington, not in London, Lima, or Lagos—where FSOs spend much of their time. Moreover, decisionmakers are often informed by analyses that are best prepared by a group that is only grudgingly tolerated by FSOs—experts with specialized knowledge and skills in, for instance, military, economic, or scientific affairs. Finally, the decisionmaking process has a distinct combative quality; an aggressive, abrasive style often prevails over a passive, compromising one. The essence of the Foreign Service, then, hinders the department's effectiveness in policy formulation and raises serious doubts about its ability and disposition to play a leading policy role.

Lack of Innovation and Risk Avoidance. The Macomber Report found that "the mores of the [Foreign] Service . . . are not conducive to creative thinking. . . . [C]onformity is prized . . . above all other qualities."[40] Presidents who seek (or say they seek) creativity, innovation, and new ideas generally report that they find them in short supply at State. Instead, they discover inertia and excessive caution. Terms like "museum-like" and "curator mentality" are bandied about. President Kennedy's oft-related remark to McGeorge Bundy that State "never come[s] up with anything new. . . . The State Department is a bowl of jelly," is not unique.[41] Jimmy Carter, after lauding Brzezinski and his NSC staff for producing "new ideas," said that he "rarely received innovative ideas" from State.[42] (Conversely, however, it is inconceivable that experienced, cautious FSOs would have agreed with Reagan NSC staffer Lieutenant Colonel Oliver North that an innovative yet disastrous NSC-supervised diversion of funds in 1986 from Iran arms sales to the Nicaraguan Contras was a "neat idea.")[43]

The historian Arthur Schlesinger, Jr. once observed that the Foreign Service officer has come to be known as a person for whom the risks always outweigh the opportunities.[44] This may relate partly to the nature of the diplomatic profession. Diplomats are expected to reflect not their own, but their government's views. Great care must be taken not to exceed one's instructions. Every word must be carefully measured.

But there is more to it than this. Prevalent norms within the State Department inhibit direct confrontation on particularly sensitive issues, incline FSOs to avoid the appearance of abrasiveness, and penalize risk-takers.[45] It can be hazardous to be creative, to go out on a limb. Initiative or premature insight may set back or destroy careers even when FSOs correctly read or predict evolving international events. An example is the fate of the department's old China hands, who were purged for submitting what are now regarded as perceptive reports on Communist China. There are many others. Officers working on arms control issues or U.S.-Soviet relations have been especially vulnerable during the transition from one administration to another. The prudent course is the cautious course. "Fitting in" has a higher value than "standing out."[46]

Management Is Merely Housekeeping. The following question is often asked: If State cannot get its own house in order, if it cannot manage itself reasonably efficiently, how can it conceivably coordinate the entire foreign affairs community? Those posing this question have two concerns—internal State Department feuding and the department's relative inattention to effective management practices. Even casual observers have at least a general awareness of fights for turf between and among various regional and functional bureaus and other departmental units, while experienced professionals describe State as deeply divided and analogize its intradepartmental bickering to tribalism and and clannishness.[48] Of course, internal spats are common to other agencies as well. But what is less frequently encountered elsewhere in the executive branch is resistance to the very notion of management and a tradition that deemphasizes the standing and importance of managers:

- *Murphy Commission:* "Traditionally the State Department, and particularly the Foreign Service, has accorded little attention to management. Indeed there is a general antipathy towards the very idea of management.[48]
- *Ronald Spiers:* "[D]uring the 31 years I've spent in this building . . . nobody ever really paid attention to management."[49]
- *William Bacchus:* "[B]ecause of insufficient attention to the need for sustained and effective management [of the personnel system] . . . the Foreign Service will not be able to function at the levels required in the future."[50]
- *Macomber Report:* "[T]he Department . . . has sometimes been disappointing in its performance of [the interdepartmental coordination] role. The principal cause of this has been its weakness in the area of management capability."[51]

Management concerns the control and direction of programs, resources, and personnel. It, therefore, bears directly on organizational effectiveness. An effective manager possesses analytical and integrative skills and talents, he is a decisonmaker, and he mobilizes subordinates' energies to carry out assigned tasks.

This is not how management or managers are viewed by the Foreign Service. Management is equated with housekeeping or (to elevate it a bit) "administration." Most FSOs, like most university professors, neither admire nor aspire to be administrators. Such attitudes mean that, despite several efforts, career development programs designed to augment State's managerial competencies have met with only limited success.[52] Moreover, only senior officials are positioned to be senior managers. If they take no personal interest in the subject and delegate this function entirely to subordinates, it will not have sufficient priority. It is particularly noteworthy that since the tenure of George C. Marshall (1947–1949)—who, among other things, revitalized an executive secretariat as a managerial tool and created the Policy

Planning Staff—few secretaries of state have paid adequate attention to managing their own department.

The State Department's Role

The State Department is so beset with problems and debilities that it cannot now or in the foreseeable future assume a central foreign policy role. This has been evident for many years. Therefore, it is time to put the illusion of a State-centered system to rest.

This does not mean that extreme centralization in the White House is an appealing alternative. Although Zbigniew Brzezinski's 1983 proposal to, inter alia, formally legitimate the NSA's policy primacy and his occasional role as a negotiator, subject him by law to Senate confirmation, and enlarge substantially the NSC staff may be more feasible than a patently unworkable State-centered system, there is little support for it in Congress or among past or present senior government officials.[53] Morever, like the highly centralized, closed NSC system of the sort that characterized all but the first year of the Nixon administration, this proposal has many faults. Kissinger himself, albeit after the fact, acknowledged shortcomings in the Nixon NSC system.[54] Among the most serious weaknesses of that kind of very centralized system are the following:[55]

- Such a system, with an NSA whose paramount role is that of presidential policy adviser rather than that of custodian-manager of the NSC system, undercuts the NSC's image as a "neutral broker" and undermines the important, legitimate policy advisory role of the secretary of state. This engenders friction between the secretary and the NSA that invariably becomes public knowledge, embarrassing the administration and confusing allies.
- Sharply elevating the NSA's policy advisory function tends to weaken the authority that the secretary of state and his department must have to carry out diplomatic duties effectively. Foreign governments discover where the real power lies and bypass or ignore the State Department. Friction and confusion are further exacerbated when the NSA assumes the mantle of chief diplomat and public spokesman for U.S.

foreign policy. Moreover, an NSA who performs all these roles has little time to manage the NSC system.

- A tightly controlled, highly centralized system run from the White House can distance the president and the NSA from the greatest repository of expertise—the permanent government. Even an NSC staff of substantial size cannot substitute for the intelligence community, the Defense Department, the State Department, and other government agencies.
- When the White House runs the show so exclusively, it may not be able to build and sustain the kind of consensus with the bureaucracy, Congress, and the public that most successful long-term policies ultimately require. Closed systems are not conducive to building confidence and trust. Indeed, there could be renewed calls to make the NSA accountable to Congress.
- The president and the NSA alone lack the time to handle all vital issues themselves, let alone secondary or tertiary ones. This inclines an administration toward a crisis or "front burner" orientation, since critical matters will claim much, if not all, of its time. Long-term problems—nuclear proliferation, Middle East peace, NATO cohesion, for example—invariably receive scant attention.

These are persuasive reasons for not creating such a system. A preferred alternative to a Nixon-Kissinger–type system, the Brzezinski option, or a State-centered system would be one roughly analogous to that in operation during much of the Ford administration, when Lieutenant General Brent Scowcroft served as NSA. Scowcroft, while an important presidential policy adviser, concentrated on performing effectively his custodial/institutional functions and on being a facilitator for and arbitrator among other senior officials. The secretary of state, ideally, would here be a significant presidential foreign policy adviser, as well as the principal negotiator and policy spokesman.

The case of President Reagan's second secretary of state, George Shultz, illustrates what is probably the maximum influence future secretaries can expect to have. Although Shultz was influential in some security-related issues such as terrorism and U.S.-Israel strategic cooperation, he never came close to eclipsing the Pentagon and Secretary of Defense Casper Weinberger in core defense policy and programmatic issues. Nor, despite his professional background in economics and prior government experience at the Office of Management and Budget and the Treasury Department, did he challenge Treasury's primacy in international economic policy. Although Shultz did become the President's leading foreign policy adviser, there is little evidence that his department's stature was elevated.

Shultz's prominence was due to an unusual combination of factors.[56] Reagan had no desire to act as his own secretary of state, no deep personal interest in international affairs, and little knowledge of the subject. Fortuitously, the secretary of state's frequent competitor, the NSA, was strapped, by presidential preference. Most of Reagan's NSAs (William Clark was one notable exception) had their policy advisory roles restricted. Some were weak and ineffectual or unschooled and inexperienced in foreign policy. Two were tainted by the Iran-Contra scandal. Despite this, by January 1982 the NSC, not State, had the primary interagency coordinative function. The NSC often performed this role inadequately—partly because of excessive decentralization of authority and partly because the Reagan administration downgraded the NSA's policy advisory role.

Moreover, Shultz was a skilled, experienced bureaucratic operator regarded highly by Congress and by many within the administration. His effectiveness was further strengthened by his self-effacing style and, later, by his enhanced stature in the wake of the Iran-Contra affair. Above all, Shultz developed a close rapport with the President. And personal compatibility with the president, as past secretaries attest, is always a crucial factor.[57]

The secretary of state can still be important. However, recent history—certainly since 1961, and probably since before then—cautions against holding out great expectations for the secretary's own department. It is not prepared to be, nor are others disposed to permit it to be, the central coordinator and director of American foreign policy. And State cannot have a high policy profile unless the secretary does. But—Catch-22—even under recent influential secretaries (Dulles, Kissinger, Shultz), departmental stature did not parallel the rising tide of secretarial status. What, then, is or can be the department's role?

Three categories of significant activities can reasonably be expected of State. Foremost among them are the implementation of foreign policy decisions and the continued fulfillment of the traditional missions of the Foreign Service: representation, negotiation, and reporting. In this diplomatic arena, the department and the Foreign Service possess unique experience and talent. Second, although less certain of realization, an influential secretary who has the president's confidence might be able to draw some of his immediate staff and perhaps two or three senior departmental officers into a closer, more comfortable relationship with the White House. This is a far cry from a State-centered system, but it expands the scope of contact. Finally, State can and must continue to contribute to the whole range of substantive foreign policy issues—in senior- and lower-level interagency committees, in less formal contexts, and through the secretary and his seventh-floor staff. But in most instances, the department will remain a contributor, not a leader, in the policy formulation process. For it to aspire to a higher role is only to court yet another blow to its prestige and reputation.

Notes

1. A condensed, less detailed treatment of this subject appeared in Duncan L. Clarke, "Why State Can't Lead," *Foreign Policy* 66 (Spring 1987): 128–42.
2. Henry B. Miller and Robert W. Miller, "The Office of Undersecretary of State of Security Assistance," in Commission on the Organization of Government for the Conduct of Foreign Policy (hereafter cited as Murphy Commission), *Adequacy of Current Organization: Defense and Arms Control*, vol. 4, Appendix K (Washington, D.C.: Government Printing Office, 1975), p. 282. See also, Graham Allison and Peter Szanton, *Remaking Foreign Policy: The Organization Connection* (New York: Basic Books, 1976), p. 121. Kissinger agrees: "The State Department is simply not equipped to handle interdepartmental machinery" (Henry Kissinger, *Years of Upheaval* [Boston: Little, Brown, 1982], p. 453).
3. John M. Collins, *U.S. Defense Planning: A Critique* (Boulder, Colo.: Westview Press, 1982), pp. 96–101; Don Oberdorfer, "Man Behind the Mask," *Washington Post*, 3 February 1986, p. Al.
4. I.M. Destler, "State: A Department or 'Something More'?" in Duncan L. Clarke, ed., *Public Policy and Political Institutions: United States Defense and Foreign Policy—Policy Coordination and Integration* (Greenwich, Ct.: JAI Press, 1985), p. 102.
5. Smith Simpson, *Anatomy of the State Department* (Boston: Beacon Press, 1967), pp. 67, 63–66; Phillip G. Henderson, *Managing the Presidency: The Eisenhower Legacy—From Kennedy to Reagan* (Boulder, Colo.: Westview Press, 1988), pp. 85–90.

6. "White House Announcement of New Procedures for Overseas Interdepartmental Matters," in *Weekly Compilation of Presidential Documents*, 7 March 1966, pp. 232–33.

7. William I. Bacchus, "Obstacles to Reform in Foreign Affairs: The Case of NSAM 341," *Orbis* 18 (Spring 1974): 266–76.

8. Quoted in Jack Anderson, "Kissinger: One-Man State Department," *Washington Post*, 18 October 1974, p. D19. Lieutenant Colonel Oliver North, Reagan NSC action officer in the Iran-Contra affair, gave the State Department the code name "Wimp" (Theodore C. Sorenson, "The President and the Secretary of State," *Foreign Affairs* 66 [Winter 1987–88]: 231).

9. Leslie H. Gelb, "Why Not the State Department?" in Charles W. Kegley, Jr. and Eugene R. Wittkopf, eds., *Perspectives on American Foreign Policy* (New York: St. Martin's Press, 1983), p. 286; Barry Rubin, *Secrets of State: The State Department and the Struggle Over U.S. Foreign Policy* (New York: Oxford University Press, 1985), pp. 76, 96, 143, 212, 259; James T. Hackett, "How the White House Can Regain Control of Foreign Policy," in *Institution Analysis* (Washington, D.C.: The Heritage Foundation, 5 March 1984); Andrew L. Steigman, *The Foreign Service of the United States: First Line of Defense* (Boulder, Colo.: Westview Press, 1985), p. 101. At least one secretary of state, John Foster Dulles, distrusted his own department and effectively cut himself off from its career staff. Kissinger, too, worked with a small number of trusted staffers when he was secretary.

10. See, for instance, Jimmy Carter, *Keeping Faith: Memoirs of a President* (New York: Bantam Books, 1982), pp. 449–50; Kissinger, *Years of Upheaval*, p.434.

11. I.M. Destler, *Presidents, Bureaucrats and Foreign Policy: The Politics of Organizational Reform* (Princeton, N.J.: Princeton University Press, 1972), ch. 9; I.M. Destler, "A Job That Doesn't Work," *Foreign Policy* 38 (Spring 1980): 80–88; Destler, "State: A Department or 'Something More'?" p. 104.

12. Destler, *Presidents, Bureaucrats and Foreign Policy*, p. 167.

13. See James W. Clark, "Foreign Affairs Personnel Management," in Murphy Commission, *Personnel for Foreign Affairs*, vol. 6, Appendix P (Washington, D.C.: Government Printing Office, 1975), p. 190; Destler, "State: A Department or 'Something More'?" p. 101.

14. Destler, "State: A Department or 'Something More'?" p. 101.

15. See Richard Brown, "Toward Coherence in Foreign Policy: Greater Presidential Control of the Foreign Policymaking Machinery," in R. Gordon Hoxie, ed., *The Presidency and National Security Policy* (New York: Center for the Study of the Presidency, 1984), p. 332; Gelb, "Why Not the State Department?" p. 286.

16. Carter, *Keeping Faith*, p. 53.

17. Ibid., p. 449.

18. Zbigniew Brzezinski, *Power and Principle: Memoirs of the National Security Adviser, 1977–81* (New York: Farrar, Straus & Giroux, 1983), p. 73.

19. Henry Kissinger, *White House Years* (Boston: Little, Brown, 1979). p. 27.

20. Destler, "State: A Department or 'Something More'?" p. 102. But elsewhere Destler writes that State Department officials seem to perform the task of relating foreign policy choices to domestic political realities "incompletely,

reluctantly, and with a sense that such 'low politics' ought not to sully the pursuit of high diplomacy" (I.M. Destler, "National Security Advice to U.S. Presidents: Some Lessons from Thirty Years," *World Politics* 29 [January 1977]: 172).

21. See Joseph G. Bock and Duncan L. Clarke, "The National Security Assistant and the White House Staff: National Security Policy Decisionmaking and Domestic Political Considerations, 1947–1984," *Presidential Studies Quarterly* 16 (Spring 1986): 258–79; Joseph G. Bock, *The White House and the National Security Assistant: Friendship and Friction at the Water's Edge* (Westport, Ct.: Greenwood Press, 1987).

22. Brzezinski, *Power and Principle*, pp. 534–35.

23. U.S. Department of State, *Diplomacy for the 70s: A Program of Management Reform for the Department of State* (hereafter cited as Macomber Report) (Washington, D.C.: Government Printing Office, 1970), p. 5.

24. Murphy Commission, *Adequacy of Current Organization*, p.36; Clark, "Foreign Affairs Personnel Management," p. 191.

25. William I. Bacchus, *Staffing for Foreign Affairs: Personnel Systems for the 1980's and 1990's* (Princeton, N.J.: Princeton University Press, 1983), p. 52. See also, Robert L. Rothstein, *Planning, Prediction, and Policymaking in Foreign Affairs: Theory and Practice* (Boston: Little, Brown, 1972), pp. 39–41.

26. Bacchus, *Staffing for Foreign Affairs*, pp. 44–47. My criticisms here and elsewhere, as well as those of virtually all other observers, are directed not at individual FSOs, but at the system. Several friends, acquaintances, and former students are FSOs. Without exception, they are remarkably capable men and women.

27. Ibid., p. 46.

28. Ibid., pp. 48–49; Edward K. Hamilton, "Summary Report," in Murphy Commission, *Case Studies on U.S. Foreign Economic Policy, 1965–1974*, vol. 3, Appendix H (Washington, D.C.: Government Printing Office, 1975), p. 9; Rubin, *Secrets of State*, pp. 133–34.

29. U.S. Congress, House of Representatives, Committee on Foreign Affairs (hereafter cited as HFAC), Subcommittee on International Security and Scientific Affairs, and Subcommittee on International Operations, *Hearings: Overview of International Science and Technology Policy*, 98th Cong., 1st sess., 1983, especially pp. 84–90; Bacchus, *Staffing for Foreign Affairs*, pp. 50–51.

30. Bacchus, *Staffing for Foreign Affairs*, pp. 59–62; quoted in John Goshsko, "Diplomats Weak in Vital Languages," *Washington Post*, 12 November 1986, p. A1.

31. The legislative history and a chapter-by-chapter analysis of the act are contained in William I. Bacchus, *Inside the Legislative Process: The Passage of the Foreign Service Act of 1980* (Boulder, Colo.: Westview Press, 1984).

32. Bacchus, *Staffing for Foreign Affairs*, pp. 221–24.

33. Ronald I. Spiers, "Managing the Department of State," *Current Policy* (U.S. Department of State), No. 747 (26 September 1985): 3; Murphy Commission, *Adequacy of Current Organization*, p. 56; testimony of Henry Kissinger, U.S. Congress, House of Representatives, HFAC, Subcommittee on International Operations, Committee on Post Office and Civil Service, Subcommittee on

Civil Service, *Hearings: The Foreign Service Act*, 96th Cong., 1st sess., 1979, p. 458; Kissinger, *Years of Upheaval*, p. 437; Bacchus, *Staffing for Foreign Affairs*, p. 58; Destler, *Presidents, Bureaucrats and Foreign Policy*, pp. 157–58. One of State's own distinguished himself by winning the North American Cow Chip Throwing Contest. Afterward, he announced to the crowd: "Ladies and gentlemen, I've worked in the State Department for years and so I have a definite advantage" (Mary Jordan, "Boren Hopes for Last Laugh on Parris," *Washington Post*, 22 September 1986, p. Dl).

34. Virtually anyone who writes (or gossips) about the Foreign Service refers to this subject. The essence of the notion is captured, although not in a particularly balanced fashion that accords sufficient weight to the importance of having informed "country advocates," by Laurence H. Silberman, "Toward Presidential Control of the State Department," *Foreign Affairs* 57 (Spring 1979): 882–83.

35. I recall vividly an incident that occurred in 1980 when I was on the faculty of the National War College in Washington. One of the twelve rather senior FSOs in that year's class felt so strongly about the pejorative implications of the term that he requested, and received, an opportunity to address the entire class (about 180, as I recall, 80 percent of whom were military officers) on the subject of the loyalty and professionalism of the Foreign Service.

36. See Chapter 6. Common congressional sentiments toward State and FSOs were expressed by Representatives Dan Mica and Olympia Snowe, chairman and ranking minority member, respectively, of the Subcommittee on International Operations, HFAC. They accused State and career diplomats of having "distaste and disdain" for Congress, of a "lack of understanding" of the legislative branch, and of feeling "that Congress is an unneeded attachment to American government . . . (and) . . . a bother" (Dan Mica and Olympia Snowe, "The State Department Created the Fix It's in," *Washington Post*, 29 October 1987, p. A25; John Goshko, "Round Two on State Department Budget," *Washington Post*, 14 January 1988, p. A25).

37. Macomber Report, p. 390; testimony of Patrick Linehan, HFAC, *The Foreign Service Act*, p. 526.

38. Donald P. Warwick, *A Theory of Public Bureaucracy: Politics, Personality, and Organization in the State Department* (Cambridge, Mass.: Harvard University Press, 1975), p. 105; Bacchus, *Staffing for Foreign Affairs*, pp. 100–103.

39. See Chris Argyris, *Some Causes of Organizational Ineffectiveness Within the Department of State*, U.S. Department of State, Center for International Systems Research, Occasional Paper 2 (Washington, D.C.: Government Printing Office, 1967); Andrew M. Scott, "The Department of State: Formal Organization and Informal Culture," *International Studies Quarterly* 13 (March 1969): 2–3; Bacchus, *Staffing for Foreign Affairs*, pp. 37–41; Steigman, *The Foreign Service of the United States*, pp. 68–69; Morton H. Halperin, *Bureaucratic Politics and Foreign Policy* (Washington, D.C.: The Brookings Institution, 1974), p. 36.

40. Macomber Report, p. 310.

41. Quoted in Arthur Schlesinger, Jr., *A Thousand Days: John F. Kennedy in the White House* (Boston: Houghton Mifflin, 1965), p. 406.

42. Carter, *Keeping Faith*, p. 53.

43. U.S. Congress, *Report of the Congressional Committees Investigating the Iran-Contra Affair* (hereafter cited as *Report: Iran-Contra Affair*), H. Rept. 100–433, 100th Cong., 1st sess., 1987, p. 271.
44. Schlesinger, *A Thousand Days*, p. 414.
45. Argyris, *Some Causes of Organizational Ineffectiveness*, p. 16; Macomber Report, p. 5; Destler, *Presidents, Bureaucrats and Foreign Policy*, p. 166.
46. Additional examples abound. Former Ambassador Robert G. Neumann relates that: "In Pakistan . . . there was always tension before the war of 1971 between the Embassy in Islamabad and the Consulate General in Dacca, East Pakistan [now Bangladesh]. When the rebellion . . . started, the Consul General in Dacca reported accurately that atrocities were committed. This was not welcome in our Embassy. That man's career did not profit from that. He spoke up" (testimony of Robert G. Neumann, HFAC, *The Foreign Service Act*, p. 238). See also, Ellis O. Briggs, "The Staffing and Operations of our Diplomatic Missions," in Henry M. Jackson, ed., *The Secretary of State and the Ambassador* (New York: Praeger, 1964), pp. 134–35; Gary Sick, *All Fall Down: America's Tragic Encounter with Iran* (New York: Random House, 1985), p. 121.
47. Destler, "State: A Department or 'Something More'?" p. 99; Destler, *Presidents, Bureaucrats and Foreign Policy*, p. 159; Bacchus, *Staffing for Foreign Affairs*, p. 69; Kissinger, *White House Years*, p. 27; Warwick, *A Theory of Public Bureaucracy*, p. 33; Rubin, *Secrets of State*, p. 245.
48. Murphy Commission, *Report* (Washington, D.C.: Government Printing Office, 1975), p. 46. See also, Warwick, *A Theory of Public Bureaucracy*, pp. 31–32.
49. Interview with Ronald I. Spiers, "Managing Adversity: The State of State," *Foreign Service Journal* 64 (February 1987): 33. See also, Ronald Spiers, "Managing the Department of State," pp. 1, 3. Spiers was Under Secretary of State for Management in the Reagan administration.
50. Bacchus, *Staffing for Foreign Affairs*, p. 91, 100.
51. Macomber Report, p. 4.
52. Bacchus, *Staffing for Foreign Affairs*, pp. 65–68; Clark, "Foreign Affairs Personnel Management," p. 203; Spiers, "Managing the Department of State," p. 1.
53. Brzezinski, *Power and Principle*, pp. 535–38. Brzezinski later significantly revised his proposal; see Zbigniew Brzezinski, "NSC's Midlife Crisis," *Foreign Policy* 69 (Winter 1987–88): 93–99.
54. Kissinger, *Years of Upheaval*, pp. 434–37.
55. This list is neither exhaustive nor unique, but it contains commonly mentioned and telling criticisms. See Murphy Commission, *Adequacy of Current Organization*, pp. 40–41.
56. See Cecil V. Crabb, Jr. and Kevin V. Mulcahy, *Presidents and Foreign Policy Making: From FDR to Reagan* (Baton Rouge: Louisiana State University Press, 1986), pp. 294–96, 300–303.
57. William O. Chittick, "The Secretaries on Continuity and Bipartisanship in American Foreign Policy," *International Studies Notes* 11 (Fall 1984): 5; Oberdorfer, "Man Behind the Mask," p. A1.

CHAPTER 4

The Department of Defense and Defense Reorganization

The principal focus of this chapter is the Goldwater-Nichols Department of Defense Reorganization Act of 1986, P.L. 99–433 (hereafter referred to as Goldwater-Nichols), especially its impact on the Joint Chiefs of Staff and the combatant commands. The Office of the Secretary of Defense and the military departments are also treated, but primarily as they are affected by this legislation. The Planning, Programming and Budgeting System and the weapons acquisition process are not addressed, except in the context of some specific provisions of Goldwater-Nichols. Finally, I do not deal with the defense agencies (Defense Mapping Agency, Defense Nuclear Agency, and so on), although they are affected by Goldwater-Nichols.

A note of caution is in order concerning verb tenses. Congress permitted the Department of Defense to take until about 1990–1991 to implement certain provisions of the act and, at any rate, considerable time must elapse before its real impact can be assessed confidently. Hence, the reader should not necessarily assume that the author's occasional use of the past tense to describe various problems that have afflicted DOD elements implies that these problems do not now exist or will not persist in the future. Conversely, of course, it may be that past problems are or will be solved or mitigated by the legislation.

Passage of Goldwater-Nichols

Goldwater-Nichols was the first major defense reorganization legislation since 1958, and the most sweeping since 1947. The Reagan administration at first ignored and discouraged congressional interest in defense reorganization and, later, opposed fundamental statutory changes until the eleventh hour. Yet, President Reagan declared Goldwater-Nichols a "milestone" when reluctantly, and without a formal signing ceremony, he signed it into law on 1 October 1986.[1] Senator Barry Goldwater, who guided the bill through the Senate while chairing the Senate Armed Services Committee, said, "It's the only goddamn thing I've done in the Senate that's worth a damn." Similarly, Congressman Les Aspin, chairman of the House Armed Services Committee, called it "one of the landmark laws of American history," and Congressman Bill Nichols, the legislation's principal architect in the House, termed it his "proudest achievement."[2]

Passage of Goldwater-Nichols was extraordinary in at least three respects. First, Congress pushed through the legislation over the united opposition of a popular president, Secretary of Defense Caspar Weinberger, all acting secretaries of the military departments, and all acting members of the JCS. The Chief of Naval Operations and the Marine Corps Commandant were particularly hostile. The Navy, as Vincent Davis rightly observes, "in more than two hundred years had never met a centralization proposal that [it] liked."[3] Second, whereas the executive branch had initiated almost all prior defense reorganizations, Congress carried the ball this time. This was a remarkable role reversal since, before the 1980s, Congress had been a prime obstacle to senior-level centralization of authority within DOD. Finally, Goldwater-Nichols had nearly unanimous congressional support. Backing for the legislation cut across party and ideological lines. The House version (H.R. 3622) was approved by a 406–4 vote. The Senate passed an amended version of H.R. 3622 by a vote of 95–0.

Four factors help explain the overwhelming congressional support for Goldwater-Nichols.

Studies. From 1944 to 1982, there were at least twenty major studies on the organization of the U.S. defense establishment.[4] Virtually all of them found that establishment's effectiveness severely impeded by weaknesses in the joint structure, and all recommended changes in the JCS. Notable studies included the Symington Report (1960), the Fitzhugh Report (1970), the Steadman Report (1978), the Odeen Report (1979), and the Brehm Report (1982).[5] But the studies had little effect on the JCS. Even with the changes implemented in 1958 and 1984, the JCS remained substantially the same institution that had been established in 1947. However, the studies, especially those since the Fitzhugh Report, fueled a momentum toward and consensus for organizational change, at least among detached civilian defense analysts and many retired military officers.

They also prepared the analytical groundwork for three subsequent studies, all of which contributed importantly to Goldwater-Nichols. A report by Georgetown University's Center for Strategic and International Studies was cited frequently and favorably during congressional hearings in 1985 and 1986.[6] It paralleled a 1985 staff report for the Senate Armed Services Committee that constituted the most thorough assessment of defense organization theretofore undertaken.[7] Many of its recommendations were incorporated into Goldwater-Nichols. The third study was President Reagan's own Packard Commission Report, which supported many key recommendations of its two immediate predecessors.[8] The Packard Commission Report's 1986 release coincided with final congressional deliberations on the legislation. Its presidential imprimatur made it difficult, and potentially embarrassing, for the White House and secretary of defense to do anything other than show greater receptivity to what by this time was a tide of congressional support for major change.

Military Operational Shortcomings. While huge cost overruns on defense contracts, inflated prices for spare parts, and outright fraud contributed importantly to the reform movement, there was another, more significant, impetus for change—growing congressional concern about the combat performance of the armed forces.[9] The planning, organizational, and execution problems of the failed 1980 Iran hostage rescue mission, the 1983 Grenada invasion, and the October 1983 terrorist attack on the Marine barracks in Beirut had a cumulative effect on Congress. The last incident was a particularly critical catalyst because it prompted many conservatives to join liberals and moderates in calling for changes in the defense establishment.[10]

Leadership from Military Officers. There was no chance of defense reform without strong backing from general and flag rank military officers. In February 1982, less than six months before his retirement, Chairman of the JCS (CJCS) General David C. Jones appeared before the House Armed Services Committee and,

almost simultaneously, published an article urging major alterations in his institution.[11] General Jones, who served on the JCS
longer than any officer in history, then launched a whirlwind of
public appearances, articles, and congressional testimony advo-
cating change. Even after retirement, General Jones lent constant
encouragement to the process that led ultimately to Goldwater-
Nichols. General Jones was joined in 1982 by an influential ally
—General Edward C. Meyer, Chief of Staff, U.S. Army. Subsequently, a vast majority of retired Army and Air Force general
officers testifying before Congress urged changes in the defense
establishment, although only a minority of senior retired Navy
and Marine Corps officers favored reform.[12] That the Navy (which
someone once characterized as an institution with 200 years of
tradition untainted by progress) would prefer the status quo of
relative service autonomy was predictable. Unlike the Army, whose
mission performance is heavily dependent on air and naval transport and combat and logistic support, the Navy has its own army
(the Marines) and air force (naval air).

Congressional Leadership.   Given executive branch opposition,
political leadership had to come from Congress. In the House, it
was provided by Les Aspin and, especially, conservative Alabama
Democrat Bill Nichols, who chaired the Armed Services Committee's Investigations Subcommittee. On the Senate side, the
initiative was carried by Barry Goldwater and the ranking minority
Armed Services Committee member, Senator Sam Nunn. Goldwater's position was pivotal. He was someone of unquestioned
integrity, universally admired by fellow legislators. He was well
versed in defense matters and a retired major general in the Air
Force Reserve. Barry Goldwater was Mr. Conservative, Mr. Republican. Moreover, and importantly, he had been instrumental
in launching Ronald Reagan's political career. At the very moment
that Senator Goldwater was about to end thirty years of public
service, Reagan could hardly deny his long-time patron what the
senator considered his crowning achievement.[13]

Evolution of American Defense Organization

The historical development of American defense organization,
here only briefly recounted, provides the backdrop for Goldwater-
Nichols. While the story predates the National Security Act of

1947 (P.L. 80–253), I begin with that seminal legislation. Goldwater-Nichols's impact on OSD and the military departments is addressed in this subsection; its importance for the JCS and combatant commands is discussed in subsequent sections.

Office of the Secretary of Defense/Military Departments[14]

1947. The National Security Act of 1947 created the position of secretary of defense to give the president a principal staff assistant in all matters relating to national security. But the act's most noteworthy feature is the power it did *not* grant the secretary. He was provided with only three special assistants, and OSD, although it necessarily evolved from the general legislation, had no specific statutory basis until Goldwater-Nichols (Sec. 131(a)). More significantly, instead of presiding over a single, unified executive branch department, as President Truman desired, the secretary headed something called the National Military Establishment. It comprised three largely independent executive departments (Army, Navy, and Air Force), each headed by a cabinet-level secretary. The secretaries of these departments were given substantial powers, subject only to the secretary of defense's authority to establish *general* policies and programs, exercise *general* direction and control over logistics, and supervise and coordinate the budget. Finally, since the roles and missions of the three executive departments were only vaguely defined, this crucial issue was later resolved by the services when the secretary of defense met with the JCS in Key West in 1948. The resulting organizational arrangement was later aptly characterized by President Eisenhower as "little more than a weak confederation of sovereign military units."[15]

1949. On President Truman's recommendation, Congress amended the National Security Act in 1949 (P.L. 81–216) to create a Department of Defense, with the secretary of defense responsible for its general direction. His special assistants became assistant secretaries, and his control over the defense budget was consolidated. The former executive Departments of the Army, Navy, and Air Force were reduced in stature to military departments of DOD. They were to be separately administered, but were now under the authority and control of the secretary of defense. The 1949 legislation unified and centralized DOD significantly, but Congress constrained the secretary in two important respects: he was prohibited from transferring, reassigning, abolishing, or consolidating the combatant functions assigned to the military departments, and the service secretaries, as well as the members of the JCS, were given the right, on their own initiative, to present budget recommendations to Congress after first informing the secretary of defense.

1953. In 1953 President Eisenhower directed the transfer of several defense functions previously outside the secretary's jurisdiction to his control and gave him six additional assistant secretaries.

1958. The Department of Defense Reorganization Act of 1958 (P.L. 85–599) amended the National Security Act to grant the secretary of defense express direction, authority, and control over his department. In addition, he gained substantial freedom to reorganize DOD (except that major combatant functions could not be transferred or abolished if disapproved by either house of Congress), his authority over defense research and development was strengthened, assistant secretaries could now issue orders to the secretaries of the military departments, and the 1949 stipulation that these departments be separately administered was relaxed to "separately organized." There were several changes in defense organization from 1958 through 1985, such as the creation of defense agencies, but no major statutory changes occurred until 1986.

1986. The thrust of Goldwater-Nichols was to expand and strengthen the roles of the CJCS and the combatant commanders and to mandate greater unification at the expense of service separatism. But the secretary of defense and military departments did not escape coverage.

The conference report states in the strongest possible terms that "[t]he Secretary has *sole* and *ultimate* power within the Department of Defense on *any* matter on which the Secretary chooses to act" (emphases added).[16] Yet, Title I of Goldwater-Nichols imposed several requirements on the secretary with the obvious intent of facilitating more cooperative relations between OSD and other DOD components. The law requires the secretary to provide annual written policy guidance to DOD components for their preparation of program and budget proposals—a practice long predating Goldwater-Nichols; with the assistance of the under secretary of defense for policy, provide annual written guidance to the CJCS for the preparation and review of contingency plans (discussed below); and inform the secretaries of military departments of military operations and other DOD activities affecting their responsibilities (Sec. 102). The law also requires the secretary to advise the president on the appropriate qualifications for DOD political appointees (Sec. 102). The clear intent here, probably too optimistically, is to encourage appointment of better qualified senior officials.

Goldwater-Nichols stripped the secretary of defense of his prior relative freedom to reorganize the department (Sec. 103) and required him, the CJCS, and the military department secretaries to conduct separate studies of the functions and organization of OSD (Sec. 109).[17] These studies—plus one by an independent contractor, which the law requires—could be used by Congress as a starting point for future reorganization of OSD since that subject received scant attention in Goldwater-Nichols.

Military Departments. Title V of Goldwater-Nichols has five major effects on the service secretaries and military departments.[18] First, the act strengthens and clarifies the service secretaries' roles and makes them the focal points for their departments in specified relationships with the secretary of defense and CJCS. Secondly, each of the military departments has two large, costly, and often duplicative staffs. (The Department of the Navy, with the Marine Corps, has three staffs). One, the civilian secretariat, is under the secretary of each service. It contains political appointees, other civilians, and military officers. The other staff, the military headquarters staff, serves the chief of the particular military service and is composed mostly of uniformed officers. Many defense reformers urged abolition or radical reduction of the civilian secretariat. But Goldwater-Nichols retains the two separate staffs in each military department, while mandating significant (not radical) reduction in their size. Among other things, the number of general and flag rank officers on each military headquarters staff is reduced by 15 percent.

Reformers had also long called for the merger/unification of the functions of the two staffs. The third effect of the act was to, in fact, unify sole responsibility for seven functions within the civilian secretariats: acquisition, auditing, comptroller, financial management, inspector general, legislative liaison, and public affairs. An eighth function, research and development, is also centralized in the civilian secretariats, but the service secretaries may assign to the military staffs those research and development duties relating to testing and establishing military requirements.

A major objective of the law was to strengthen civilian control by enhancing the power of service secretaries. This could be effectuated only through genuine integration of civilian secretariat and military headquarters staff functions. By 1987 the Department of the Army was moving in this direction, but the Department of the Air Force was not. Instead, the Air Force had merely "consolidated," not "integrated," certain functions—acquisition, comptroller, and financial management—thereby leaving the service, not the Air Force secretary, effectively still in charge. This prompted a letter from Congressmen Aspin and John Dingel to Secretary Weinberger charging the Department of the Air Force with "bureaucratic abdication" of its responsibilities under Goldwater-Nichols, hearings by Congressman Nichols's investigations subcommittee, and an examination of the matter by the General Accounting Office.[19]

Fourth, Goldwater-Nichols addresses the enduring problem of information exchange between the chiefs of staff and the service secretaries. Since the act's language here is qualified, it remains to be seen whether the problem will be eased. The chiefs are required, with some exceptions, to inform the service secretaries of significant military operations and other matters affecting their military departments.

Finally, the Navy lost its former statutory authority over three roles and missions: naval reconnaissance, antisubmarine warfare, and protection of shipping. This was one of the most controversial provisions of the House bill. Congress feared that retention of this legal authority could be used by the Navy to argue that units engaged in these activities should not come under a unified combatant commander, thereby undermining an essential goal of the legislation.[20]

Joint Chiefs of Staff/Combatant (Unified and Specified) Commands[21]

1947. The National Security Act of 1947 created the JCS as a permanent body. Its members were the Army Chief of Staff, the

Chief of Naval Operations, the Air Force Chief of Staff, and the Chief of Staff to the Commander in Chief (a position never filled and abolished in 1949). The JCS was given the Joint Staff: 100 officers drawn from the military departments and headed by a director appointed by the JCS. The corporate chiefs were designated as the principal military advisers to the president and secretary of defense. They were also charged with preparing strategic plans and providing for the strategic direction of the military forces, preparing joint logistic plans and assigning the military services logistic responsibilities, coordinating military education, and reviewing major material and personnel requirements of the military forces. A final JCS duty was the establishment of unified commands in strategic areas, subject to the direction of the president and secretary of defense.

A unified command has forces assigned from two or more services; specified commands consist of forces from a single service. By 1987 there were eight unified commands (the European Command, the Pacific Command, and so on) and three specified commands (for example, the Strategic Air Command). Throughout this chapter, the terms *unified* and *specified* commands are used interchangeably with the term *combatant* commands. Similarly, unified and specified commanders are combatant commanders or commanders in chief (CINCs).

1949. The 1949 amendments to the National Security Act created the position of JCS chairman and enlarged the Joint Staff to a maximum of 210 officers. The chairman was to be appointed by the president and confirmed by the Senate and would serve a two-year term—with one reappointment possible. But Congress distrusted even a moderately powerful CJCS and emphatically rejected President Truman's proposal that the CJCS serve as the principal military adviser to the president and secretary of defense. Congress also prohibited the chairman from exercising command authority and limited him to presiding over JCS meetings as a nonvoting member, providing agendas for those meetings, and reporting disagreements to the president and secretary of defense. Truman's desire to have an independent chairman who could rise above the service-controlled joint structure was thwarted. JCS plans and advice continued to be dominated by individual service interests.

1953. Two changes occurred in 1953. First, President Eisenhower issued an executive order requiring that (1) the selection and tenure of the director of the Joint Staff be subject to the secretary of defense's approval; (2) the selection and tenure of Joint Staff officers be subject to the approval of the CJCS; and (3) responsibility for managing the Joint Staff be transferred from the corporate JCS to the chairman. This strengthened the chairman's authority, but the JCS as a corporate body continued to control the Joint Staff and assign tasks to it.

The second change involved a major adjustment in the chain of command. (The phrase *chain of command* refers to the hierarchy of responsible parties through which orders run for carrying out military missions.) Eisenhower's 1953 directive sought greater civilian control over the chain of command by requiring the secretary of defense to designate a military department, not a service chief, as the executive agent for each command. But this arrangement soon proved unwieldy and ineffective, prompting Eisenhower to again address the issue in 1958.

1958. The Department of Defense Reorganization Act of 1958 made the commandant of the Marine Corps a JCS member (when Marine Corps–related issues were under consideration) and instituted important changes in the Joint Staff. In his 1958 message to Congress, Eisenhower stressed the importance of placing the Joint Staff directly under the chairman's authority so that it could transcend parochial service interests and offer a unified national perspective on military matters.[22] But while Congress permitted the chairman to vote in JCS proceedings for the first time and raised the statutory limit on the size of the Joint Staff to 400 officers, it undermined the president's objective by circumscribing the CJCS's authority. The JCS was allowed to retain its prerogative, parallel to the chairman's, to assign duties to the Joint Staff; the chairman could select the Joint Staff director, but only in consultation with the JCS; and the chairman's previously exclusive right to manage the Joint Staff was now constrained by the phrase "on behalf of the Joint Chiefs of Staff." In short, the essential nature of the joint system was not altered in any fundamental respect. It continued to function as a loosely coordinated committee in which the special interests of the services prevailed over a unified national perspective.

President Eisenhower's message to Congress included this often quoted passage:

[S]eparate ground, sea, and air warfare is gone forever. If ever again we should be involved in war, we will fight it in all elements, with all services, as one single concentrated effort. Peacetime preparatory and organizational activity must conform to this fact. Strategic and tactical planning must be completely unified, combat forces organized into unified commands . . . singly led and prepared to fight as one, regardless of service.[23]

To accomplish this goal, Eisenhower proposed clearer functional distinctions between the military services and the combatant commands. The respective services would be responsible for the maintaining functions: recruiting, organizing, training, and equipping the forces. The unified and specified commands would command and operate the forces. Congress facilitated this objective by repealing the service chiefs' statutory authority to command forces; giving the president, acting through the secretary of defense, authority for establishing unified and specified commands; and assigning the combatant commanders full operational control over their forces. The military services were to have only administrative, not operational, responsibility for deployed forces.

With this legal foundation, the secretary of defense issued Department of Defense Directive 5100.1[24] in 1958, creating two command lines: one for administrative and support activities, the other for operational direction of the forces. The administrative/support chain of command ran from the president to the secretary of defense to the service secretaries and, lastly, to the service components of each combatant command. The operational chain of command ran by statute from the president to the secretary of defense to the unified or specified commander. The JCS was clearly and purposefully outside the operational chain of command. But Directive 5100.1 permitted the JCS to "advise" the secretary on military operations and, unlike the legislation, stated that the operational chain of command ran "through" the JCS. It was widely understood at the time that the word *through* indicated that the JCS would be merely transmitters, not originators, of command orders. But that interpretation was not congenial to the chiefs, and in practice, the distinction between the operating and maintaining functions often broke down. Hence, the services continued to dominate the operating functions, thereby subverting Eisenhower's central goal of unified operational command.[25]

Subsequent Developments. There were some changes in the JCS and combatant commands after 1958. For instance, each chief (other than the CJCS) was given a single four-year term in 1967, the Marine Corps commandant became a full participating JCS member in 1979, and legislation in 1984 (discussed below) gave the chairman some new authority. But the essential features of the system were in place by 1958. Twenty-eight years elapsed before Goldwater-Nichols challenged that system.

Joint Chiefs of Staff

The CJCS is the highest ranking officer in the armed forces. But before 1986 he had relatively little independent authority apart from the corporate chiefs. Indeed, two of his most important duties were performed in behalf of his fellow chiefs: participating in National Security Council meetings as a statutory military adviser to the president and managing the Joint Staff. Within the Joint Staff there was a small unit of between six and nine officers who worked directly for the chairman. The Joint Staff prepared plans and reports for the JCS. It was headed by the Joint Staff director (a three-star officer), and its elements included the following directorates: manpower and personnel (J-1); intelligence —the Defense Intelligence Agency (DIA) (J-2); operations (J-3), which assisted the JCS in carrying out its operational responsibilities as the military staff in the chain of command; logistics (J-4); plans and policy (J-5), which prepared strategic plans and studies, provided political-military advice, supported JCS participation in international negotiations and assisted the JCS and CJCS in addressing programmatic and budgetary matters; and Command, Control, and Communications (C^3) systems, which gave C^3 support to unified and specified commands for joint military operations.

The corporate JCS performed three central functions: advising, strategic and contingency planning, and providing operational direction to combatant commands as a de facto—if not statutorily sanctioned—link in the chain of command. The first two functions are treated below; the third is discussed later, in the section on combatant commands.

Advice

Senior policymakers in OSD, the NSC, and elsewhere generally give high marks for the quality of advice they receive *personally* (and often confidentially) from the chairman and *individual* service chiefs. However, since the 1940s policymakers have almost uniformly faulted the institutional views and products of the JCS corporate body. That advice is criticized for papering over issues that cut across service lines, lacking precision, and having taken too long to be formulated. The result, as former Secretary of Defense James Schlesinger said, was that JCS advice "is generally irrevelant, normally unread, and almost always disregarded."[26] Therefore, OSD civilians had to make decisions on military issues without the potentially vital input of joint military advice. There was broad agreement that this situation was caused by the nature of the JCS system itself.[27] Following are some causes of poor joint military advice.

Service Chiefs' Dual, Conflicting Responsibilities. The central feature of the JCS system was the dual responsibility (often called "dual-hatting") of each service chief. A chief played two inherently conflicting roles. First, he headed his own service and was expected to be a vigorous defender of its interests. He was also a member of the corporate JCS, in which capacity he was expected to rise above parochial service interests in order to provide policymakers with unified national military advice. Said General David Jones:

Chiefs are judged by their peers and services on their success in obtaining funding for their own major systems and on protecting service interests in . . . meetings. . . . Furthermore, a service chief, who is a service advocate in one hat and supposedly an impartial judge of competing requirements in his other hat as a member of the Joint Chiefs of Staff, has a fundamental conflict of interest.[28]

This conflict of interest was endemic to the system and has been recognized as a core problem by every major study of DOD organization since 1947.[29] A chief who subordinated his service's needs to the larger joint interest would lose the respect and dedication of his service. As a result, dual-hatting yielded watered-down JCS advice that merely reflected whatever level of compromise was necessary to obtain the unanimous agreement of the four services. Moreover, since the chiefs—few of whom had a strong prior background of joint service—accorded primacy to service interests, they often lacked the time and/or inclination to devote sufficient attention to JCS matters.

Chairman's Limited Independent Authority. The chairman, alone among the chiefs, is positioned to offer advice unconstrained by service constituencies. But prior to Goldwater-Nichols, his authority to offer independent advice was severely limited. He was only one of five equals, and he could not speak authoritatively for the JCS without its approval. His influence stemmed in large measure from his ability to persuade, not direct, his colleagues. The CJCS controlled few resources, no promotions, and (until 1984) few assignments. Of course, some past chairmen were influential, but their influence depended largely on their personalities and the inclination of some to quietly ignore the statutory provision prohibiting them from offering advice independent of the JCS.[30]

Desire for Unanimity. The JCS had a strong proclivity for offering unanimous advice to policymakers. In part, this reflected a belief that recommendations carried more weight if all the chiefs were in agreement. But consensus was reached only by avoiding the tough issues, such as potential conflicts over roles and missions. Therefore, the imperative for unanimity resulted in whatever recommendations the services could, in fact, agree upon. This generally yielded bland advice. The secretary of defense was thereby deprived of a range of diverse, pointed alternatives to consider.[31]

The Joint Staff. Unanimity of advice was reinforced by the workings and character of the Joint Staff. Its procedures, said the Fitzhugh Report, were based on service concurrence; they "maximize the opportunities for compromise."[32] Each service had a veto at every step of the process, something that drove staff recommendations to the lowest common level of assent. Joint Staff practices, concluded the Brehm Report, "seek unanimous consensus among the Services."[33]

The quality of the Joint Staff itself was criticized repeatedly. While officers serving on the staff were generally capable, few of the services' most talented officers elected a Joint Staff assignment. Among the reasons for poor staff quality were the following:

- The services themselves had little interest in improving staff quality since an ineffective Joint Staff permitted service interests to dominate.[34]
- Although after 1984 the services took some steps to enhance advancement opportunities for their officers on the Joint Staff, historically, Joint Staff officers were not as successful as many of their peers in receiving promotions and choice assignments upon completion of this joint tour of duty. This was a major disincentive to seeking an assignment to the Joint Staff.[35]
- The services tended to keep the best officers on their own staffs or assign them to more important joint posts, like OSD.[36]
- The widely held perceptions that the Joint Staff had little real influence, that its cumbersome staffing procedures were unproductive, and that independently minded Joint Staff officers risked intimidation by their service deterred promising officers from volunteering.[37]
- An officer assigned to the Joint Staff generally wanted to "punch his ticket" and return to his service as soon as possible. Consequently, there was a rapid turnover rate, and the staff had little corporate memory. The average tour for Joint Staff officers was less than thirty months. General and flag rank officers changed every twenty-four months.[38] Since most staff officers lacked previous joint experience or education, they often had difficulty dealing effectively with Joint Staff responsibilities.[39]

Effects of Goldwater-Nichols on the JCS

In considering significant changes to the JCS system, Congress faced essentially three choices. It could adopt one of two "radical" alternatives—abolish the JCS and replace it with either a national (joint) military advisory council[40] or a general staff system.[41] The remaining option was to retain the JCS while strengthening its chairman and joint institutions. Each of the first two proposals had some articulate advocates, such as General Edward Meyer for a national military advisory council and former Secretary of Defense Harold Brown for a general staff system, but neither proposal attracted much legislative support. Most civilians and retired military officers appearing before congressional committees favored the latter, more incremental approach.

Appointment and Duties of JCS Chairman. Goldwater-Nichols (Sec. 152(a)) allows the president to extend the chairman's term by reappointing him to a third two-year term. Before being appointed CJCS, an officer must first have served as vice chairman of the JCS, service chief of staff, or unified or specified commander—although the president may waive this requirement (Sec. 152(b)).

None of the chairman's new duties were more important than his greatly enhanced advisory role. Since Congress rejected revolutionary change and, instead, elected to retain the JCS, the only way to provide more effective representation of the joint military perspective was to elevate the authority of the one senior officer uniquely situated to offer that perspective. Therefore, the statutory proscription against the CJCS offering his own advice, independent of the corporate chiefs, was repealed. The chairman (not the corporate chiefs) is now the *principal* military adviser to the president, the NSC, and the secretary of defense (Sec. 151(b)(1)). While the other JCS members retain an advisory role and the CJCS must consult with them (and the combatant commanders) and seek their advice (Secs. 151(b)(2), 151(c)(1), 151(e)), this could reduce significantly the tendency for unanimous JCS advice. This prospect is further enhanced by the requirement that the CJCS inform policy officials of the range of military advice on a matter and of the views of JCS members who disagree with him (Secs. 151(c)(2), 151(d)(1).

Goldwater-Nichols reaffirmed the long-standing practice of the chairman's attendance at and participation in NSC meetings, subject to the president's desire and, very importantly, transferred responsibility for the duties theretofore performed by the corporate JCS to the chairman (Secs. 151, 153). Moreover, those duties are updated and expanded. (They are discussed later in this chapter). However, one seemingly innocuous, yet potentially pyrotechnic, provision is mentioned here. The act requires the chairman to prepare a report every three years on the roles and missions of the armed forces in which he "shall consider," among other things, "unnecessary duplication of effort among the armed forces" (Sec. 153(b)). Nothing is more sensitive than the services' well-guarded respective roles and missions. The report will surely attract their undivided attention.

The JCS Vice Chairman. Prior to Goldwater-Nichols, the CJCS was the only senior DOD military or civilian official without a deputy. When the chairman traveled away from Washington (a common occurrence), his duties devolved to the service chiefs on a rotating basis. This caused considerable discontinuity since the post of acting chairman would sometimes change hands several times within a matter of days. A new system was instituted in 1982 whereby the service chiefs rotated this responsibility every three months. But this somewhat improved procedure had serious weaknesses:

- Continuity still suffered. There were four different acting chairmen every year.
- Acting chairmen lacked the time to inform themselves about and perform the duties of the chairman while still fulfilling their normal responsibilities.
- Some acting chairmen used their new temporary hat to improperly further their own service's interests, while others employed their own service staff, rather than the Joint Staff, to support them in this capacity.

This situation was clearly unsatisfactory. A permanent JCS vice chairman could provide needed continuity, which was particularly essential in times of crisis when the chairman was away. He might also function as the chairman's alter ego and ally on the JCS, as he would be free of conflicting service responsibilities and be a JCS member himself. Moreover, if he was made the second-ranking officer in the armed services, just below a greatly strengthened chairman, the position would attract high-caliber officers.[42]
Goldwater-Nichols created a new four-star position of JCS vice

chairman and made him the second highest ranking military officer. He must be from a different service than the chairman and may serve up to three two-year terms. The vice chairman is acting CJCS in the absence of the chairman and a nonvoting participant in JCS meetings. He is a voting member when acting as chairman. Goldwater-Nichols requires, subject to presidential waiver, that an officer have the joint specialty (discussed below) and have served in at least one joint duty assignment as a general or flag rank officer in order to be appointed as vice chairman. Finally, the vice chairman is to perform whatever duties the CJCS may assign him (Sec. 154).[43]

Joint Staff. The Joint Staff no longer reports to the corporate JCS. Instead, it is now entirely the creature of the chairman. It is under his authority, direction, and control. He manages it and determines its duties and procedures (Sec. 155(a,c)). For the first time, the CJCS has it in his power to end the lowest-common-denominator consensus recommendations that characterized past service-dominated Joint Staff practices and products.[44] He can do this by, for instance, ensuring that vital issues are addressed regardless of their sensitivity for a particular service and by insisting that the secretary of defense receive a more sharply defined diversity of viewpoints.

The Joint Staff, whose combined permanent military and civilian personnel can total up to 1627, should become a much more interesting and attractive place to work. It should, therefore, attract high-quality officers. This prospect is reinforced by Goldwater-Nichols's emphasis on joint assignments as a precondition for promotion to senior ranks, reduction in the size of service staffs, the loss of key functions by the service chiefs, and the CJCS's right to select Joint Staff officers from lists submitted by the military departments containing the names of the services' "most outstanding officers" (Sec. 155(a)(3)).

By 1987 and 1988, it was clear that assignment to the Joint Staff (and to some other joint units, such as the unified command staffs) was indeed being actively sought by many promising officers. Moreover, CJCS Admiral William J. Crowe, Jr., advanced key objectives of Goldwater-Nichols when he employed his new authority over the Joint Staff to order significant organizational changes. An Operational Plans and Interoperability Directorate (designated J-7) was created, with responsibility for the functions of joint exercises and training; joint doctrine; joint education; joint tactics, techniques, and procedures; readiness; consolidated operational planning; and hardware interoperability. This constituted the first *potentially* viable organizational focus in U.S. history for resolving fundamental problems impeding effective unified action by American armed forces. The Joint Staff organization was further changed by the addition of a new Force Structure, Resource, and Assessment Directorate (designated J-8), with responsibility for preparing force and budget analyses, evaluating acquisition programs, and conducting net assessments.[45]

Joint Officers Personnel Policy. In 1984, the Department of Defense Authorization Act for FY 1985 (P.L. 98–525) sought to upgrade joint duty assignments. Among other things, it required the CJCS to select officers to be assigned to the Joint Staff, encouraged longer tenure for some Joint Staff officers, and directed the secretary of defense to see that Joint Staff officers received equitable treatment in promotions and subsequent assignments. Two years later, Goldwater-Nichols sharply escalated the importance of joint duty assignments.

The Brehm Report in 1982 first recommended establishment of a cadre of joint duty career specialists with the ability, education, and background to provide better continuity, objectivity, and experience in handling joint matters.[46] Goldwater-Nichols adopted this proposal by creating an occupational category called the "joint speciality" for the management of officers trained in and oriented toward joint matters.[47] Joint speciality officers are selected by the secretary of defense (who must establish career guidelines for them), on the advice of the CJCS, from nominees submitted by the secretaries of the military departments. An officer cannot be selected for the joint specialty until he first completes an approved joint education program and, thereafter, completes a tour in a joint duty assignment. To guard against these officers becoming isolated from their parent service, they must return periodically to that service for field assignments. The legislation also stipulates that 50 percent of the joint duty officers or nominees in grades above captain/navy lieutenant be joint specialty officers. A personnel category designated by the secretary of defense as "critical joint duty assignments" must be filled exclusively with joint specialty officers (Sec. 661).[48] Goldwater-Nichols's obvious objective is to attract outstanding officers to important, career-enhancing joint positions that are reserved, in whole or in substantial part, for them.

The act has major implications for joint military education programs, officer assignments from joint colleges, and "jointness" overall. In the past, few officers on joint duty assignments knew much about the several branches of their own service, let alone the other services. Moreover, few graduates of the two senior joint colleges were assigned to joint duty immediately upon completion of their education, and, in fact, joint service was defined so loosely that, as Harold Brown said, "almost anything" qualified.[49] No more. The joint colleges[50]—primarily the three National Defense University schools under the control of the CJCS: the National War College, the Industrial College of the Armed Forces, and the Armed Forces Staff College—must periodically revise their curricula to strengthen officer education in joint matters; all joint specialty officers and more than 50 percent of other officers graduating from a joint school must receive immediately a joint duty assignment; and only specifically enumerated assignments qualify as joint duty assignments. Moreover, joint duty tours must be two years in length for general and flag rank officers, and at least three years for other officers (Secs. 663(b-d), 664, 668(b)). Under the original Goldwater-Nichols legislation, these joint duty tours were, respectively, three and three-and-a-half years in length. But the services lobbied Congress successfully in 1987 and 1988 to reduce officers' time in the joint environment.[51]

Congress was concerned about the limited joint experience of many general and flag rank officers, including most service chiefs. Therefore, from now on—subject only to a waiver by the secretary of defense—*no* officer can be promoted from colonel to brigadier general or from navy captain to rear admiral without at least one genuine joint duty assignment. All officers promoted to general or flag rank must take an education course (called CAPSTONE) on working with the other services. Finally, the secretary of defense must advise the president on the qualifications needed by officers to serve in three- and four-star positions, and the CJCS must evaluate the joint duty performance of officers recommended for these ranks (Secs. 403, 404, 663(a)).

Before Goldwater-Nichols, the services dominated absolutely the promotions and assignments of officers, including those on joint duty assignments. This meant, in the words of a Senate Armed Services Committee report, that "[j]oint thinkers [were] likely to be punished, and Service promoters [were] likely to be rewarded. This system of punishments and rewards must be changed."[52] And changed it was. For the first time, the services, while still very influential in promotions and assignments, lost some of their control over the careers of all officers. Goldwater-Nichols made the secretary of defense and, especially, the CJCS, guardians of the careers of joint duty officers. It did so with elaborate precision. Henceforth, all promotion boards considering officers who have served in joint duty assignments must include at least one joint duty officer designated by the CJCS. The secretary of defense, with the chairman's advice, is charged with overseeing and monitoring the promotions and career assignments of such officers (Secs. 402(a)(c), 665). The promotion review process for officers who are serving or have served in joint duty assignments (Secs. 402, 662):

- requires the secretary of defense to furnish guidelines to the military departments to ensure that promotion boards give appropriate consideration to joint duty performance;
- directs the CJCS to review promotion board reports before they are submitted to the secretary of defense;
- authorizes the secretary of a military department, upon determination by the CJCS that a promotion board acted contrary to the secretary of defense's guidelines, to return the report to the promotion board for further proceedings;
- directs the secretary of defense to take appropriate action to resolve any remaining disagreement between the secretary of a military department and the CJCS; and
- requires the secretary of defense to ensure that the qualifications of officers assigned to joint duty assignments are such that, as a group, they are promoted at a rate not less than the rate for officers of the same service in the same grade and competitive category who are serving on, or have served on, their service's headquarters staff.[53]

Strategic and Contingency Planning: Strategic Planning. The strategic planning process—linking national objectives set by policy officials with the military forces, weapons, and capabilities developed by the military departments—suffered in the past from the ineffectual institutional role of the JCS. The individual service chiefs were deeply involved in DOD's resource allocation process, but the corporate JCS exerted little influence over the composition of DOD's budget. The JCS did not recommend to civilian policymakers cross-service priorities for allocating defense resources. Instead, service parochialism prevented the JCS from doing much other than call for across-the-board budget increases for all of the services. These fiscally unconstrained, "blue sky" proposals inevitably meant that JCS documents (the Joint Strategic Planning Document) urged far larger and more expensive peacetime forces than any administration was willing to sustain. Hence, they were regularly discounted as unrealistic by the secretary of defense, and he had to rely almost entirely on his civilian staff to see that service programs were balanced and consistent with national priorities. Nor could the CJCS be of much assistance to the secretary since he lacked the staff resources and statutory authority to offer independent budget recommendations on the vast spectrum of pertinent subjects. The absence of effective joint military input into the strategic planning and budgeting process resulted in disjointed military strategies among the respective services and permitted them to spend money on their own priorities, often at the expense of essential national requirements.[54]

Goldwater-Nichols addressed this situation by sharply augmenting the authority and duties of the chairman in strategic planning, programming, and budgeting. He is, among other things, responsible for:

- preparing strategic plans that conform with resource levels projected by the secretary of defense (that is, preparing fiscally constrained plans);
- performing net assessments (comparing the capabilities of U.S./Allied armed forces with those of potential adversaries);
- advising the secretary on the conformance of fiscal year program and budget recommendations by the military departments and other DOD components with the priorities established in the strategic plans;
- submitting to the secretary fiscally constrained, alternative program and budget proposals, under guidance from the secretary; and
- assessing military requirements for defense acquisition programs (Sec. 153(a)(1–2, 4)).

The law also requires the CJCS to develop joint military doctrine for the employment of the armed forces (as well as to formulate policies for joint training and the coordination of military education) (Sec. 153(a)(5)). This was a much-needed reform because the JCS had largely ignored the development of joint doctrine. For instance, the JCS had never published a doctrine to integrate the operations of tactical air and land forces. Consequently, the services, each of whom had different approaches to military operations, dominated operational doctrine. This had serious and negative ramifications when U.S. armed forces were employed in combat.[55]

Contingency Planning. Senior policymakers understandably take an interest in nuclear war plans. Presidents and secretaries of defense are briefed regularly on the Single Integrated Operational Plan (SIOP). The president approves general strategic guidance, and Defense, with JCS advice, prepares the more detailed policy guidance—the Nuclear Weapons Employment Plan (NUWEP)—for preparation of the SIOP.

However, prior to Goldwater-Nichols, other contingency plans for the use of force—which were prepared by the combatant commanders within and through the JCS system and the Joint Staff —were jealously guarded from civilian intrusion. These plans suffered from several deficiencies. First, the services' almost exclusive focus on resource issues meant that contingency planning (which was unconnected with the resource allocation process) was not among their central concerns. Second, these plans usually said little about operational strategy, and the strategy called for was rarely subjected to periodic review. Finally, and most significantly, only the secretary and (occasionally) the deputy secretary of defense had access to these plans, and then only upon request. There was no effective procedure whatsoever for providing civilian guidance in developing the plans. This lack of policy guidance and nonparticipation of civilians meant that military contingency plans ran a high risk of being rejected by policymakers in times of crisis because of their inattention to political (as well as diplomatic and economic) factors.

Only once did a secretary of defense attempt to provide adequate guidance. Secretary Harold Brown issued the Planning Guidance for Contingency Planning (PGCP) in 1980. It was designed to align contingency planning with broad national policy and the secretary's own defense guidance. Brown directed the under secretary of defense for policy to oversee and review JCS contingency plans. But this commendable practice and the PGCP itself were discontinued by the Reagan administration. In the Reagan years, the secretary was once again briefed on contingency plans in an ad hoc fashion, and only upon request.[56]

Goldwater-Nichols requires the under secretary of defense for policy to assist the secretary in preparing written policy guidance for the preparation and review of contingency plans and in reviewing such plans (Sec. 134). In conformance with this guidance, the CJCS is to prepare and review contingency plans and advise the secretary of critical deficiencies in force capabilities that are identified through this process. The chairman is also to establish and maintain a uniform system of evaluating the preparedness of the combatant commands for carrying out their missions (Sec. 153(a)(3)). This could give contingency planning greater salience and align the plans' political assumptions with national policy. It may also encourage a healthy questioning of assumptions and move contingency planning closer to the resource allocation process.

Combatant Commands

President Eisenhower knew that modern warfare requires the effective integration of land, sea, and air forces under a single command authority. Indeed, creation of unified combatant commands was a central objective of his 1958 reforms. But the reforms failed. The unified CINCs had insufficient authority to effectively carry out their assigned missions because the services continued to dominate the commands in three ways.

First, the service chiefs, through their membership on the JCS and under the ambiguous language of DOD Directive 5100.1, were in the de facto chain of command. A committee, such as the corporate JCS, is, by its very nature, an ineffectual mechanism for providing crisp, decisive, time-urgent direction.[57] But the chiefs exerted substantial influence on the CINCs through their role in the chain of command.

Second, the services controlled crucial matters internal to the unified commands. Within the unified commands are single-service component commands corresponding to the military departments (Army, Navy, Air Force) from which forces are drawn. The CINCs had full operational authority over their forces, but only through these component commands. Moreover, the services effectively dominated the unified commands through their control of the administrative chain of command that ran through the military departments to the component commands. Hence, on nonoperational matters—procurement, logistics, maintenance, and training—the component commanders bypassed the CINCs and reported directly to their respective military departments. Consequently, the CINCs had limited influence over the readiness, composition, and structure of the forces for which they were operationally responsible. This fragmentation of authority below the level of the unified commander substantially impeded preparations for and conduct of joint military operations.

Finally, Eisenhower's reforms did not eliminate the close association of each command with a particular service. So, for example, the Navy effectively dominates the Atlantic Command, the Army the Southern Command, and so forth.[58]

In addition to these problems, the unified commanders had little influence on the allocation of resources either to or within their commands. There was a natural tension between the service chiefs, who were responsible for providing the resources (weapons, trained personnel, and so on), and the unified commanders, who were responsible for war-fighting. The unified commanders are primarily concerned with readiness; they get nervous when they see readiness traded off for future force structure or modernization. Yet, their voices were scarcely heard in such decisions.[59] In 1984 the CINCs were permitted to participate in the deliberations of the Defense Review Board, but, at best, this only slightly ameliorated the problem.[60]

Effects of Goldwater-Nichols on Combatant Commands

Chain of Command. Since Article II of the Constitution designates the president as commander in chief of the armed forces, it is debatable whether Congress can restrict his command authority by statutorily specifying the chain of command.[61] Mindful of this, Congress set forth the chain of command in Goldwater-Nichols so as to afford the president maximum freedom of action. The chain of command, unless otherwise authorized by the president, runs from the president to the secretary of defense to the unified or specified commanders (Sec. 162(b)). At the president's election, authorized orders from him or the secretary of defense may be "transmitted through" the CJCS, and the chairman may "assist" the president and secretary of defense in performing their command functions (Sec. 163(a)). But Congress was emphatic, in its conference report, that even if the CJCS should perform these functions, he "would not be part of the chain of command."[62]

CINCs' Authority over Their Commands. Absent a presidential waiver, an officer must have the joint specialty and have served in at least one joint duty assignment in order to be selected as a CINC (Sec. 164(a)). The act dramatically elevates the CINCs' authority over their commands and gives them a powerful ally and advocate—the CJCS. Goldwater-Nichols:

- Authorizes the secretary of defense to assign the CJCS authority for overseeing the activities of the combatant commands and specifies that the CJCS is the spokesman for the combatant commanders, especially concerning their operational requirements (Sec. 163(b)). Moreover, the secretary, in consultation with the chairman, "shall ensure" that combatant commanders have sufficient command authority over their forces, and should a combatant commander at any time consider his command authority to be insufficient, the commander "shall promptly inform the secretary of defense" (Sec. 164(c)(2–3)).
- Specifies the CINC's command authority so as to give him, subject only to the direction of the president and secretary of defense, unquestioned control over all subordinate commands and forces assigned to his command (Sec. 164(c-d)).
- Authorizes the secretary of defense to assign authority to the CINCs for those aspects of administration and support that the secretary deems necessary to accomplish their missions. The military departments may retain some responsibility for administration and support if the secretary, on the advice of the CJCS, deems this appropriate (Sec. 165).
- Requires subordinate elements of a combatant command and other DOD elements to communicate with each other (on matters for which the CINC has been assigned authority), according to procedures established by the CINC. Moreover,

the CINC may direct subordinate elements within his command to advise him of all communications to and from other DOD elements on matters for which he has *not* been assigned authority (Sec. 164(d)(2–4)).
* Requires the CINC's concurrence in the selection of his subordinate commanders and staff members, as well as his evaluation of the performance of the subordinate commanders. The CINC is further authorized to suspend from duty any officer assigned to his command (Sec. 164(e-g)).

CINCs' Resource Allocation Role. Through their patron, the CJCS, the CINCs' impact on the resource allocation process was increased. After conferring with the CINCs, the chairman is to advise the secretary of defense on the priorities of the requirements identified by the CINCs and the extent to which the program and budget proposals of other DOD elements conform to these priorities (Secs. 153(a)(b)(B-C), 163(b)(2)). In addition, after consultation with the CJCS, the secretary must include in his annual defense budget request to Congress a separate budget proposal for those activities of the unified and specified commands that he determines to be appropriate (Secs. 153(a)(4)(D), 166). This latter statutory provision was not followed in 1987. Secretary Weinberger refused to submit a separate budget request for unified and specified command activities, a clear case of noncompliance with the specific language of Goldwater-Nichols.[63]

In sum, Goldwater-Nichols shifts the balance of power decisively away from the services and toward the CINCs and the CJCS. There was early evidence that many of the reforms to strengthen the CINCs were taking hold. For instance, the December 1986 revisions to a crucial JCS war-fighting document (Unified Action Armed Forces) implemented the CINC's authority under Goldwater-Nichols to organize and employ *all* of his assigned forces. In addition, Admiral Crowe, General George B. Crist, CINC, U.S. Central Command, and other senior military officers spoke positively in 1987 and 1988 about the reforms' impact on U.S. military operations in the Persian Gulf region.[64] *If* they choose to exercise it, the CINCs now have the legal authority to rival or surpass the service chiefs in prominence and to become the most powerful leaders of deployed American forces since World War II.

Conclusion

Few U.S. national security institutions have more doggedly and successfully resisted organizational reform than the Pentagon. Perhaps this is why the architects of Goldwater-Nichols were so elated when it was finally enacted into law.

For now, however, Goldwater-Nichols deserves only two cheers. The implementation phase will be long and arduous. History amply demonstrates the services' agility in skirting reform legislation. Moreover, some provisions of the act will require adjustment, and serious unforeseen problems may well be encountered. Much depends on OSD's vigor in monitoring the services' compliance with the legislation and the attitudes and actions of the CJCS and the CINCs toward their new, vastly increased powers. Secretary Weinberger and Deputy Secretary of Defense William Taft IV seemed uninterested in and uncommitted to full and timely implementation.[65] Frank Carlucci, a member of the Packard Commission and a supporter of much of the defense reform movement, was Weinberger's successor in the Reagan administration's last year. Carlucci was much more cooperative. But it may take both a secretary with a receptive attitude and a new administration before the potential of the act is wholly realized, just as it took a Secretary Robert McNamara in 1961 to utilize the powers granted by the Defense Reorganization Act of 1958. Also, the act's impact may not be fully evident until at least 1990 or 1991 since the drafters wisely established a set of deadlines for implementation.

The broad bipartisan congressional coalition for defense reorganization, if it remains intact, promises a high degree of interest in and oversight of Goldwater-Nichols. Pentagon subversion of congressional intent could, therefore, entail some risks. Furthermore, while government reorganization is no panacea for improved cost-effectiveness or efficiency,[66] the act affords the armed forces an opportunity to, themselves, address grave and long-standing problems. If the opportunity is seized, the nation's defense establishment and defense effort should be well served. If, instead, the military services see Goldwater-Nichols as a threat to be resisted, public and congressional confidence in and support of the services will likely decline. Then, a much exercised Congress and/or a reform-minded president, perhaps aided by a Robert McNamara–type secretary of defense, might reach for the big gun of "radical" reform. A general staff system was not adopted in 1986. But it has much to commend it, as well as some distinguished proponents. It could be taken off the shelf.

Notes

1. White House press release, 1 October 1986.
2. Quoted in George Wilson, "Defense Reorganization Enacted," *Washington Post*, 18 September 1986, p. A15.
3. Vincent Davis, "Organization and Management," in Joseph Kruzel, ed., *1987–1988 American Defense Annual* (Lexington, Mass.: Lexington Books, 1987), pp. 171–73.
4. They are listed in Department of Defense (hereafter cited as DOD), *Current News* 844 (21 April 1982): 48. There also have been numerous studies by individuals, such as Lawrence J. Korb, *The Joint Chiefs of Staff: The First Twenty-Five Years* (Bloomington: Indiana University Press, 1976); John G. Kester, "The Future of the Joint Chiefs of Staff," *AEI Foreign and Defense Policy Review* 2 (1980): 2–23; William J. Lynn, "The Wars Within: The Joint Military Structure and Its Critics," in Robert J. Art, Vincent Davis, and Samuel P. Huntington, eds., *Reorganizing America's Defense: Leadership in War and Peace* (Elmsford, N.Y.: Pergamon-Brassey's, 1985), pp. 168–204; and Archie D. Barrett's excellent *Reappraising Defense Organization: An Analysis based on the Defense Organization Study of 1977–1980* (Washington, D.C.: National Defense University Press, 1983). For a summary of the arguments against reform, see Victor H. Krulak, *Organization for National Security: A Study* (Washington, D.C.: United States Strategic Institute, 1983); Alan R. Millet, et al., *The Reorganization of the Joint Chiefs of Staff: A Critical Analysis* (Elmsford, N.Y.: Pergamon-Brassey's, 1986), pp. 1–60; MacKubin Thomas Owens, "The Hollow Promise of JCS Reform," *International Security* 10 (Winter 1985–86): 98–111.
5. *Report on Reorganization of Department of Defense* (hereafter cited as Symington Report), 1960, reprinted in U.S. Congress, House of Representatives, Committee on Armed Services (hereafter cited as HASC), Investigations Subcommittee, *Hearings: Reorganization Proposals for the Joint Chiefs of Staff*, 97th Cong., 2d sess., 1982, pp. 636–42; U.S. Department of Defense, Blue Ribbon Defense Panel, *Report to the President and the Secretary of Defense on the Department of Defense* (hereafter cited as Fitzhugh Report) (Washington, D.C.: Government Printing Office, 1970); DOD, *Report to the Secretary of Defense on the National Military Command Structure* (hereafter cited as Steadman Report), 1978); President's Reorganization Project, *National Security Policy Integration* (Odeen Report, September 1979); Chairman's Special Study Group, *The Organization and Functions of the JCS*, Report for the Chairman, Joint Chiefs of Staff (hereafter cited as Brehm Report, April 1982).

6. *Toward a More Effective Defense* (hereafter cited as CSIS Report) (Washington, D.C.: Center for Strategic and International Studies, Georgetown University, 1985), reprinted in Barry M. Blechman and William J. Lynn, eds., *Toward a More Effective Defense: Report of the Defense Organization Project* (Cambridge, Mass.: Ballinger, 1985), pp. 1–39.

7. U.S. Congress, Senate, Committee on Armed Services (hereafter cited as SASC), *Defense Organization: The Need for Change*, Staff Report, S. Prt. 99–86, 99th Cong., 1st sess., 1985.

8. President's Blue Ribbon Commission on Defense Management, *A Quest for Excellence: Final Report to the President* (Packard Commission Report) (Washington, D.C.: Government Printing Office, June 1986).

9. Brad Knickerbocker, "Pressure Grows for an Overhaul of Pentagon's Management Machinery," *Christian Science Monitor*, 6 December 1984, p. 1.

10. SASC, *Defense Organization*, pp. 359–70; George C. Wilson, "Mr. Reliable Becomes Mr. Fix-It," *Washington Post*, 7 August 1986, p. A21. See also, Edward N. Luttwak, *The Pentagon and the Art of War* (New York: Simon & Schuster, 1984).

11. David C. Jones, "Why the Joint Chiefs of Staff Must Change," *Directors and Boards* 6 (Winter 1982), reprinted in *Armed Forces International* (March 1982): 62–72. General Jones got the ball rolling, but it rolled slowly at first. For why this was so, see Louis J. Moses, *The Call for JCS Reform: Crucial Issues* (Washington, D.C.: National Defense University Press, 1985), pp. 45–50.

12. However, it was a substantial and articulate Navy and Marine Corps minority, which included Admiral Harry D. Train, Vice Admiral Thor Hansen, and General Wallace M. Greene.

13. See Davis, "Organization and Management," pp. 182–83. There is another factor not to be overlooked—superior staff work on both the House and Senate sides. In particular, Archie Barrett of Congressman Nichols's subcommittee staff knows more about defense organization than anyone. Before retiring from the Air Force, he worked on this subject in DOD during the Carter administration and wrote a superior book on same (see note 4). Barrett, who has a Ph.D. from Harvard, often questioned witnesses appearing before the subcommittee. While the political credit for Goldwater-Nichols rightly goes to those two men, in another sense, the act might be titled "Jones-Barrett."

14. For the 1947–1985 period, see generally SASC, *Defense Organization*, pp. 49, 379–414; Office of the Secretary of Defense, Historical Office, *The Department of Defense: Documents on Establishment and Organization, 1944–1978* (hereafter cited as OSD Historical Office, *DOD Documents*) (Washington, D.C.: Government Printing Office, 1978).

15. President Eisenhower's Message to Congress of 3 April 1958, in OSD Historical Office, *DOD Documents*, p. 177.

16. *Congressional Record—House*, 12 September 1986, p. H6859. The conference report (*Conference Report on H.R. 3622*, H. Rept. 99–824, 99th Cong., 2d sess., 1986) is contained in *Congressional Record—House*, 12 September 1986, pp. H6830–76.

17. Reducing the secretary's authority here is probably unwise. But some mem-

bers of Congress distrusted Secretary Weinberger and feared he might abuse his authority by weakening provisions of Goldwater-Nichols. The studies of OSD were forwarded to Congress by October 1, 1987, as required by law.

18. On the many problems and debilities of the service secretaries, see John G. Kester, "Do We Need the Service Secretary?" *Washington Quarterly* 4 (Winter 1981): 150–67.

19. Letter from Congressmen Les Aspin and John Dingel to Secretary of Defense Caspar Weinberger, 26 March 1987 (mimeo); letter from Congressman Les Aspin, 7 August 1987 (mimeo); U.S. General Accounting Office (hereafter cited as GAO), *Reorganization of the Military Departments: Financial Management Structures*, GAO/T-NSIAD–88–12 (Washington, D.C.: GAO, 1988).

20. HASC, News Release, 11 September 1986, p. 4.

21. For the 1947–1979 period, see generally SASC, *Defense Organization*, pp. 139–47, 275–78; OSD Historical Office, *DOD Documents*.

22. OSD Historical Office, *DOD Documents*, pp. 175–86.

23. Ibid., p. 175.

24. Ibid., pp. 316–24.

25. Lynn, "The Wars Within," pp. 178–79.

26. SASC, *Hearings: Organization, Structure and Decisionmaking Procedures of the Department of Defense*, 98th Cong., 1st sess., 1983, Part 5, p. 187.

27. See Fitzhugh Report, p. 34; Brehm Report, pp. 27–28.

28. Testimony of General David C. Jones, SASC, *Hearing: Structure and Operating Procedures of the Joint Chiefs of Staff*, 97th Cong., 2d sess., 1982, p. 21.

29. For example, see SASC, *Defense Organization*, pp. 166–71; Symington Report, p. 6; Steadman Report, p. 53; CSIS Report, p. 12.

30. SASC, *Defense Organization*, pp. 171–73.

31. Ibid., pp. 173–74; Steadman Report, p. 52; testimony of General Jones, *SASC, Structure and Operating Procedures*, p. 22.

32. Fitzhugh Report, Appendix N, p. 14.

33. Brehm Report, pp. 47–48.

34. Kester, "The Future of the Joint Chiefs of Staff," p. 17.

35. Brehm Report, p. 44.

36. Steadman Report, p. 51.

37. Brehm Report, p. 9; testimony of Admiral Harry D. Train, U.S. Navy (Ret.), HASC, Investigations Subcommittee, *Hearings: Reorganization of the Department of Defense*, 99th Cong., 2d sess., 1986, pp. 161, 164.

38. Brehm Report, p. 42.

39. Ibid., pp. 7, 43.

40. For descriptions and assessments of this option, see Lynn, "The Wars Within," pp. 191–95; SASC, *Defense Organization*, pp. 188–89, 203–13.

41. For descriptions and assessments of this option, see William J. Lynn and Barry R. Posen, "The Case for JCS Reform," *International Security* 10 (Winter 1985–86): 86–89; SASC, *Defense Organization*, pp. 203–205, 228–37; Robert L. Goldrich, "The Evolution of Congressional Attitudes Toward a General Staff in the 20th Century," in SASC, *Defense Organization*, pp. 244–74.

42. SASC, *Defense Organization*, pp. 191, 217–22; HASC, *Reorganization of the Department of Defense*, pp. 158–59, 849.

43. Congress expected that the vice chairman's duties might include partici-pation in the acquisition and procurement process. But the conference report cautioned that neither the chairman nor vice chairman "should . . . partic-ipate too deeply in the defense acquisition process" (*Congressional Record—House*, 12 September 1986, p. H6861).
44. CJCS Admiral William J. Crowe, Jr. apparently had not fully exercised this new authority as of late 1987.
45. See James Locher, "Organization and Management," in Joseph Kruzel, ed., *1988–1989 American Defense Annual* (Lexington, Mass.: Lexington Books, 1988), pp. 178, 180.
46. Brehm Report, Appendix E, pp. E1–E5. The proposal was later endorsed by the CSIS Report (pp. 14–15), which was particularly influential with Congress.
47. Proponents of the joint specialty denied that it created an elite corps, or "royalty corps," of purple-suited (joint service) officers (HASC, *Reorgani-zation of the Department of Defense*, pp. 541, 855).
48. The legislation does not clearly define "joint duty assignment." But in 1987 Secretary Weinberger issued lists setting forth 8235 joint duty positions and 1000 critical joint duty assignments (OSD, Joint Duty Assignment List, July 1987 [mimeo]).
49. HASC, *Reorganization of the Department of Defense*, p. 287. A year before Goldwater-Nichols was enacted, Secretary of Defense Caspar Weinberger belatedly sought to address some of these problems via an internal directive (see SASC, *Defense Organization*, pp. 199–210, 226).
50. An internal 1987 DOD report recommended that in the future about 25 percent of the students at the Army, Navy, and Air war colleges be drawn from other services, and that service war colleges then be designated "joint colleges." Its clear purpose was to circumvent the intent of Goldwater-Nichols. An informed source commented, "The report is self-serving and poorly done. Congress will be very critical" (confidential interview with the author, 27 August 1987).
51. HASC, *HASC Tasks*, 100–13, July 1988; GAO, *Military Personnel: Proposals to Modify the Management of Officers Assigned to Joint Duty*, GAO/NSIAD–88–78BR (Washington, D.C.: GAO, April 1988); Congressman Bill Nichols, letter to Admiral William J. Crowe, Jr., 18 May 1987 (mimeo).
52. SASC, *Defense Organization*, 224.
53. The law also requires the secretary of defense to submit an annual report to Congress that, among other things, details the promotion rates for officers serving in joint duty assignments, and if their promotion rates are lower than other officers, the secretary must provide an explanation of corrective actions he has taken or plans to take (Sec. 667).
54. Lynn and Posen, "The Case for JCS Reform," pp. 77–79; Steadman Report, pp. 52–53; SASC, *Defense Organization*, pp. 160–162.
55. SASC, *Defense Organization*, p. 165. General David Jones said: "We do not reward strategists enough. . . . [I]f Clausewitz were in the U.S. military he would retire as a colonel and go to work for a think tank. . . . You can be a service strategist, but we really need some broad-thinking [joint] strate-

gists" (Testimony of General Jones, HASC, *Reorganization of the Department of Defense*, p. 541). Goldwater-Nichols required the president to submit to Congress an annual report on "the national security strategy of the United States" (Sec. 603). Since the United States has rarely had a reasonably coherent, clearly identifiable peacetime national security strategy, the utility of this report—which is unlikely to do anything to change this—is questionable.

56. Robert W. Komer, "Strategymaking in the Pentagon," in Art, Davis, and Huntington, *Reorganizing America's Defense*, pp. 215–17. The conference committee report on Goldwater-Nichols expressed "continuing concern over the absence of effective civilian oversight of the contingency planning process" (*Congressional Record—House*, 12 September 1986, p. H6859). The Odeen Report makes a strong case for much more interagency participation in contingency planning than has been or is now the case (pp. 33–40). On overall problems with contingency planning, see also Kester, "The Future of the Joint Chiefs of Staff," p. 12; SASC, *Defense Organization*, pp. 184–87.

57. See testimony of Lieutenant General John H. Cushman, U.S. Army (Ret.), HASC, *Reorganization of the Department of Defense*, p. 559.

58. Lynn, "The Wars Within," pp. 179–80; Lynn and Posen, "The Case for JCS Reform," p. 83; SASC, *Defense Organization*, pp. 303–309, 312–19, 327–28, 331–33, 348–50.

59. See testimony of Admiral Train, HASC, *Reorganization of the Department of Defense*, p. 159.

60. Testimony of Lawrence J. Korb, ibid., p. 275.

61. For contrasting views, see John G. Kester, "The Constitution and the Chain of Command," in ibid., pp. 755–64, and Raymond J. Celada, "The Military Chain of Command," in SASC, *Defense Organization*, pp. 371–77.

62. *Congressional Record—House*, 12 September 1986, pp. H6863–64.

63. Confidential interview with the author, 27 August 1987.

64. Locher, "Organization and Management," pp. 178–79.

65. Many close observers held this view. For instance, John Kester stated that "reference to 'OSD's vigor' these days is an oxymoron; in fact, the services run the place to the small extent it is run at all. The biggest problem Goldwater-Nichols faces . . . is that it is very difficult for Congress . . . to shape up the management of an executive agency when the boss of that agency is hostile. It is hard to think of a more hostile department head than Caspar Weinberger, or one less interested or skilled in management" (John Kester, letter to the author, 17 September 1987).

66. James G. March and Johan P. Olson, "Organizing Political Life: What Administrative Reorganizations Tell Us About Government," *American Political Science Review* 77 (June 1983): 281–96.

CHAPTER 5

The Intelligence Community:
Coordination, Policy, and the Director
of Central Intelligence

Within the national security bureaucracy, only the Defense Department, which employs the largest number of intelligence personnel and spends the lion's share of the intelligence budget, rivals the intelligence community in organizational size and complexity. Any condensed treatment of intelligence, even one focusing primarily on coordination, must be selective. This chapter, after discussing various relationships between the consumers and producers of intelligence,[1] and then the role of the president and National Security Council in setting intelligence policy, concentrates on the Director of Central Intelligence (DCI), particularly his coordinative functions within the community. Attention is also given to national intelligence.[2] Next are sketches of each DCI, emphasizing their roles in national intelligence, and finally, a condensed assessment of the Defense Intelligence Agency.

It is important to stress that, with the partial exception of the Central Intelligence Agency and the DIA, this chapter does not address the functions or organizational makeup of the respective members of the intelligence community. This has been done quite ably by others.[3] Nor does it examine—except very briefly and selectively—what many consider to be the most significant process-related issue: the procedures and mechanisms for executive branch oversight of the community (such as the Intelligence Oversight Board) and the equally important subject of congressional oversight. This subject, too, has been treated repeatedly and exhaustively by others.[4]

Consumer-Producer Relations

Since the late 1940s, most serious students of intelligence community processes have dealt in one way or another with aspects of the relationship between consumers and producers of intelligence. Yet, with some notable exceptions—like Richard Betts, Hans Heymann, and Arthur Hulnick—few recent writers have analyzed the subject systematically.[5] This is unfortunate. The ultimate function and purpose of the intelligence process is linked intimately to this relationship.

It seems appropriate to begin where many others do, with the "intelligence cycle."

The Intelligence Cycle

The concept of the intelligence cycle—that is, those processes by which information is acquired, converted into intelligence, and made available to consumers—traditionally has been presented as a sequence of rational and logical steps, each dependent on the previous step:[6]

1. *Direction:* Consumers advise intelligence community managers of their informational needs. These needs are then translated into specific *requirements* by senior intelligence community managers, who then assign ("task") the collection of the needed information to appropriate intelligence collection entities.
2. *Collection:* Resources are allocated to the collection units, the needed information is collected, and the raw data are translated into a report (which also assesses the reliability of the informational sources).
3. *Analysis:* Analysts or analytic teams, who supposedly understand the original requirement, compare the raw report or data to the existing data base and make judgments about its meaning.
4. *Production:* Analysts convert these "facts" and judgments into a finished intelligence product; that is, an evaluated product whose contents may include information from any classified or unclassified source.
5. *Dissemination:* The intelligence product is distributed to consumers.

The Real World

The actual intelligence production process differs substantially from this traditional portrayal.[7]

1. *Direction.* Deputy Director of Central Intelligence Robert M. Gates lamented in 1987 that "policymakers in successive administrations have largely abdicated their intelligence-guidance responsibilities. For many years, trying to get senior policy principals to attend meetings to discuss longer-range intelligence requirements has been an exercise in frustration."[8] In practice, then, intelligence requirements are usually generated by community analytic elements or collection managers, not policymakers. This is so because consumers often do not know precisely what information they need, lack the time to reflect upon, define, and clearly communicate their needs, or are unfamiliar with existing data and collection capabilities. Moreover, the needs of various consumers may conflict with one another, and requirements may change, sometimes suddenly, with crises or shifts in an administration's foreign policy.

Some of the most constant and important consumer requirements are readily discernible and are translated into so-called "standing intelligence requirements." But many requirements are not so evident. They, therefore, reflect what intelligence managers think consumers need and what they think their organizations can provide. In addition, as we will see, there have been problems coordinating the requirements-setting process among collection organizations. Finally, many, probably most, consumer information needs give rise to requirements not for collection of new data, but for analysis, research, and evaluated information.

2. *Collection.* Collecting intelligence is not an automatic process. There are many kinds, sources, and methods of collection, each of which raises unique issues and, often, difficulties. The desired information may be unavailable—or available at an unacceptable cost. Or perhaps years would be required to develop the technical or human capability to acquire it. The enormous volume of collected information must be sorted, processed, and converted into raw intelligence reports, ideally, according to established priorities. In addition, some "analysis" occurs at this step in the process in order to, for example, place raw data in a usable format and appropriate perspective, or to remind analysts and sometimes consumers (who often receive raw intelligence) of existing reports. Collection units like the National Reconnaissance Office, the National Security Agency, and the CIA's clandestine arm—the Directorate of Operations (DDO)—do not produce finished intelligence. But the distinction between raw and finished intelligence is frequently obscured in practice. So, for example, the National Security Agency's Signals Intelligence (SIGINT) reports often incorporate data from other sources, and the National Photographic Interpretation Center's basic imagery reports often include collateral intelligence information.

3–4. *Analysis /Production.* A senior CIA official stated in 1987 that "the National Security Agency often labels certain raw intelligence as 'technical,' not 'substantive,' and withholds it from the CIA. There are problems of information exchange."[9] This is but one illustration of why the analysis and production phases are more complex, "political," and judgmental than the traditional explanation suggests. Many analysts are generally involved in producing finished intelligence. The perspectives, assessments, and interests of these analysts and their respective organizations often differ. This can materially affect the content, phrasing, and format of the final product. In addition, various finished intelligence products, like National Intelligence Estimates (NIEs), Special National Intelligence Estimates (SNIEs), and Interagency Intelligence Memorandums (IIMs), are designed to serve policymakers in distinct ways. And there are other kinds of intelligence products besides estimative and raw intelligence. They, too, serve different consumer needs.

5. *Dissemination.* The dissemination phase entails more than mechanically sending a report forward to consumers. First, except for the most sensitive information, raw reports are distributed much more widely than finished reports. Second, care must be taken that reports go in a timely fashion to properly cleared consumers. Third, intelligence producers may seek to "market" their product, that is, actively call it to the attention of important consumers. Lastly, the intelligence report may be presented to consumers in written form or (often most effectively) in an oral briefing.

6. *Evaluation.* Whether evaluating the utility of intelligence collection and intelligence products should be a regularized component of the intelligence process or independent from it can be debated. But it is an important function. Prior to at least the mid-1970s, this function was performed haphazardly or not at all.

Today, evaluative mechanisms are in place, but it seems probable that this is an area requiring continued attention.

The traditional description of the intelligence cycle is a "rational actor" explanation. As such, it oversimplifies, ignores the impact of organizational and individual behavior on the process, and fails to address the multiple demands and constraints on consumers, collectors, and producers. It also assumes incorrectly that consumers and producers interact only at the beginning and end of the cycle.

Classic Dilemma: Distance or Closeness to Policy?

Intelligence producers must be close enough to consumers to to provide an adequate informational base for decisionmaking, one that is responsive to policy needs. But if producers are too close to consumers, intelligence runs a risk of being corrupted by the very process it is expected to serve.

Many who address this dilemma contrast two schools of thought—the so-called traditionalists, who incline toward some distance from policy, and an opposing school (usually un-labeled) that favors a closer relationship. Unfortunately, the traditionalists are too often set up as strawmen, who are then easily knocked down. Kenneth deGraffenreid, for instance, portrays traditionalists—Sherman Kent being among the more prominent—as those who supposedly "neglect the connection between policy and intelligence," view the producer-consumer relationship "as similar to that between librarian and reader," and hold that "the intelligence community determines what information should be available to the president."[10] There is an element of truth to this, but it overstates the case. Sherman Kent, while staunchly maintaining that considerable distance from policy was essential for the protection of independent judgment, stated expressly in his earliest writing that intelligence must be close enough to the policy process to receive guidance.[11] Indeed, when Kent later became concerned that intelligence products were becoming insufficiently responsive to policymakers' needs, he suggested moving toward a closer consumer-producer relationship.[12]

The nontraditionalist school favors a close consumer-producer linkage, a sort of symbiotic relationship. But even the most ardent members of this group acknowledge the importance of retaining sufficient producer independence to ensure the integrity of the intelligence product.[13]

Differences between the two schools of thought should not be drawn too starkly, but neither should they be denied and dismissed as posing a "false problem."[14] There are real differences in emphasis and tone. Each group tilts toward one prong of the dilemma. But since dilemmas are situations that seemingly defy an obviously satisfactory solution, perhaps the most that can be expected is a reasonable balance between two vital considerations. Assuming there is reciprocal respect for one another's essential needs, there is no inherent reason why there cannot be both a functional separation and a continuous mutual dialogue between intelligence producers and consumers. Of course, two questions will always remain open to debate: How separate? How mutual? A natural tension will always exist between policy and intelligence. There would be reason for alarm if it were absent.

Politicization of Intelligence. Next to losing their heads, intelligence producers most dread the "politicization" of intelligence.[15] Indeed, these two fears may be related. Analysts who too vigorously resist consumer pressures to alter objective intelligence analyses may well be putting their figurative heads (careers) on the line.

In the largest sense, the intelligence function is permeated with things political. This is most evident when intelligence units serve as operational arms of policy—for example, covert actions/"special activities."[16] Producers, too, serve policy, hopefully through the presentation of "objective" information. But when policymakers exert pressure on producers to "bend" their objective analysis to "fit" existing or preferred policy directions, intelligence is corrupted, "politicized." Producers must be sensitive to policy without being consumed by it. Says Richard Betts of the consumer-producer relationship: "[P]olitical promiscuity is destructive but political virginity is impossible."[17]

Captain George Thibault, U.S. Navy (Ret.), former Special Assistant to DCI Stansfield Turner, states:

A frequent politicization occurs simply as a result of an intelligence organization being part of a policymaking organization (DIA, NSA, etc.).

Even when intelligence professionals work to avoid bias, the fact that they cannot help but see collected raw intelligence and issues being analyzed through their organization's eyes, injects a disposition to bias. To a DOD person, the issues which are important are not the same as the . . . [ones that the] State Department sees as important. The same "fact"/raw intelligence is seen differently, analyzed differently, given a different weight of consideration. The only intelligence agency which [is] not [within a policymaking] executive department is the CIA. They [CIA] are usually accused of having whatever bias is in vogue in academe . . . but not of being [unduly] influenced by policy (until Casey I would say).[18]

Politicization may be subtle or overt. Direct, unambiguous pressure on intelligence producers is unusual. More common is indirect pressure—consumer actions and attitudes that are seen by producers as indirect pressure. Robert Gates asserted:

Policymakers have always liked intelligence that supported what they want to do, and they often try to influence the analysis to buttress the conclusions they want to reach. They ask carefully phrased questions; they sometimes withhold information; they broaden or narrow the issue; on rare occasions they even try to intimidate. The pressures can be enormous.[19]

When intelligence producers sense they are working in a hostile environment or that intelligence that contravenes an established or preferred policy course will not be well received, they do not necessarily tailor their intelligence to please, although this is not unknown. But they may either avoid treating difficult issues or phrase their analyses so as to tone down its variance with the policy course.[20]

In the mid-1980s, motivated in large part by the "political activities" of DCI William Casey—the first DCI to hold cabinet rank—Senators Barry Goldwater and Daniel Moynihan introduced a bill (S. 3019) that would have required the DCI to be appointed from among career civilian or military intelligence officers.[21] The bill did not become law, but the issue may reappear. This measure, which is contrary to the recommendation of the Rockefeller Commission (1975) that the president should retain the option to appoint a DCI "from outside the career service of the CIA," would be unwise.[22] Not only might it restrict the president's freedom to select someone with whom he has good rapport and in whom he has confidence, but outsiders (like James Schlesinger) may sometimes be better positioned to institute internal change desired by the president than insiders, who may feel circumscribed by their organizational affiliation. Few DCIs have been more universally acclaimed than professional military officer General Walter Bedell Smith, and noncareerists George Bush and William Webster played useful stabilizing roles during difficult periods for the intelligence community.

Attitudes of Policymakers

The attitudes that policymakers and intelligence producers tend to have about one another suggests why their relationships are often tense.

Intelligence Increases My Uncertainty. Most presidents and other senior political leaders rise to high levels by being self-confident and decisive, not self-doubting, introspective, and reflective. They want "answers" to guide them through the foreign policy thicket, not qualified "on the one hand . . . but on the other hand . . ." type reports. They find many intelligence analyses (especially political intelligence) "soft" and couched in carefully phrased, often ambiguous words that increase rather than reduce their uncertainty about international events.

The CIA sometimes has provided policymakers with precise, day-to-day political intelligence to inform decisionmaking—concerning, for example, the 1980 imposition of martial law in Poland, or the 1986 electoral irregularities in the Philippines.[23] However, intelligence forecasts usually can only alert consumers to the spectrum of uncertainties they confront when dealing with complex issues by identifying various outcomes, their relative probabilities, and their possible implications. This rarely pleases policymakers. But the alternative—oversimplifying reality by superficially and speciously resolving ambiguities—would ill serve the consumer and the nation.[24]

Where Does This Stuff Come From? Policymakers rarely have an understanding of how the information is acquired, or how estimates, forecasts, and judgments are arrived at, by the intelligence community.[25] The more senior the policy official, the less likely it is that he knows the key intelligence officers who participated in the process that produced the report. The credibility of these anonymous officers, then, may be suspect, particularly if their judgments run counter to declared policy, clash with firmly held beliefs of policymakers, or pertain to subjects on which the policymaker himself has, or thinks he has, considerable expertise.[26]

Yet policymakers understand enough about the intelligence community to know that the word *community* is a misnomer. Intelligence reports are sometimes viewed suspiciously solely because of their origin in this so-called community: an agglomeration of competing, turf-conscious, querulous institutions whose collective behavior manifests all the usual features of bureaucratic politics. Most intelligence analysts usually consider themselves objective truth seekers when conducting their own analyses. But when they must defend their work against competing viewpoints within the community, they can become fiercely "political" creatures. There is nothing necessarily improper or unprofessional about such behavior. The point is that the coordinative process for producing an NIE, for example, can affect its contents. And policymakers know this.[27]

I Have Other Sources of Information.   Consumers are inundated with mountains of information from outside the intelligence community (newspapers, foreign leaders, congressmen, and so on) that can supplement intelligence. It can even supplant intelligence when, for instance, it is or seems more germane to a particular issue than intelligence reports, is more supportive of some consumers' preferred positions, or when certain consumers are denied intelligence because of its classification level. Moreover, within the intelligence community itself there is usually a smorgasboard of viewpoints. This invites or allows policymakers to pick and choose. Indeed, this is probably one reason why policymakers are rarely tempted to exert crude pressure on producers to skew their analyses. If the CIA holds that the Soviets could deploy 45,000 tanks against NATO, someone can probably be found in Army Intelligence or the DIA who puts the figure at 65,000.[28]

My Beliefs and Values Have Served Me Well.   We all acquire certain beliefs and values over time. These beliefs tend to be resistant to change, certainly to sudden change. Senior policymakers are reluctant to alter belief systems that they feel have served them well and have helped bring them to positions of great responsibility. Among the reasons why sound intelligence does not necessarily translate into sound policy is the common tendency of policymakers to reject or ignore information that is inconsistent with their preformed political and normative conceptions. The impact of preconceptions is particularly profound when, as is often the case, consumers receive ambiguous intelligence reports.[29]

Intelligence Restricts and Undercuts My Policies. One reason why every president since Dwight Eisenhower expressed dissatisfaction with intelligence is illustrated by Lyndon Johnson's remark: "Policy making is like milking a fat cow. You can see the milk coming out . . . and just as the bucket is full, the cow with its tail whips the bucket and all is spilled. That's what the CIA does to policy making."[30] The CIA's estimates during the Vietnam conflict, while generally accurate, were not well received in the White House. Johnson wanted intelligence that would help him *win* the war. Intelligence professionals regularly confront proposed policy initiatives with analyses showing how enemies will counter them, allies will resist them, and others will be generally obstreperous. Policymakers naturally conclude that intelligence constrains their freedom of action.

More than this, because Congress receives a vast quantity of intelligence, executive policymakers often suspect that the CIA consciously uses this congressional channel to sabotage certain administration policies. When legislators do exploit this situation through the selective use of intelligence that supports their positions, or when controversies within the intelligence community over, say, Soviet compliance with arms control agreements enter the public realm by way of Congress or some other route, an administration is embarrassed and its policies are undercut. And an administration that attempts to use intelligence as an instrument of public persuasion runs a risk that this tactic will backfire for any of several reasons.[31]

Attitudes of Intelligence Producers

Intelligence producers are expected to be balanced, objective, independent professionals whose meticulously drafted analytical products differentiate between the known and the unknown so that the level and range of uncertainty is adequately communicated. Producers have identifiable sets of attitudes toward those whom they serve.

I Am Criticized for Doing What I Must Do. Producers can, at best, reduce uncertainty and construct plausible hypotheses about the capabilities, intentions, and activities of foreign powers on the basis of what is almost always partial and often conflicting evidence. When evidence is ambiguous, analytical integrity and accuracy allows no alternative but ambivalence. Ambiguity must be reflected in careful separation of "fact" from judgment and in refined usage of language, something that is often unappreciated by consumers. Worse still, consumers may ignore estimative intelligence altogether, rely primarily on raw intelligence or current intelligence (journalistic summaries and analyses of recent events),[32] and assume—usually incorrectly and at considerable risk—that they are their own best intelligence analysts.[33]

Consumers must understand both the limits of intelligence and what it can do for them. Otherwise, disappointment is inevitable.[34] Indeed, while there are, of course, intelligence failures for which the intelligence community can be faulted, Richard Betts has argued persuasively that most so-called intelligence failures are usually policy failures.[35] Policy failures occur for multiple reasons, but one factor can be the misuse or nonuse of intelligence by policymakers.

Consumers Keep Me in the Dark. Not only do consumers often fail to inform intelligence managers of their *informational* needs, but even the DCI is sometimes uninformed of *policy* developments that bear directly on the community's ability to produce useful, timely reports. William Colby relates that many CIA analyses were less helpful for policy than they could have been because several of Henry Kissinger's most secret and important negotiations with Soviet, North Vietnamese, and Middle Eastern leaders were not reported to the CIA.[36]

Some Consumers Don't Really Use Thoughtful, Relevant Intelligence Reports. A 1981 survey by the Intelligence Community (IC) Staff found that consumers value intelligence "on the basis of brevity, timeliness and relevance *in that order*." These priorities tend to be reversed by intelligence producers.[37] That policymakers, especially senior ones, sometimes do not read intelligence analyses with an eye toward their relevance for policy issues (or do not read them at all) may be frustrating for analysts, but it is not surprising. Time is a policymaker's most precious commodity. Even a "reading president" like John F. Kennedy had to be selective in what he read. For Ronald Reagan, who had a short attention span, intelligence reports were kept very brief (and frequently took the form of videotapes). Lengthy estimates languish at the bottom of in-boxes.

On the other hand, this often means that the staffs of senior policy officials and mid-level policy officers are especially important consumers. They are generally the ones who digest intelligence reports for their superiors, and they are also probably the only policy officials who follow developments regularly in a particular country or region. Mid-level consumers are important in another respect—they provide useful feedback and advice to producers about their products.[38]

The President and Intelligence Community Management

All intelligence activities should either enlighten the president's decisions or (as with covert operations, for example) advance his policies. Several entities separate from the DCI assist—or, potentially, might assist—the president in managing or directing the intelligence community. Three such entities are the NSC, the Office of Management and Budget, and—at a distinctly tertiary level of importance—the President's Foreign Intelligence Advisory Board (PFIAB).

The National Security Council

The NSC is the highest executive branch unit providing direction to the intelligence community. The National Security Act of 1947 charges the DCI with making recommendations to the NSC on the coordination of intelligence activities that relate to national security. But the NSC's intelligence agenda has been dominated over the years by the consideration of proposed covert actions and other special activities, rather than by management and coordination concerns. Indeed, prior to the 1970s, NSC committees were concerned almost exclusively with covert operations.[39] However, before the Reagan administration's Iran-Contra affair, it appears that no NSC staffer had ever been personally and intimately involved in a sustained manner in the actual *execution* of a major covert action. This function, of course, properly belongs to the operational arm of the CIA.

Various NSC committees have dealt with intelligence and, since the early 1970s, some have addressed such matters as establishing intelligence requirements and priorities, reviewing intelligence expenditures, and assessing the quality of intelligence products.[40] The activity level of those committees not dealing with covert operations has varied. The Nixon administration's Intelligence Committee met only once or twice. Others, like the Carter administration's Policy Review Committee (PRC) (which usually dealt with defense and foreign policy, not intelligence, issues) and the Reagan administration's Senior Interagency Group for Intelligence (SIG/I), were more active. Major new initiatives and reorganizations have generally come through executive orders, NSC Intelligence Directives (NSCIDs), and other executive branch documents, rather than through legislation. The NSCIDs, among other things, have established guidelines for the dissemination of intelligence information and have delegated specified authority to the DCI.[41]

The Office of Management and Budget

OMB is not an audit agency—it does not establish intelligence policy, nor does it perform an oversight function. However, on infrequent occasions OMB has influenced intelligence community management. In 1960, for example, the Bureau of the Budget organized a group that recommended to President Eisenhower that he take several measures to strengthen intelligence management, including stronger control by the National Security Agency of the cryptologic agencies. Similarly, in 1971, President Nixon implemented many of the recommendations of Assistant OMB Director James Schlesinger to improve the quality of the intelligence product and to better control the community's budget.[42]

OMB has a budgetary role. The Intelligence Branch of OMB's National Security Division receives the National Foreign Intelligence Program (NFIP) budget (discussed later) from the DCI. OMB reviews and evaluates this request and gives the president a final recommendation, which is subject to appeal by the concerned agency. OMB sometimes requires, or attempts to require, the intelligence community to, for instance, justify procurement of costly new technical collection systems on the basis of their likely contribution to the analytic product.[43]

Prior to about 1976–1977, the effectiveness of OMB's budget review was severely constrained: it was often uninformed of covert actions, it had imperfect control of the CIA's Contingency Reserve Fund, it had much less impact on DOD's intelligence budget than on the CIA's, and it had great difficulty monitoring budget execution.[44] Although OMB was somewhat more active in the intelligence area during the Carter years and Congress has scrutinized covert operations and intelligence expenditures much more closely since the late 1970s, OMB was curbed sharply under the Reagan administration. Its Intelligence Branch was cut from a barely adequate five or six analysts to just three. These three were responsible for examining the entire NFIP budget, a prima facie impossibility. Moreover, the budget of the military services' intelligence units is handled separately by OMB as part of the larger DOD budget.[45]

Since the Reagan administration slashed OMB's professional national security staff at a time when the intelligence community's budget increased dramatically, and since the primary defense function of OMB during this period was to champion, not question, DOD programs, it is clear that the quality of OMB's budgetary review of the intelligence community—especially Defense intelligence—suffered accordingly. Indeed, even before the Reagan years OMB could usually do no more than dent the budget requests of Defense intelligence elements like the National Security Agency.[46] And the Reagan OMB, according to a senior member of the IC Staff, had "little or nothing to do with intelligence."[47]

There are persuasive reasons for the president to increase the authority and staff capability of OMB in this area. First, intelligence expenditures are massive (an estimated $24 billion in FY 1987, one-half of which went to the NFIP),[48] and they represent one of the few "controllable" program areas of the federal budget. Second, OMB is the only executive unit independent of the intelligence community with the *potential* authority and ability to insist upon sound budgetary and managerial practices. Finally, despite successive executive orders strengthening the DCI's authority, management authority within the intelligence community remains excessively fragmented.

The President's Foreign Intelligence Advisory Board

The PFIAB is a body of private citizens charged with advising the president on select intelligence issues.[49] Since its establishment in 1956 by President Eisenhower (when it was titled the Board of Consultants on Foreign Intelligence Activities), the PFIAB has had a mixed history and record. By the late Eisenhower administration, it was essentially defunct. It was revived by President Kennedy, abolished by President Carter, and resurrected by President Reagan. The board is *not* a watchdog of the intelligence community, but it has on rare occasion made some useful recommendations concerning the organization, management, and quality of intelligence.

The PFIAB's most controversial initiative was the famous, or infamous, B Team exercise in 1976, which most CIA analysts considered to be a counterproductive experience in allegedly "competitive" analysis. In the annual estimate of Soviet strategic forces (NIE 11-8-76), CIA professionals (the "A Team") were—at the urging of the PFIAB, with the consent of President Ford—pitted against a "B Team" whose members were known for their hawkish views: General Daniel Graham, William Van Cleave, Seymour Weiss, Paul Nitze, and others. There was no "C Team" of doves. Not surprisingly, the final B Team report concluded that the CIA had underestimated the military capabilities and intentions of the Soviet Union.[50]

The PFIAB has suffered from several limitations:

- Its members are political appointees, some of whom lack pertinent government or professional experience.
- DCIs often have been reluctant to provide the PFIAB with sufficient information for it to offer helpful advice.
- Busy board members cannot devote full-time attention to PFIAB activities.
- It is dependent on the president's need and desire for its counsel.
- Budget and staff resources have sometimes been inadequate.

- The board's mandate frequently has been both vague and limited.

It's a close call whether future presidents should retain the PFIAB. If the board is to provide the president with confidential, thoughtful, outside advice on those matters it seems most suited to address—*broad* questions of intelligence policy, quality, and management—its effectiveness would be enhanced if most members had high-level defense, foreign affairs, or intelligence experience, membership was politically more diverse, the board had adequate staff support, and above all, its chairman had access to and the confidence of either the president or the president's National Security Assistant.

Director of Central Intelligence

No senior government position is more sensitive than that of DCI. Many directors either have been forced to resign or have become objects of bitter criticism. Some of the reasons for this are unique to the circumstances or the individual. But more fundamental is the natural, predictable tension between the necessarily secretive nature of intelligence and the values and requisites of a free, open society. The DCI and his agency, the CIA, are bound to be on a hot seat, especially if they are involved heavily in covert actions.

This section spells out the DCI's basic functions. Subsequent sections treat individual DCIs and the director's coordinative roles in specific areas.

Legal Authority

The DCI's principal roles are set forth in loosely defined fashion in the National Security Act of 1947. He is head of the CIA; he is authorized "to make recommendations to the National Security Council for the coordination of such intelligence activities of the departments and agencies of the government as relate to the national security"; and he is "to advise the National Security Council in matters concerning such intelligence activities of the government departments and agencies as relate to national security."[51] The DCI, then, directs an important agency, coordinates various community intelligence activities (but without specific *statutory command* authority), and—by law and several executive orders— is the president's primary foreign intelligence adviser.

Directors often have performed these functions ineffectively. Most DCIs either have delegated to deputies major authority for managing most internal CIA matters or have concentrated their attention on the agency's Directorate of Operations (DDO) and its covert activities, rather than on the agency's scientific and analytic directorates. Resistance to the DCI's responsibility for community coordination, especially from Defense intelligence units, has persisted since 1947. And some DCIs have had little influence with the president and, sometimes, minimal access to him.

DCI as Head of the CIA: Can He Be Impartial?

The DCI's dual roles as intelligence community leader and CIA director may conflict. When he tries to be an impartial community leader, he risks distancing himself from his essential support base and the only agency he fully controls—the CIA. By stressing his community duties (and, perhaps, involving himself deeply in the president's political agenda), he may neglect his responsibilities as manager and defender of the agency. On the other hand, there has always been concern, especially among Defense intelligence units, that the DCI/CIA director cannot be a neutral arbiter when important differences arise among community members.

The DCI has, indeed, sometimes sided with the CIA on re-source allocation issues or in the development of NIEs, but at other times he has opposed his own agency's position. Allegations of partiality on these kinds of questions are usually overdrawn, yet the *perception* persists. Moreover, the perception acquires considerable poignancy when DCIs, like Allen Dulles and William Casey, become intimately involved in and personally committed to various clandestine activities. This risks eroding the director's credibility as an impartial community arbiter, objective presidential adviser, and effective spokesman to Congress.[52]

Remove One of the DCI's Hats?   This problem led Senator Arlen Specter, former DCI Stansfield Turner, and others to propose removing the DCI from direct responsibility for clandestine activities. Likewise, the Church Committee found this proposal worthy of serious consideration.[53] One of several variants of the proposal would split the current DCI's functions between two officials, each of whom would be subject to Senate confirmation. One official would be Director of National Intelligence (DNI) and would serve as community coordinator and senior presidential adviser. The other would be director of the CIA.

The primary advantage of this measure is that it removes the DCI from a potential conflict-of-interest situation engendered by his wearing the two hats of DCI and CIA director and (the real issue) by his close association with clandestine activities. It is also sometimes asserted that the new DNI's direct tie to the president would facilitate NSC oversight of covert actions, clarify lines of authority within the community, and enable the DNI to better perform his communitywide management functions.[54]

But the DNI concept has encountered sustained, broad-based opposition from most policymakers and former senior intelligence officials because of its several serious disadvantages:[55]

- Severing the DCI's (DNI's) direct link to the CIA would necessitate his establishing an analytic support organization of substantial size. Otherwise, he would be a mere figurehead wholly dependent on other agencies for information and analyses.
- Implementation of this proposal would needlessly enlarge the intelligence bureaucracy and sharply *worsen* intracommunity coordination and management by adding yet another intelligence actor. The DNI would lose two key levers that today afford the DCI influence with both the intelligence and policy communities—the superior analytic backing of the CIA's Directorate of Intelligence (DDI) and command authority (under the president) over the agency's clandestine services.
- By removing the DCI/DNI from the detached environment of the CIA, there is much greater likelihood that he will be drawn into White House politics to an unhealthy extent.
- There is no evident reason why the new DNI would necessarily either increase or decrease the degree of NSC oversight of covert actions.

Concern about the DCI's sometimes detailed immersion in covert action programs is legitimate. The president, and perhaps

Congress, should insist that he not become so involved in such activities as to neglect and jeopardize his other major roles. Thus far, no administration has seriously considered instituting a DNI-type proposal, and wisely so. Some have suggested making DDO a separate entity directly accountable to the NSC. But this, too, seems counterproductive. It would, inter alia, exacerbate the usually strained communication links between CIA analysts and covert operators while complicating the DCI's access to the kind of intelligence that only the clandestine service can provide.[56]

DCI as Coordinator

It was recognized from the beginning that the DCI's major limitation was his weak statutory authority to coordinate intelligence.[57] Absent supportive executive orders (and even this may be insufficient), he can only recommend, not direct, intelligence organizations other than the CIA to institute various coordination and management measures. The 1947 National Security Act reflects an uneasy and perhaps unresolvable tension between two basic considerations: (1) the need for centralized coordination of disparate intelligence activities under a strong DCI in order to serve national-level consumers in the most cost-effective manner, and (2) the need for the various intelligence entities to retain some degree of independence from the DCI in order to meet unique departmental requirements, and the further recognition that an all-powerful "intelligence czar" could unwisely deprive consumers of a broad spectrum of viewpoints and (sometimes) healthy competitive analyses on intelligence issues. Although the DCI's coordinative authority has gradually increased since the mid-1970s under successive executive orders, he continues to preside over intelligence units that are reluctant to surrender prerogatives to him. Hence DCIs must generally coordinate and lead through consensus-building.

Lacking a sweeping, authoritative legal mandate for community coordination, most DCIs prior to the 1970s concentrated on their more clearly defined and less contentious responsibilities. What limited communitywide management that did occur was handled largely by the United States Intelligence Board (USIB) and its many subcommittees. The USIB, which was chaired by the DCI, was created in 1958 to coordinate the setting of intelligence requirements, approve NIEs, and generally supervise the intelligence agencies' activities. It tended to operate on a consensual basis. The real power to allocate resources and set intelligence requirements remained decentralized and in the hands of the principal collectors. Said the Church Committee: "[the USIB] had no budgetary authority; nor did it provide the DCI with any direct control over the components of the intelligence community. The separate elements of the community continued to function under the impetus of their own internal drives and mission definitions."[58]

This state of affairs began to change somewhat with James Schlesinger's brief tenure as DCI in 1973. Today, in addition to retaining his long-standing role as coordinator of national intelligence production, the director performs important community coordination functions in such areas as the development of the NFIP budget and the preparation of guidance to and execution of national intelligence collection plans.

The DCI currently has various mechanisms to assist him in performing communitywide functions.

The Intelligence Community Staff. The IC Staff, established in 1972, is a management body, not a collector or producer of intelligence. It assists the DCI in the development, review, and approval of the NFIP budget and in community collection, planning, and other activities. The IC Staff (which totalled 246 in FY 1987) has some permanent personnel, but most are detailed from various intelligence elements, especially Defense intelligence.[59]

The IC Staff clearly cannot be more assertive than a DCI wishes it to be. But this has not been the problem. Rather, some DCIs, like Stansfield Turner, report that the IC Staff "has not been adequate, and [the DCI] has had to rely on his CIA staff for much of his preparatory work and for keeping him informed of what takes place throughout the Community."[60] The IC Staff may have improved its ability to assist the DCI in The Reagan administration, but William Casey elected not to play as active a communitywide role as Turner. Certainly, a persistent weakness of the IC Staff has been the quality of some of the military intelligence officers detailed to it. The IC Staff has been considered a dumping ground for mediocre officers. Indeed, the services resist sending promising officers to the IC Staff precisely because they fear this will *strengthen* the DCI's hand vis-à-vis DOD intelligence units.[61]

National Foreign Intelligence Board (NFIB). The NFIB, first publicly recognized in President Carter's Executive Order 12036 in 1978, is a descendant of the old USIB. It is chaired by the DCI and comprises all the principal intelligence components. The NFIB advises the director on the production, review, and coordination of national foreign intelligence and on other matters of community concern, such as the protection of sources and methods, interagency exchanges of intelligence information, and intelligence arrangements with foreign governments.[62]

National Foreign Intelligence Council (NFIC). The NFIC was created in 1981 to deal with national foreign intelligence priorities and budgets. It concentrates more on management than on analytical issues. It, too, is chaired by the DCI and has broad community membership.[63]

National Intelligence Council (NIC). The NIC (not to be confused with NFIC) was formed in 1980 as a collegial body of National Intelligence Officers (NIOs), their assistants, and its Analytic Group (NIC/AG) to coordinate major interagency intelligence production, serve as a contact point with senior consumers, and advise the DCI on analytic and collection issues.[64]

Individual DCIs: From the Truman through the Reagan Administrations

The CIA's first three years were difficult ones for the fledgling agency and for the first DCI, Rear Admiral Roscoe Hillenkotter. Hillenkotter had spent most of his naval career at sea and resumed sea command when he left the CIA in 1950. He lacked the experience, instincts, and rank to deal effectively with senior government officials. Hillenkotter chaired the community's principal coordination committee—the Intelligence Advisory Committee (IAC), established in 1947—which suffered many of the infirmities of its successor body, the USIB. Although Hillenkotter briefed President Truman daily, the CIA's efforts to produce coordinated estimative intelligence were undermined by the DCI's failure to assert the agency's authority, the CIA's lack of an independent capability to analyze military data, and the determined resistance of the military services and Pentagon intelligence units.[65]

General Walter Bedell Smith, 1950–1953

An ineffective DCI and CIA became increasingly intolerable, especially with the outbreak of the Korean War. This situation was rectified in October 1950 with the appointment of one of the most forceful DCIs in the agency's history—General Walter Bedell ("Bedell") Smith. General Eisenhower's former chief of staff, called the "American Bulldog" by Winston Churchill, was universally admired and almost as universally feared. This assertive, bureaucratically savvy, senior-ranking military officer commanded the attention of top military officers and civilian officials. He put the CIA squarely on the map, and its work was used at the highest levels of government. Smith instituted sweeping administrative changes within the agency, many of which remain in place today. His presence was felt throughout the intelligence community, and he had sufficient stature to insist that the military intelligence services attend meetings he convened. Yet personal influence rather than recognized authority defined this DCI's coordinative role. Even before Smith's departure, it was evident that basic coordination problems remained intact.[66]

Perhaps Bedell Smith's major legacy is the establishment of the CIA's leading analytical role, particularly regarding estimative intelligence. He moved to implement the recommendation of five separate study groups that the DCI have more centralized authority over long-term estimates. In 1950, Smith created the Office of National Estimates (ONE) and its Board of National Estimates, both housed in the CIA, to manage the agency's and community's production of NIEs. He saw that DOD cooperated in NIEs on military subjects, and he began to build the CIA's own capability to independently assess military issues.

Smith was the first in a long line of DCIs to consider NIEs *his* estimates. He made it known that he would be free to emphasize, add, or delete viewpoints and judgments. The degree to which a DCI should exert such personal prerogatives was to become a matter of considerable controversy. Such authority was implied in the original concept of the NIEs and in the roles of the IAC and its descendants, the USIB and the NFIB, in which bodies the director was seen as (at least) first among equals. No president has expressly forbidden the DCI from assuming this role. Most, but not all, DCIs have exercised this prerogative with caution and restraint.[67]

Allen Dulles, 1953–1961

The CIA's first civilian director was experienced in espionage and foreign affairs. Because of Allen Dulles's deep personal interest and involvement in the details of clandestine activities, he was known within the agency as the "Great White Case Officer." The CIA's clandestine service—then the Directorate of Plans (DDP) —acquired a preeminent position within the agency, the CIA's image was increasingly identified with covert actions, and 54 percent of its budget from 1953 to 1961 went for clandestine collection and covert actions. Dulles's absorption in clandestine activities meant that he largely ignored community coordination functions and gave little personal attention to the analytic side of the agency. But he had the confidence of President Eisenhower (who distrusted the objectivity of many military intelligence products) and enjoyed an unusually effective conduit to the White House through his brother, Secretary of State John Foster Dulles. Moreover, he had many personal acquaintances in the White House and elsewhere in government. While Dulles was reluctant to offer Eisenhower policy advice, there was no such reticence when it came to private conversations with his brother.[68]

Partly because he disliked and avoided personal confrontation, Dulles failed to provide leadership in coordinating intelligence community activities. He was notably hesitant to challenge military intelligence units. Hence, an unusual opportunity to exert centralized authority in behalf of better community management procedures was lost. DOD's role, especially in technical collection programs, thereby became firmly entrenched, making later attempts at coordination much more difficult.[69]

Under Dulles, the CIA did consolidate its centrality in the NIE process. By 1956 the agency had sufficient resources to end the Pentagon's dominance of estimates concerning Soviet strategic nuclear weapons (the "strategic estimates"). The CIA drafted its own position as the main text of both strategic and nonstrategic NIEs, while military and other intelligence units were relegated to footnoted dissents.

But Dulles let ONE, its Board of National Estimates, and the CIA's analytical directorate, the DDI, essentially run themselves. He paid little attention to the texts of draft NIEs. While he communicated informally with CIA estimators, he did not formally review NIEs until the completion of the final draft and just prior to a USIB or NSC meeting. When he chaired USIB meetings on NIEs, Dulles—apparently alone among prior or succeeding DCIs—was a consistent advocate for the CIA's position, thereby fueling concern about the DCI's objectivity.[70]

Many NIEs had a policy impact during the Eisenhower years. They were integrated systematically into the NSC policy paper process and were utilized by the NSC's Planning Board. Dulles briefed the full NSC very effectively on intelligence issues, including new NIEs.[71]

John McCone, 1961–1965

After the Bay of Pigs failure, President Kennedy replaced Dulles with a corporate manager who had no prior intelligence experience —John McCone. A factor in McCone's appointment was Kennedy's expectation that he would address matters of community management/coordination, an area neglected by Dulles. But despite Kennedy's January 1962 letter to McCone charging him with, among other things, "the coordination and effective guidance of the total U.S. foreign intelligence effort," and despite McCone's vigorous pursuit of this objective, he had only marginal success.[72] McCone's real interests were in analysis and technical collection. Nonetheless, clandestine activities continued to claim most of the DCI's time, 55 percent of the CIA's full-time personnel, and 52 percent of the agency's total annual budget between 1962 and 1970.[73]

Kennedy was interested in intelligence even when it contained unwelcome information. The DCI had access to the President, and Ray Cline, head of DDI, met two or three times a week with NSA McGeorge Bundy in the White House. McCone would offer a personal or political opinion only if asked directly by the President to do so. After Kennedy's assassination, there was a notable change. Lyndon Johnson was less tolerant of intelligence officers who brought bad news. McCone was excluded from important policy meetings and eventually resigned from government.[74]

McCone had an active interest in estimative intelligence and the NIE process. He demanded analytical rigor, but let the production process run its own course until a final draft NIE reached his desk. Then he scrutinized it closely. When he differed with the CIA draft, he did not change it; instead, McCone let it go forward to the USIB, where he encouraged active debate and a hearing for all viewpoints. At USIB meetings, he sometimes sided with a military intelligence service and against the CIA.[75]

Vice Admiral William Raborn, Jr., 1965–1966

William Raborn had little impact during his one year as DCI. He was clearly unsuited for the position, as the following exchange, related by a former associate, suggests:

Raborn: "I've told you. I want those cryptonyms translated!"
CIA aide: "But, Admiral, I've done it."
Raborn: "No, you haven't!"
CIA aide: "I'm sorry if I haven't. If you show me where, I'll translate it."
Raborn: "What is this KUWAIT?"[76]

Richard Helms, 1966–1973

When Raborn became DCI, Richard Helms became his deputy. President Johnson told Helms that he would succeed his boss. Helms, a veteran of the clandestine service, was the first professional CIA officer to become director. Internal CIA matters and covert operations, not community management, consumed most of his time. Helms was forced to resign in 1973 for refusing to cooperate with the White House Watergate coverup.[77]

DCI Helms had reasonably good relations with Lyndon Johnson and attended Tuesday Lunch Group meetings where major policy issues, particularly concerning Vietnam, were discussed. He scrupulously limited his advice to intelligence and never volunteered opinions on policy matters. But Helms walked a narrow, difficult line between retaining the President's confidence by being a "team member" and giving him unwelcome intelligence. His relations with the White House deteriorated in the Nixon years. President Nixon saw the CIA as a haven for liberal Ivy League intellectuals and distrusted both the agency and its director. Except for NSC meetings, from which he was initially excluded, Helms rarely saw the President. His dealings with the White House were with Kissinger (and Alexander Haig), and it was Kissinger, not Helms, who briefed Nixon on intelligence matters. Indeed, no other NSA was more deeply and personally involved in the intelligence process. Kissinger and his NSC staff monitored key intelligence reports, and the NIEs—despite their accuracy on Vietnam—fell into comparative neglect and disrepute.[78]

While Helms considered an NIE his "piece of paper," he distanced himself from the drafting process until just before or at USIB meetings.[79] At those meetings, he played an active role on nonstrategic NIEs, especially concerning Southeast Asia, but apparently never overruled the CIA's position in the strategic NIEs.[80]

James Schlesinger, February 1973–June 1973

Many intelligence professionals viewed James Schlesinger as Nixon's revenge on a CIA that refused to do his bidding in Watergate and that resisted Kissinger's real or supposed attempts to politicize intelligence. Schlesinger had a solid background in national security affairs and came to the CIA from OMB, where he had written a report critical of the agency. About 1500 employees, two-thirds from the covert side, were soon either fired or forced to resign or retire early. He initiated reforms in community management and acquired new authority over intelligence community budgets, but his five-month tenure was too short to see them through.

Schlesinger changed the format of the NIEs and determined that ONE and the Board of Estimates should be abolished (a move later implemented by William Colby). He was intimately involved in the drafting of strategic NIEs (in which area he possessed considerable expertise), and he encouraged the development of new and innovative methodologies in this area. At USIB meetings, he invited competitive debate and participated actively in it.[81]

William Colby, 1974–1976

William Colby, whose background was in the clandestine service, became DCI at a difficult time in the agency's and the nation's history. Richard Nixon resigned in disgrace, and the CIA became a focus of press and congressional inquiries. Colby was the most open and public DCI. He cooperated fully with the Rockefeller Commission's investigation and with congressional investigatory committees, and he oversaw the compilation of the CIA's own self-critical "Family Jewels" report.

Most of his time was spent responding to revelations about

improper or illegal intelligence community activities. As DCI, Colby saw himself as a manager, not a clandestine operator, although 37 percent of the CIA's budget in 1975 went to clandestine activities.[82] Since President Ford was running for election from the moment he assumed office, the President distanced himself from the agency that had become a political pariah. When Ford entered the election year, Colby was replaced. "I had great respect for President Ford," said Colby, "and he fired me."[83]

For reasons discussed later, Colby abolished ONE and the Board of National Estimates and created a new system for producing NIEs. He took an active interest in their drafting, especially concerning nonstrategic NIEs, and managed USIB debates (which reached a high pitch at this time) in an equitable manner.[84]

George Bush, 1976–1977

George Bush had no prior intelligence experience, yet he played an important role during the last year of the Ford administration. Bush put his political ambitions aside and concentrated successfully on restoring CIA morale, ensuring the independence and objectivity of its estimates, and establishing a better relationship with a Congress that was moving toward acquiring a new and far more assertive intelligence oversight role.[85]

Admiral Stansfield Turner, 1977–1981

President Carter's Executive Order 12036 gave DCI Stansfield Turner unprecedented coordinative authority in community affairs. Turner's major contribution was to exert that authority vigorously, especially concerning the NFIP budget and the setting of national collection requirements.

Yet Turner was perhaps the least popular of DCIs among CIA professionals. There were several reasons for this: he was sometimes tactless in dealing with subordinates; CIA civilians were uneasy about the several Navy officers who served on his staff (although some, like George Thibault, were highly competent); many believed he made up his mind without adequately considering what CIA officers had to say; and his handling of the agency's clandestine side (DDO) was a source of resentment. This last issue was particularly important. The number of authorized personnel billets in DDO fell by 820, mostly through normal attrition. But what rankled CIA people was the impersonal manner in which 17 officers were fired and 147 others were forced into early retirement.[86]

Turner briefed the President weekly until 1979, and biweekly thereafter. But he did not have a close personal relationship with Carter and had relatively restricted access to him. Zbigniew Brzezinski, not Turner, gave a morning intelligence briefing to the President, and Brzezinski was almost always in attendance when Carter met with the DCI. Turner attended NSC meetings, but was excluded from the important Friday Breakfast session, when senior policy advisers met informally with the President. He generally refrained from offering unsolicited policy advice to the President, but sometimes found this to be, in his words, "very difficult."[87]

After ONE was abolished, the NIE process was afflicted with serious problems, some of which pertained to the resulting diminution of the CIA's role in the production of estimative intelligence. In early 1979 Turner wisely reconstituted the collective NIE review function within the CIA and its DDI. But several NIEs were not completed on schedule, and the total annual number produced fell to less than half the annual average prior to 1977. These problems were finally addressed through major, positive procedural changes that, unfortunately, were not implemented until the last year of the Carter administration.

Turner's highly personal, direct, and rather abrasive approach toward those involved in the NIE process elicited considerable criticism. He made his own systematic, substantive inputs into the strategic NIEs especially, sometimes writing entire sections himself. Moreover, although he insisted upon affording dissenting views greater prominence in the NIEs, unlike prior directors he did not use NFIB (USIB's successor) as a forum for debate or for final deliberations. Instead, NFIB meetings were conducted brusquely.[88]

William Casey, 1981–1987

William Casey will be remembered principally for his involvement in the "extra-legal" Iran-Contra affair.[89] But even before this scandal came into public view in November 1986, Casey had established himself as the most controversial DCI in history. Most of the controversy focused directly or indirectly on his handling of covert operations and on his alleged politicization of intelligence. (Although there were other issues, such as Casey's treatment of his personal finances.)

Casey had been long active in Republican Party politics and was Ronald Reagan's campaign manager in 1980. He had served in the Office of Strategic Services (OSS) during World War II. Like Allen Dulles, he had an avid interest in clandestine activities. Many CIA officers were uneasy from the start about the wisdom of pressing forward with those covert operations that held little promise of garnering broad-based public or congressional support.[90] But with the President's enthusiastic support and encouragement (the rather vague "Reagan Doctrine"), he implemented several substantial covert operations in Latin America, the Middle East, Africa, and Asia.

Political fallout was not long in coming, and not just from liberal Democrats. For example, in 1984 the chairman of the Senate Intelligence Committee, who was also the respected dean of congressional conservatives, Senator Barry Goldwater, released to the press a letter he had written to Casey. Goldwater, in his usual no-nonsense manner, stated that he was "pissed off" at not being adequately informed of the CIA's mining of Nicaraguan harbors.[91] Casey's relationship with this committee and much of the rest of Congress was exceedingly strained. Legislators complained that he misrepresented and withheld intelligence information.[92]

No DCI ever had easier access to the president, and Casey was the first DCI to be given cabinet status. But unlike virtually any other DCI, he was a *frequent* participant in high-level *policy* deliberations. His policy advice to Reagan extended well beyond Central America and Iran-related issues to other subjects, such as, for example, arms control. Casey's deep immersion in policy matters about which he often held strong views raised, said Secretary of State George Shultz (whom Casey had advised Reagan to fire), "grave doubts about the objectivity and reliability of some of the intelligence" both he and the President were receiving.[93] The majority report of the congressional committees that investigated the Iran-Contra affair concluded that during this episode, Casey "tailored intelligence reports to the positions he advocated [and] the . . . President believed and acted on these erroneous reports."[94] The crucial distinction between policy and intelligence adviser was blurred and, almost as disturbing, was perceived as being blurred by many inside and outside government. More than a year before the Iran-Contra story broke, an American Bar Association committee, all but one of whose members were former CIA officials, expressed concern about "the apparent drift of the CIA . . . towards assuming an institutional policymaking role in foreign affairs, a development encouraged by giving cabinet-level status to the DCI and appointing a political confidante of the president to that position."[95]

Concern about the too intimate tie between intelligence and policy was further fueled by the selective release of intelligence to bolster the President's political agenda with Congress and the public. Other administrations, of course, have done this, but it is a risky tactic that, among other things, invites this kind of disquieting remark, made by the House Intelligence Committee in 1982: "[T]here have been a few products whose *primary* purpose appears less to inform policy choices than to help mobilize support for policy."[96]

Controversy also spilled over into the NIE process. Much of it focused on the director's now well-established practice of claiming a personal prerogative to add, delete, or redraft various sections. One senior CIA analyst, John Horton, resigned because he believed Casey's alterations or pressures for alterations were unsupported by the evidence and were motivated by a desire to bolster the President's announced or preferred policies. The result, it was claimed, was to politicize the estimates.[97]

But the independence and analytical rigor of the NIE process— while tested—remained intact. In fact, as is discussed later, there were substantial improvements in that process. Although greatly concerned about the DCI's questionable pressures, Horton later reportedly acknowledged, as did others, that the NIE that prompted his resignation (concerning Mexico) in the end had retained its integrity.[98] Indeed, there were several NIEs that squarely challenged the soundness of administration policies and Casey's own personal policy preferences concerning, for instance, the Marcos regime in the Philippines, various Middle East matters, alleged Soviet support of international terrorism, Nicaragua, and Angola.[99] A senior official in the CIA's DDI who has a reputation for analytical integrity said that Casey drew a sharp line between his personal views and those of "the organization." Casey, he stated, "would not change the product."[100] This was confirmed by a well-informed, independent-minded congressional staffer: "Estimates under Casey *were* credible and quality *greatly* improved over the Turner years."[101]

The CIA's Robert Gates agrees that Casey separated his personal views from the estimates themselves and that "more than once" he signed an NIE with which he personally disagreed. But Gates goes further. He feels that it should not "raise eyebrows" when a DCI "in policy discussions . . . expressed his own views, which . . . differed from the agency analysis." Sometimes, says Gates, a "director's personal view is insightful and correct."[102] Yes, at times it is. And yes, it may be appropriate for a DCI to offer his personal views to policymakers on *intelligence* matters—provided that his agency's position is fully and fairly presented. But when he acts regularly as a de facto senior *policy* adviser and cabinet member who rivals even the secretary of state on some policy issues, it is another kettle of fish.[103] The threat and perceived threat of intelligence corruption then looms large. It was this, not Casey's supposed "cooking of the books" (forcing estimative intelligence reports to be rewritten to fit his policy preferences), that was the central problem.

Finally, concerning the DCI's community coordination role, Casey adopted a less assertive approach than Admiral Turner. If he had wished to expand the DCI's coordinative authority, which he apparently did not, he probably had sufficient influence with the President to have done so. That such authority went unexercised during an era of rapid budget growth is especially unfortunate.

William H. Webster, 1987–

"Judge" William Webster's principal task, certainly in his first year as DCI, was to clean up Casey's mess. He came to the agency after nine years as Director of the Federal Bureau of Investigation (FBI), where he retained his reputation for personal integrity, honesty, and (with some exceptions) sensitivity to civil liberties. He moved quickly to strengthen internal controls on convert operations, discipline seven CIA employees involved in the Iran-Contra affair, and improve the CIA's credibility with Congress.

Concerning the NIEs, Webster said: "They can be ignored, or torn up, or thrown away [by policymakers], but they may not be changed."[104]

The DCI's Coordinative Authority: Budgets[105]

We turn now to the DCI's coordinative authority in specific areas, beginning with resource allocation.

The Church Committee found that, through the Ford administration, DCIs were never "able to define priorities for the allocation of intelligence resources," and absent such authority, they could not "insure that unwarranted duplication and waste were avoided."[106] Indeed, prior to 1971, when President Nixon directed DCI Helms to prepare recommendations to the President for a consolidated NFIP budget, there was no identifiable national intelligence budget. The DCI had, and continues to have, independent authority only over the CIA's budget, which is a small part of the NFIP budget and an even smaller fraction of total intelligence community expenditures. Before the Carter administration, the DCI functioned essentially in an advisory capacity concerning those portions of the NFIP budget contributed by DOD and other non-CIA intelligence units, and he never had much influence over tactical intelligence budget resources.

Tactical intelligence generally refers to intelligence that supports military plans and operations at the military unit level. Tactical and national intelligence differ in scope, level of employment, and point of view. Still, the distinction between them has always been blurred. This has become increasingly so with advances in areas like automatic data processing, communications support technology, and real-time intelligence.

Total intelligence community resources are divided into two broad categories—the NFIP budget and the Tactical Intelligence and Related Activities (TIARA) program budget. The former includes all intelligence activities designed to serve the foreign intelligence and counterintelligence needs of policymakers. The latter is designed to meet the needs of military commanders in the field and is part of the annual Department of Defense Authorization Bill.[107] The TIARA budget probably constitutes at least 50 percent of total intelligence community expenditures.

Although DCIs have made NFIP budget recommendations since

1971, they had little real authority over that budget until President Carter's Executive Order 12036 in 1978, which gave the DCI unprecedented "full and exclusive authority over approval of the National Foreign Intelligence Program Budget submitted to the President." The order empowered the DCI to provide guidance to department/agency heads and program managers. They, in turn, had to submit their program and budget proposals to DCI Turner for approval. The NFIB could only offer advice to the director; final decisional authority, below the White House level, was his.[108] For the first time, the director's communitywide budgetary authority matched, or came close to matching, his assigned responsibilities.

Stansfield Turner exerted this authority, and the IC Staff was greatly enlarged with the addition of new budget, program, and policy specialists. Senior Defense intelligence officials initially resisted the DCI's new authority, but their resistance gradually eased when they found that the DCI could often be a valued ally in support of larger military intelligence budgets. Says Turner, "though [Defense intelligence units] lost some budgetary authority to the DCI, they gained the support of someone who was more sympathetic to their needs than were their military superiors."[109]

By 1981 the Defense intelligence units had grudgingly come to accept the DCI's enhanced position. Nonetheless, while retaining the essence of the DCI's new NFIP budget authority, President Reagan's Executive Order 12333 diluted it somewhat.[110] Moreover, the authority of the IC Staff was reduced. Former Senate Intelligence Committee staffer Stephen J. Flanagan concluded that the diminished central guidance and less systematic program review of the Reagan administration's NFIP budget process invited "imprudent duplication of effort . . . and neglect of important national concerns."[111]

The DCI's Coordinative Authority: The Requirements Process

The DCI usually issues guidelines to community collection and production elements concerning the kind of information that should be collected and the issues of primary interest to consumers that should be addressed in reports. But before 1971 he had no express authority to establish national intelligence collection or production requirements and little capability to monitor or assess compliance with his guidelines. Although the DCI received firmer formal authority over requirements in 1971 and the IC Staff was created to assist him, in practice, there was no improvement in either his *real* authority or in the quality of guidance received from policymakers concerning their intelligence needs.[112]

William Colby attempted to better focus community collection and production assets on policymakers' intelligence needs in a new guidance document—the Key Intelligence Questions (KIQs)—which identified issues of importance to consumers that collection and production managers could consider in developing their plans. But the KIQs proved ineffective, primarily because of a familiar reality—the DCI's limited authority over most of the community.[113]

President Carter's 1978 executive order gave the DCI greater coordinative authority over collection and production. It also established the National Intelligence Tasking Center (NITC), chaired by the DCI, to coordinate and task national foreign intelligence collection activities. But the NITC encountered determined resistance from Defense intelligence units (which largely ignored it). The DCI's authority over these activities was reduced by President Reagan's 1981 executive order; the NITC was abolished, and no formal successor body was created. Today, as in the past, the DCI lacks decisive authority, outside of the CIA, to set national collection and production priorities for the community. National requirements will therefore almost certainly continue to be neglected.[114]

One of the weakest and most difficult areas in the entire intelligence effort is the systematic, efficient, and meaningful establishment of requirements for collectors. The present decentralized collection system encourages the inefficient utilization of billions of dollars of collection resources, to the detriment of policymakers' national intelligence needs. Yet the obstacles to improving this situation are formidable.

Experienced collectors have a good idea about which collection resources are worthwhile and which are not, but they will not jeopardize their own programs by volunteering this information.[115] The military intelligence organizations, with their own tactical intelligence needs, jealously guard their independence. Moreover, policymakers are notoriously lax in giving collectors a clear indication of their intelligence needs. Indeed, they often do not know what these needs might be. In practice, then, the setting of requirements devolves to the collecting agencies themselves. A third problem is inherent in the requirements process itself. If the intelligence officer (or policymaker) drafts a list of requirements that addresses all the specific questions he would like answered, it would be so lengthy as to offer little practical guidance. But a short general list provides little real guidance to anyone. Yet another factor (and this hardly exhausts them) is that, while recent executive orders have given the DCI considerable authority to task collection efforts (his ability to *enforce* tasking is something else), they have not given him clear authority to control the dissemination of raw intelligence to consumers. Presidents have been reluctant to do this since they value multiple sources of raw intelligence, especially that which comes from the National Security Agency. There is, then, no easy or obvious "solution."[116]

The DCI and Covert Actions

The National Security Act of 1947 does not grant the CIA express authority to conduct covert actions.* However, it does charge the CIA with performing such "additional services" and "other functions and duties" as the NSC may direct, and this language was interpreted as authorizing such actions. This authority and the DCI's coordinative role in this area have been confirmed in a series of NSCIDs and executive orders. The Church Committee documented several serious problems that existed prior to the mid-1970s concerning, among other things, the NSC's role (or nonrole) in covert actions, the overall policy approval process, oversight, coordination, and the monitoring of ongoing covert actions.[117] Most of these problems were substantially rectified in the Ford and Carter administrations, although there has probably never been a completely adequate mechanism and procedure for ongoing review of the way covert operations are implemented.[118]

In the Reagan administration, while DCI Casey was deeply involved in covert actions and retained substantial coordinative authority, the White House moved aggressively into this area. By the second Reagan term, important interagency management responsibility for covert actions apparently passed from the DCI to the "208 Committee," which was housed in the Old Executive

---

*This section, "The DCI and Covert Actions," is short and incomplete. Only select issues are raised.

Office Building and was chaired by an NSC staffer. Major decisions were made or considered by the senior-level National Security Planning Group (NSPG), which was chaired by the President and composed of his key security advisers. Before a proposed covert action could proceed, it had to be approved by the President through the issuance of a presidential "finding."

However, in the Iran-Contra episode—which apart from intelligence problems was a monumental *policy* failure—responsible management, direction, and oversight of covert actions collapsed: the findings process was circumvented and abused; some covert actions proceeded without any presidential finding; other actions went forward after CIA personnel drafted findings in such a broad, open-ended manner as to effectively defeat the notion of presidential accountability; congressional intelligence committees were not informed of presidential findings or proposed covert actions in a full and timely manner; even very senior policymakers, including the President, were sometimes uninformed of important operations; and key NSC staffers were deeply, personally, and dangerously involved in major covert actions. This debacle was shrouded in a secrecy that, in the words of the congressional investigating committees, "was used not as a shield against our adversaries, but as a weapon against our own democratic institutions."[119] The committees' majority report made twenty-seven recommendations, most of which would not require additional legislation, to improve the handling and oversight of covert operations.[120]

The CIA has primary operational responsibility for covert actions, but the military services have their own independent capabilities for "special operations." There is little public information about the DCI's involvement in or influence over the military's covert operational activities, but this might be a problem area. The Church Committee was silent on this subject, although it noted in passing that the DDO and the CIA's chief of station in foreign countries exercised lax supervision over the military's covert operations.[121] It is uncertain whether procedures for approval and accountability within the executive branch are adequate here.[122] This matter may require clarification.

A perennial problem area is internal to the CIA. At various times in the agency's history, especially since the mid-1970s, the deputy director of intelligence has been informed by DDO of new covert activities. But generally, despite repeated efforts to bridge the gap, the clandestine service's acute concern for security has inclined it to shun a close, effective working relationship with the analysts. DDI, therefore, has often been unaware of sensitive DDO operations. This complicates and sometimes undermines the production of accurate finished intelligence. It also encourages a potentially unhealthy aura of separateness for DDO. Stansfield Turner reports, for example, that "the espionage branch wouldn't abide by the overall CIA regulations."[123] Turner is convinced that unless DDO and DDI are merged into a single unit, a move he advocates, these problems will persist to the detriment of the U.S. intelligence effort.[124] Except for the Iran-Contra matter (and probably other instances as well), there was somewhat better coordination between these two directorates during much of the Reagan administration. Robert Gates reported that "senior officials in the analysis directorate review and comment on covert action proposals."[125]

National Intelligence Estimates

As the president's principal foreign intelligence adviser, the DCI has as one of his primary functions the coordination and management of the production of finished national intelligence. The most important national intelligence products are the NIEs. They represent a coordinated community assessment of the situation in a particular country or on a specific issue and project likely trends or possible reactions to U.S. policies. Differences of opinion are expressed in footnotes or parallel texts. Some NIEs, like the estimate of Soviet strategic nuclear forces, are issued annually; others are issued or updated as the need arises. Additional national intelligence products include the Special National Intelligence Estimates and Interagency Intelligence Memorandums. SNIEs generally address specific, time-urgent problems. IIMs usually do not have a predictive character.

Policy Impact of NIEs. The influence of NIEs on policy has varied considerably, yet it has usually not been commensurate with the time, effort, and expense that go into what are supposed to be the community's premier products.[126] Bedell Smith's stature in the Truman years did give the NIEs a policy impact,[127] and the influence of some estimates has been discernible.[128] But more commonly the linkage between finished national intelligence and policy decisions is either murky or nonexistent. This is so for many reasons, some of which were mentioned early in the chapter:

- NIEs may be, or may appear to be, bland or ambivalent to consumers looking for concrete guidance.
- They may reflect divergent viewpoints. This invites the consumer to either discount them or choose the most congenial viewpoint.
- Presidents and other policymakers have preconceived notions that tend to be highly resistant to information that challenges their soundness.
- NIEs must compete with other sources of information and analysis available to policymakers.
- Consumers may believe that they, not intelligence professionals, are the best analysts of intelligence.
- NIEs are often not read by busy senior policy officials, or they are read and ignored, or they are read and used only by those whose views they buttress.
- A president may distrust the CIA.
- NIEs may not be produced in a timely enough fashion to be useful.

Office of National Estimates

The sole mission of ONE from 1950 until its abolition in 1973 was the production of NIEs. It had two components: the Board of National Estimates and the drafting staff. The board, unofficially called the College of Cardinals, was composed of about twelve senior generalists. After consultations with policymakers and various intelligence units, it developed an annual NIE production plan. Individual board members also reviewed initial staff drafts and negotiated the final language of the estimate. From 1952 to 1968, the board was chaired by Sherman Kent, who is still held in the highest esteem by CIA analysts. Kent's insistence on rigorous, balanced analysis and his almost allergic sensitivity to improper political pressure on producers became an ingrained feature of the CIA's culture. ONE's drafting staff, drawn largely from the CIA, solicited information from analytical units throughout the community and prepared initial draft NIEs. Outside consultants reviewed these drafts and advised the board on various matters.

A member of the board would begin the NIE process by distributing "terms of reference," which outlined the subject and scope of the estimate and designated offices that were to contribute to it. These contributions were assembled by the staff, which then wrote the first draft. A board member reviewed this draft, and it was then rewritten in consultation with contributing agencies. The final draft went to the USIB (earlier, to the Intelligence Advisory Committee), where additional changes were usually made. The role of the DCI in this process, as we have seen, varied. But the finished NIE was (and is today) issued under his signature as representative of the entire intelligence community's position.[129]

The accuracy of the NIEs during this and subsequent periods was inevitably uneven, given the inherent uncertainties of the enterprise. Still, ONE's overall predictive record was probably about as good as could be expected, and its estimates were analytically rigorous products of independent judgment. But by the late 1960s, there were complaints about the allegedly excessive isolation of ONE from the needs of policymakers. Moreover, Defense intelligence units had always viewed NIEs as essentially CIA, not community, products, and there were long-standing differences of opinion over the estimates' format.[130]

These considerations and others contributed to Colby's decision to dismantle ONE in 1973. He faulted the board's "ivory tower" aura that supposedly "separated [it] from the rough and tumble of the real world." The board, said Colby, tended "to be institutionally committed to an approach." To counter this, he sought a system that stressed "*individual* . . . responsibility" for draft estimates. "That," said Colby, "is my main problem with the Board, that it diffuses responsibility."[131] By emphasizing individual rather than corporate responsibility for the draft estimates, he hoped they would be more responsive to policymakers' precise needs, instead of reflecting the carefully couched judgements of what the community could agree upon.[132] Colby also sought a system that would increase the Pentagon's input to the first draft—which, in fact, did occur after his reorganization.[133]

There is another factor in ONE's demise, one that remains a matter of controversy. Some former ONE members argued that the office was not dismantled because of "unresponsiveness" or poor quality estimates, but because of what some NIEs *said*. That is, Kissinger wanted an organization that was more supportive of his policy stances.[134] Colby denies this: "[T]he move was not the result of any direct or even indirect hint from either President Nixon or Kissinger."[135] On the other hand, both Kissinger and Nixon distrusted the CIA, and before Colby became DCI, Schlesinger (who weakened ONE by depleting its ranks) and Kissinger had concluded that ONE should be replaced.[136] In 1969 Kissinger *did* pressure Helms to change an NIE's assessment of the Soviet Union's SS-9 ICBM capability, although ONE stood its ground against what it considered an inappropriate attempt to politicize intelligence.[137]

The evidence that ONE's abolition was motivated partly out of a desire for "intelligence to please" remains circumstantial. Yet there are lingering doubts. The line between responsiveness to consumer needs and corruption of intelligence can be delicate. One reason for creating a corporate ONE was precisely to deter policymakers from exerting political pressure on vulnerable individual officers. With ONE gone, this concern reappeared. The increased role of Defense intelligence in the estimative process also raised the potential of politicization as Defense elements often had particular programs and policies to protect. In addition, ONE's elimination aroused other concerns. It threatened the quality of future NIEs by removing the relatively few specialists with unique skills in drafting and reviewing estimates and by disbanding the DCI's only staff component for coordinating substantive community work.[138]

A New NIE Process

The new process revolved around individual National Intelligence Officers, originally about eleven in number. A majority of NIOs were, and are today, CIA professionals, but others are military officers or come from elsewhere in government. Each NIO serves the DCI as senior adviser and coordinator for community national intelligence production and related activities in his respective functional or geographic areas. They are also principal intermediaries between consumers and producers of intelligence and are charged with determining policymakers' informational needs and seeing that they receive relevant intelligence. Over the years, NIOs have advised DCIs on various production and collection priorities, the satisfaction of requirements by community elements, and resource allocation issues. But they were severely strapped in the first few years by not having an NIE drafting staff of their own. Instead, they were expected to assign the drafting of papers to experts throughout the community.[139]

The way in which the NIO system operated from 1973 to 1980 seemed to vindicate those critical of ONE's elimination. Veteran intelligence professional Richard Lehman, the first chairman of the National Intelligence Council, concluded that "the NIO system was more of a success in providing intelligence support to the policymaker than it was in providing National Estimates."[140] Lehman and others pointed to the generally lower quality of NIEs during this period. A major reason for this was the lack of an organized, systematic drafting process and the absence of a staff of trained, experienced estimate writers. NIEs lacked the kind of broad, integrated perspective ONE had provided. NIOs were burdened with multiple demands on their time, and instead of being the sort of community officers Colby had envisaged, they relied heavily on the CIA's DDI for analytic support. As a result of these developments, annual NIE production dropped dramatically— from about fifty prior to 1973 to as few as twelve by the late 1970s. Some NIEs were delayed for years, and their influence deteriorated.[141]

However, the estimates regained much of their former stature in the Reagan years, partly because of reforms instituted in the last year of the Carter administration, which were continued and refined by William Casey. The National Intelligence Council was formed in 1980. It is a corporate body resembling ONE in many respects.[142] Under Casey, the NFIB was a more active, open forum for debating and discussing NIEs among intelligence community principals than it had been under Turner. More NIOs were added (for a total of between fifteen and seventeen), there was greater interaction among NIOs than in the past, and procedures for coordinating NIEs were better regulated. While NIOs do not have the kind of collective responsibility for finished national intelligence that ONE's Board of National Estimates had—thereby upholding Colby's conception of their role—there is the Senior Review Panel of experts that, with outside consultants, reviews draft estimates. Most significantly, the NIC acquired a drafting staff—

the Analytic Group—similar to, but smaller than, the ONE drafting staff. It drafts a significant percentage of the estimates and coordinates these drafts with analysts throughout the community. The members of the NIC/AG are drawn from various intelligence agencies, from other governmental units, and from outside of government. It has been a major factor in the improved quantity (more than 100 in 1986, for example), quality, and timeliness of the estimates.[143]

Appropriate procedures and organizational mechanisms for producing NIEs are in place. In addition, of course, to high-caliber people of integrity, what is most needed is stability in the present structures. Future administrations should be cautious about making wholesale organizational changes here. However, one measure might be helpful. Casey often did not spend much time on NIC activities. A DCI could bolster the stature and perceived independence of the NIE process if he turned more openly to the Senior Review Panel and analogized it and the NIC, perhaps publicly, to the old Board of National Estimates and ONE.

The Defense Intelligence Agency

Although it does relate to consumer-producer relations and community management and coordination, this section stands somewhat apart from the rest of the chapter.

The Defense Intelligence Agency has received scant public attention or scholarly scrutiny even though, in William Kaufmann's words, it "cries out for reform."[144] Others echo this view. But despite several internal reorganizations, most of DIA's problems remain substantially intact.

Establishment of DIA

The agency was created by neither lesislation nor executive order, but by the direction of Secretary of Defense Robert McNamara (DOD Directive 5105.21) in 1961. McNamara was concerned that his responsibility for most U.S. intelligence collection programs was not coupled with sufficient means to coordinate either these programs or the production of Defense intelligence. He hoped that a central coordinating agency with a strong bond to OSD policymakers and planners would fill this gap. He also hoped the agency would improve the allocation of Defense intelligence resources and eliminate duplicating facilities and organizations. But the Joint Chiefs of Staff fought to retain the independence of service intelligence units. The chiefs wanted the new agency to be completely subordinate to them. The DIA was a compromise between these two positions: it reported to the secretary of defense, but did so through the JCS. DOD Directive 5105.21 granted the agency full authority for assembling, integrating, and validating all DOD intelligence requirements, for producing all finished Defense intelligence products, and for setting the policy and procedures for collecting data. The services retained resources for collecting and processing intelligence, but under the supervision and coordination of DIA. Yet despite this broad grant of authority, DIA has never fulfilled McNamara's hopes, largely because of the compromise that gave it birth.[145]

Two Masters

That compromise placed the director of DIA—always a lieutenant general or vice admiral—in what President Nixon's Blue Ribbon Defense Panel (Fitzhugh Report) termed "an impossible position" because one of the agency's "principal problems" is that it has "too many masters."[146] The DIA director provides staff assistance on intelligence to both civilian officials in OSD and military officers in the JCS. But because OSD and the JCS differ on a range of programmatic, budgetary, and policy issues, and because the two have different intelligence needs (that is, broad, national-level, political-military insights versus narrower, tactical-level, more specific factual data), DIA finds itself at times caught between these two masters.[147] And the agency's oft-noted reluctance to challenge the services' intelligence units in the latters' areas of specialization clouds its credibility with the secretary and other policy and intelligence officials.[148]

DIA is supposed to coordinate and supervise the processing and collection of intelligence by the military services, yet its director reports to a JCS (and since 1986, to the JCS chairman) that controls the assignment and promotion of military officers serving in his agency. In addition, the chiefs tend to protect and nurture *their* intelligence organizations. As a consequence, concluded the Fitzhugh Report, "the 'supervision' by the DIA of intelligence collection and processing by the Services, and DIA's fiscal control is largely impotent."[149]

The Defense intelligence community remains poorly coordinated, fragmented, and without centralized management. While DIA was created primarily to consolidate Washington-based Defense intelligence activities, the service intelligence units are substantially larger today than before 1961, and they are engaged in some activities clearly assigned to DIA. The services justify the retention of DIA-assigned activities by arguing that DIA lacks the capability to provide the intelligence they require.[150]

Personnel

DIA has an image problem, which is grounded in its propensity for threat inflation (discussed below) and in the quality of its personnel. Particularly in recent years, the agency *has* had some good and dedicated people, but it continues to have difficulty attracting and retaining them. Military officers rotate in and out of DIA, and many civilians leave or, if they stay, become frustrated by the practices and ambiance of this essentially military organization.[151]

DIA's difficulty in attracting military talent partly reflects a larger problem within the military profession. Many officers avoid and intelligence career because it lacks the prestige of plans/operations and offers fewer opportunities for promotion to the highest ranks. Since the mid-1970s, promotion prospects for middle-grade intelligence specialists within individual services have approximated those of officers with other specializations, but this has not been so for those with DIA. Also, while this may be changing somewhat, field commanders have traditionally shunted a fair number of mediocre men and women into intelligence. And apart from this larger problem, the services tend to retain their best intelligence people within their own intelligence units. These people do not receive a joint assignment to DIA, although this practice may well change because of provisions of the Goldwater-Nichols Department of Defense Reorganization Act of 1986 (see Chapter 4).[152]

More than one-half of DIA's professional personnel are civilians, many of whom are retired military officers. Their quality, especially in the middle and upper echelons, has been repeatedly questioned. Patrick McGarvey, writing in the early 1970s, called DIA's civilian staff "second rate." Similar characterizations were made by the Church Committee and, in the mid-1980s, by Stansfield Turner and (indirectly) by the Senate Intelligence Committee.[153] The tone of the work environment is set by the agency's military leadership. It sometimes stifles initiative and independent, original thought and inculcates a "go along to get along" approach. This atmosphere is not appealing to bright, ambitious analysts with intellectual integrity.[154]

Unlike their counterparts in the CIA and the National Security Agency, DIA civilian personnel were subject to Civil Service regulations before 1984. This made it difficult to fire unproductive people and properly reward outstanding performance. To permit such flexibility, section 501 of the FY 1985 Intelligence Authorization Act exempted DIA from Civil Service classification provisions.[155] But as the Church Committee said in 1976, it is doubtful that "removing Civil Service constraints would in itself suffice to bring about the needed degree of improvement in performance" because DIA's basic problems would remain substantially unaffected.[156]

Quality of Analysis

Former DIA Director Major General Daniel O. Graham wrote in 1973:

Military professionals . . . through . . . downgrading the role of intelligence in general and sometimes abusing the intelligence process, have . . . produced the best argument for taking the responsibility for threat description out of military hands. . . . The basic problem is one of confidence in the military intelligence product. . . . To put it bluntly, there is a considerable body of opinion among decisionmakers, in and out of the DOD, which regards threat estimates prepared by the military as being self-serving, budget-oriented and generally inflated. . . .

DIA was plagued by the prevalent notion, even in the DOD staff, that the agency could not be counted upon for an objective threat assessment. . . . But . . . the military intelligence *user* must take his lumps as well. Too often the user has not been content with an objective judgment from his intelligence officer—he has wanted the answer that "supports the program." . . . When intelligence yields to consumer pressure, it cannot remain credible.[157]

After this withering attack on his own agency, General Graham added that this "dismal picture . . . has brightened measurably" since 1970.[158] But this is disputed by others. For instance, Stansfield Turner agrees with the Church Committee's conclusion that DIA "analyses [are] often biased to reflect the views of the services. When evidence is doubtful, the services have incentives to tilt an intelligence appraisal in a direction to support their own budgetary requests to justify existing operations and proposed new ones."[159] The problem with the quality of DIA analyses— which is more pronounced with some threat estimates and DIA contributions to certain NIEs than it is with the details of enemy weaponry, order of battle, and so on ("bean counting")—is generally seen as a combination of an insufficient number of competent analysts and an inability to withstand pressures to support DOD and service programs, budgets, and policies.[160] Military officers on a tour of duty with DIA know their promotions and future assignments are determined—or, since 1986, largely determined—by their parent service. It can be dangerous, therefore, to take a position contrary to that of a service and/or its intelligence unit. And inflating threat estimates of, say, Soviet air or sea capabilities has been a customary way to induce Congress to increase annual Air Force and Navy appropriations.[161]

This does not mean that DIA products are invariably "wrong"—although some of them are viewed suspiciously by both consumers and civilian intelligence units. It should also be acknowledged that much (certainly not all) of this criticism comes from the agency's frequent competitor, the CIA. Additionally, DOD claims—as do others sometimes, like Schlesinger and Kissinger—that the CIA has a liberal bias (which claim would, no doubt, shock many liberals).[162] While assertions of bias in one direction or another are partly reflective of Graham Allison's dictum that where you stand depends on where you sit, they are overdrawn in the case of the CIA. Admiral Turner relates that he occasionally saw some "liberal" CIA political analysis of the sort "in vogue in the academic community," but "there were about as many instances of bias in the opposite direction."[163] My personal experience is that most CIA analysts (covert operators are often another breed) run the gamut from moderate conservative to moderate liberal and, as a group, are conscientious seekers of "objectivity." DDI is not a place for ideologues.[164] Over the years,

CIA estimates of, say, Soviet defense expenditures, ICBM deployment rates, and petroleum production have been both "high" and "low." And, importantly, neither job security nor the DDI's budget are dependent on coming up with a high or low estimate.

Prescriptions for Reform

There are at least five evident paths toward reform. First, try to upgrade the caliber of DIA's personnel and intelligence product within the *present* organizational arrangement. This is the course that has been followed since about 1970. But it cannot alter the fundamental difficulty—the agency's relationship with the services. Therefore, under this course of action it will, as the Murphy Commission said, "be difficult to achieve a substantially better performance."[165]

Options two, three, and four will be difficult to implement politically and bureaucratically. In particular, options two and three—abolishing either the four service intelligence units[166] or DIA[167]—face certain and probably fatal bureaucratic resistance. Moreover, eliminating one or the other may reduce whatever organizational duplication there may be, but probably at considerable cost in functional capabilities. While continued service control over the community's tactical intelligence assets impedes efficient community management, the services have an undeniable need for such assets. It is uncertain whether DIA alone could meet this need adequately. Conversely, DIA is the Pentagon's primary organization for strategic intelligence matters and its principal participant in the NIE process. It is also the validating authority for much of the work done by service intelligence components and performs other functions that probably could not be performed effectively by the independent services.[168]

The fourth alternative is favored by the Church Committee and William Kaufmann.[169] It has DIA reporting exclusively to the secretary of defense and places it within OSD. This would end the "two masters" problem and open the way to genuine improvement in the quality of analysis. DIA would concentrate heavily on national and OSD intelligence needs. Service intelligence units would have primary responsibility for tactical intelligence that supports service missions, although the secretary must ensure their full coordination and sharing of information with his

DIA. However, this option could again raise the very dispute that divided Secretary McNamara and the JCS in 1961.

A fifth option has received little attention, yet it could be the most appealing: retain DIA and the service intelligence units and require DIA to report exclusively to the chairman of the JCS as his J-2 (intelligence directorate). But DIA would be removed from direct involvement in the NIE process, and it would no longer attempt to service OSD's unique intelligence needs. Those needs would be performed instead by a small new office within OSD somewhat analogous to the State Department's Bureau of Intelligence and Research. This option also eliminates the "two masters" problem, and unlike option four, it is sensitive to the importance of DIA to the military services. In addition, it should encounter far less bureaucratic resistance than option four. The problems with Defense intelligence today are so pervasive and so evident that a secretary of defense should be able to garner both presidential and congressional support for implementing this proposal.

Conclusion: A Legislative Charter?[170]

Several bills were introduced between 1977 and 1980 with the collective purpose of providing a comprehensive statutory charter for all components of the intelligence community. By 1979—with the Soviet invasion of Afghanistan, the Iran hostage crisis, and other developments—the necessary political support for such reform had evaporated. Yet the substantive case for a comprehensive charter was and is persuasive. Many Reagan administration actions abroad and at home in the intelligence/secrecy areas, including especially the Iran-Contra affair, further buttress this case.

In the late 1980s some legislators were again questioning the principal arguments against a comprehensive charter: namely, the supposed need of the president and DCI for flexibility, particularly in clandestine activities, and the assertion that existing legislation and executive orders were sufficient deterrents to abuse. The Reagan administration clearly abused its prerogatives in the conduct of some covert activities. The Iran-Contra episode revealed, among other things, that the Intelligence Oversight Act of 1980 was deficient in the clarity of its language. A comprehensive charter would sharply upgrade the quality of congressional oversight of the intelligence community.

Neither DIA nor the National Security Agency have a statutory foundation. The National Security Act of 1947 (as amended) is a vague, ambiguous, open-ended legal charter for the CIA, one that reflects a bygone era in executive-legislative relations. A new charter that sets forth in some specificity the missions and responsibilities of the various actors in the intelligence field would reaffirm the principle that the United States is a nation of laws. It could thereby provide a means for maintaining public and congressional confidence in the intelligence community, without which the community cannot be effective. A charter would also serve to protect the CIA and other governmental units engaged in intelligence from being asked to undertake questionable activities. Regrettably, however, Congress is not presently inclined to again consider adopting a comprehensive charter.

Notes

1. The term *consumers* (users) is here employed to refer primarily to senior- or junior-level executive officials engaged in formulating or implementing policy. There are, of course, other consumers, including various congressional committees, certain executive oversight and advisory bodies, and the intelligence community itself. *Producers* refers to those within the intelligence community who create either raw (unevaluated) or finished (evaluated) intelligence reports.
2. *National intelligence* can be defined as foreign intelligence produced under the aegis of the DCI and intended primarily for the needs of the president, the National Security Council, and other federal officials involved in the formulation and/or execution of *national* security, foreign political, and/or economic policy.
3. For excellent treatments of this subject, see Jeffrey T. Richelson, *The U.S. Intelligence Community*, 2d ed., (Cambridge, Mass.: Ballinger, 1988); Tyrus G. Fain, ed., *The Intelligence Community: History, Organization and Issues* (New York: R. R. Bowker, 1977).
4. See U.S. Congress, *Report of the Congressional Committees Investigating the Iran-Contra Affair* (hereafter cited as *Report: Iran-Contra Affair*), H. Rept. 100–433, 100th Cong., 1st sess., 1987, pp. 375–86, 423–27; Cecil V. Crabb, Jr., and Pat M.Holt, *Invitation To Struggle: Congress, The President, And Foreign Policy*, 3d ed. (Washington, D.C.: Congressional Quarterly Press, 1988), pp. 163–92. Gregory F. Treverton, *Covert Action: The Limits of Intervention in the Postwar World* (New York: Basic Books, 1987), pp. 222–63; American Bar Association (hereafter cited as ABA), *Oversight and Accountability of the U.S. Intelligence Agencies: An Evaluation* (Washington, D.C.: ABA, 1985); John M. Oseth, *Regulating U.S. Intelligence Operations* (Lexington: University of Kentucky Press, 1985); George Pickett, "Congress, the Budget, and Intelligence," in Alfred C. Maurer, Marion D. Tunstall, and James M. Keagle,

eds., *Intelligence: Policy Process* (Boulder, Colo.: Westview Press, 1985), pp. 157–75; Duncan L. Clarke and Edward L. Neveleff, "Secrecy, Foreign Intelligence and Civil Liberties: Has the Pendulum Swung Too Far?" *Political Science Quarterly* 99 (Fall 1984): 493–513; Gary Schmitt, "Oversight—What for and How Effective?" in Roy Godson, ed., *Intelligence Requirements for the 1980s: Intelligence and Policy* (Lexington, Mass.: Lexington Books, 1986), pp. 119–148; U.S. Congress, House of Representatives, Permanent Select Committee on Intelligence (hereafter cited as HPSCI), *Hearings: Congressional Oversight of Convert Activities* 98th Cong., 1st sess., 1983.

5. See Richard K. Betts, "Analysis, War, and Decision: Why Intelligence Failures are Inevitable," *World Politics* 31 (October 1978): 61–89; Hans Heymann, "Intelligence/Policy Relationships," in Maurer, Tunstall, and Keagle, *Intelligence*, pp. 57–66. My treatment of this subject was especially influenced by Arthur S. Hulnick, "The Intelligence Producer–Policy Consumer Linkage: A Theoretical Approach," *Intelligence and National Security* 1 (May 1986): 212–33.

6. For example, see U.S. Congress, House of Representatives, Committee on Foreign Affairs (hereafter cited as HFAC), Subcommittee on International Security and Scientific Affairs, *Hearings: The Role of Intelligence in the Foreign Policy Process*, 96th Cong., 2d sess., 1980, p. 234; Amos A. Jordan and William J. Taylor, *American National Security: Policy and Process*, rev. ed. (Baltimore, Md.: Johns Hopkins University Press, 1984), p. 131. Unlike some others, Jordan and Taylor acknowledge that "in the real world, things simply are not so tidy" (p. 132).

7. See Hulnick, "The Intelligence Producer–Policy Consumer Linkage," pp. 218–23, 227; Stephen J. Flanagan, "The Coordination of National Intelligence," in Duncan L. Clarke, ed., *Public Policy and Political Institutions: United States Defense and Foreign Policy—Policy Coordination and Integration* (Greenwich, Ct.: JAI Press, 1985), pp. 162–65; U.S. Congress, Senate, Select Committee to Study Governmental Operations with Respect to Intelligence Activities (hereafter cited as Church Committee), *Foreign and Military Intelligence*, 94th Cong., 2d sess., 1976, Book I, pp. 18, 346–47; Loch K. Johnson, "Decision Costs in the Intelligence Cycle," in Maurer, Tunstall, and Keagle, *Intelligence*, pp. 181–98. The production process and the consumer-producer relationship varies considerably with the intelligence product. This discussion deals primarily with finished or estimative intelligence.

8. Robert M. Gates, "The CIA and American Foreign Policy," *Foreign Affairs* 66 (Winter 1987–88): 226.

9. He added that there was virtually no exchange of personnel between the two agencies (Confidential discussion with the author, 28 April 1987).

10. Kenneth deGraffenreid, "Intelligence and the Oval Office," in Godson, *Intelligence Requirements for the 1980s*, p. 14. In 1982, when respected intelligence professional Admiral Bobby Inman was Deputy Director of Central Intelligence, he urged (unsuccessfully) the removal of the relatively inexperienced deGraffenreid as Reagan NSC staffer for intelligence (Bob Woodward, *Veil: The Secret Wars of the CIA, 1981–1987* [New York: Simon & Schuster, 1987], pp. 201–203).

11. Sherman Kent, *Strategic Intelligence for American World Policy* (Princeton, N.J.: Princeton University Press, 1966), p. 180.
12. Ibid., p. 167.
13. deGraffenreid, "Intelligence and the Oval Office," pp. 9–40.
14. John W. Huizenga, "Comments on 'Intelligence and Policymaking in an Institutional Context'," in Commission on the Organization of Government for the Conduct of Foreign Policy (hereafter cited as Murphy Commission), *Intelligence Functions Analyses*, vol. 7, Appendix U (Washington, D.C.: Government Printing Office, 1975), p. 42.
15. A committee of the ABA headed by former CIA General Counsel David Silver posed several queries to twenty-six past and present senior intelligence officials. No issue elicited greater agreement than the importance of protecting intelligence agencies from "undue political pressures" (ABA, *Oversight and Accountability*, p. 35).
16. Covert actions, euphemistically called "special activities" in President Reagan's Executive Order (E.O.) 12333 are defined in that E.O. as
    activities conducted in support of national foreign policy objectives abroad which are planned and executed so that the role of the United States Government is not apparent or acknowledged publicly, and functions in support of such activities, but which are not intended to influence United States political processes, public opinion, policies, or media and do not include diplomatic activities or the collection and production of intelligence or related support functions (Sec. 3.4(h), 46 *Federal Register* 59, 941 (1981)).
17. Testimony of Richard Betts in HFAC, *The Role of Intelligence*, p. 22.
18. George Thibault, written communication to the author, 12 April 1987.
19. Gates, "The CIA and American Foreign Policy," p. 228.
20. Richard Giza, "The Problems of the Intelligence Consumer," in Roy Godson, ed., *Intelligence Requirements: Analysis and Estimates* (Washington, D.C.: National Strategy Information Center, 1980), p. 204; testimony of John Huizenga in Church Committee, *Foreign and Military Intelligence*, p. 82. See also, Stansfield Turner, *Secrecy and Democracy: The CIA in Transition* (Boston: Houghton Mifflin, 1985), pp. 240–42.
21. U.S. Congress, Senate, Select Committee on Intelligence (hereafter cited as SSCI), *Report*, S. Rept. 98–665, 98th Cong., 2d sess., 1985, p. 28.
22. Commission on CIA Activities Within the United States (hereafter cited as Rockefeller Commission), *Report to the President* (Washington, D.C.: Government Printing Office, 1975), p. 17. See also, Turner, *Secrecy and Democracy*, p. 278.
23. Gates, "The CIA and American Foreign Policy," p. 221.
24. Hans Heymann, "Intelligence/Policy Relationships," in Maurer, Tunstall, and Keagle, *Intelligence*, pp. 60–62; Hulnick, "The Intelligence Producer–Policy Consumer Linkage," p. 215; Betts, "Analysis, War, and Decision," p. 69; Church Committee, *Foreign and Military Intelligence*, p. 272.
25. Conversely, Robert Gates reports that "CIA officers can describe in excruciating detail how foreign policy is made in every country in the world save one—the United States" (Gates, "The CIA and American Foreign Policy," p. 219).

26. See Hulnick, "The Intelligence Producer–Policy Consumer Linkage," p. 215.
27. Bruce D. Berkowitz, *American Security: Dilemmas for a Modern Democracy* (New Haven, Ct.: Yale University Press, 1986), pp. 237–38; Thomas L. Hughes, "The Power to Speak and the Power to Listen," in Thomas M. Franck and Edward Weisband, eds., *Secrecy and Foreign Policy* (New York: Oxford University Press, 1974), pp. 15, 19.
28. Berkowitz, *American Security*, pp. 224, 248; Hulnick, "The Intelligence Producer–Policy Consumer Linkage," pp. 215–16.
29. Heymann, "Intelligence/Policy Relationships," pp. 59–60; Gates, "The CIA and American Foreign Policy," p. 227; Robert Jervis, *The Logic of Images in International Relations* (Princeton, N.J.: Princeton University Press, 1970), p. 132; Robert Jervis, *Perception and Misperception in International Politics* (Princeton, N.J.: Princeton University Press, 1976), ch. 4; Robert Jervis, Richard Ned Lebow, and Janice Gross Stein, *Psychology and Deterrence* (Baltimore, Md.: Johns Hopkins University Press, 1985).
30. Quoted in Henry Brandon, *The Retreat of American Power* (Garden City, N.Y.: Doubleday, 1973), p. 103.
31. Heymann, "Intelligence/Policy Relationships," pp. 62–65; Gates, The CIA and American Foreign Policy," pp. 224–25.
32. Policymakers' "preoccupation with current reporting," says Robert Gates, "is a major problem . . . . One of the CIA's greatest concerns . . . has been the unwillingness or inability of most policymakers to spend much time on longer-range issues. . . . [T]he CIA has struggled, largely in vain, to get policy officials to devote time to intelligence issues other than those directly related to a crisis" (Gates, "The CIA and American Foreign Policy," p. 226).
33. See Ray S. Cline, "Policy Without Intelligence," *Foreign Policy* 17 (Winter 1974–75): 133.
34. Church Committee, *Foreign and Military Intelligence*, pp. 267–68; Hulnick, "The Intelligence Producer–Policy Consumer Linkage," pp. 216, 229; Helene L. Boatner, "The Evaluation of Intelligence: How Well Do We Do?" (Paper presented at International Studies Association Convention, Atlanta, Georgia, March 1984), p. 11.
35. Betts, "Analysis, War and Decision," p. 88; Richard K. Betts, *Surprise Attack* (Washington, D.C.: The Brookings Institution, 1982), pp. 104–108, 120–49.
36. William Colby, *Honorable Men: My Life in the CIA* (New York: Simon & Schuster, 1978), pp. 356–57. See also, Church Committee, *Foreign and Military Intelligence*, p. 268; Cline, "Policy Without Intelligence," pp. 132–33. Senior intelligence officers in the Nixon administration might identify with what an NSC staffer told me in 1971: "Working for Henry is like being a mushroom. He keeps you in the dark, dumps horse manure on you, and then cans you."
37. Reported in Hulnick, "The Intelligence Producer–Policy Consumer Linkage," p. 227.
38. See Walter Laqueur, *A World of Secrets: The Uses and Limits of Intelligence* (New York: Basic Books, 1985), pp. 99, 101.
39. Jeffrey T. Richelson, *The U.S. Intelligence Community* (Cambridge, Mass.:

Ballinger, 1985), p. 275; Flanagan, "The Coordination of National Intelligence," p. 166; Church Committee, *Foreign and Military Intelligence*, pp. 42–61.

40. See Richelson, *The U.S. Intelligence Community*, pp. 275–78; Church Committee, *Foreign and Military Intelligence*, pp. 42–62.

41. Flanagan, "The Coordination of National Intelligence," pp. 166–67; Church Committee, *Foreign and Military Intelligence*, p. 62.

42. Church Committee, *Foreign and Military Intelligence*, pp. 65–66.

43. Mark L. Lowenthal, *U.S. Intelligence: Evolution and Anatomy* (New York: Praeger, 1984), pp. 85–86; Flanagan, "The Coordination of National Intelligence," p. 170.

44. Church Committee, *Foreign and Military Intelligence*, pp. 60–61, 66–68. See also, Victor Marchetti and John D. Marks, *The CIA and the Cult of Intelligence* (New York: Alfred A. Knopf, 1974), p. 336.

45. Lowenthal, *U.S. Intelligence*, p. 85; OMB official, confidential interview with the author, April 1987.

46. Richard A. Stubbing, *The Defense Game* (New York: Harper & Row, 1986), pp. 81–82.

47. Confidential discussion with the author, 28 April 1987.

48. Patrick E. Tyler, "How the U.S. Cloaks a $24 Billion Budget," *Washington Post*, 26 March 1986, p. A17.

49. See generally Flanagan, "The Coordination of National Intelligence," pp. 168–70; Chester A. Crocker, "The President's External Advisors in Foreign Policy," in Murphy Commission, *Advisory Panels*, vol. 6, Appendix S (Washington, D.C.: Government Printing Office, 1975), pp. 419–22; ABA, *Oversight and Accountability*, p. 108; Church Committee, *Foreign and Military Intelligence*, pp. 63–64, 114; Rockefeller Commission, *Report to the President*, p. 73; Jim Anderson, "Books Hits Regan on Spy Board Purge," *Washington Post*, 15 May 1988, p. A7 (cf., Leo Cherne, "Discussion," in Godson, *Intelligence Requirements for the 1980s*, pp. 32–35).

50. On the Team B exercise, see John Prados, *The Soviet Estimate: U.S. Intelligence Analysis and Russian Military Strength* (New York: Dial Press, 1982), pp. 248–57. The conservative former CIA Deputy Director for Intelligence, Ray Cline, called the B team group a "kangaroo court" (p. 253).

51. National Security Act of 1947, 50 U.S.C. Sec. 403 (d).

52. Church Committee, *Foreign and Military Intelligence*, pp. 94–95, 125, 433; Flanagan, "The Coordination of National Intelligence," pp. 179–80; Turner, *Secrecy and Democracy*, p. 273; HPSCI, *Staff Report: U.S. Intelligence Performance on Central America: Achievements and Selected Instances of Concern*, 97th Cong., 2d sess., 1982, pp. 22–23.

53. Church Committee, *Foreign and Military Intelligence*, pp. 449–50; SSCI, *Hearings: National Intelligence Reorganization and Reform Act of 1978*, 95th Cong., 2d sess., 1978, pp. 860–74; Turner, *Secrecy and Democracy*, pp. 273–74; Walter Pincus, "Specter Urges Splitting Top CIA Post, Tougher Penalty for Lying," *Washington Post*, 28 October 1987, p. A4. See also, Taylor B. Belcher, "Clandestine Operations," in Murphy Commission, *Intelligence Functions Analyses*, p. 72; Allan E. Goodman, "Reforming U.S. Intelligence," *Foreign Policy* 67 (Summer 1987): 129–30.

54. SSCI, *National Intelligence Reorganization and Reform Act of 1978*, p. 13; Church Committee, *Foreign and Military Intelligence*, p. 450.
55. SSCI, *National Intelligence Reorganization and Reform Act of 1978*, pp. 46–47, 52–59, 99–100, 222–25; Flanagan, "The Coordination of National Intelligence," p. 180. Cf., Church Committee, *Foreign and Military Intelligence*, p. 450.
56. Graham Allison and Peter Szanton, *Remaking Foreign Policy: The Organizational Connection* (New York: Basic Books, 1976), pp. 202–203; Flanagan, "The Coordination of National Intelligence," p. 182.
57. Church Committee, *Foreign and Military Intelligence*, p. 72.
58. Ibid., pp. 25, 115. See also, Robert M. Macy, "Issues on Intelligence Resource Management," in Murphy Commission, *Intelligence Functions Analyses*, p. 53.
59. SSCI, *Report: Authorizing Appropriations for Fiscal Year 1987 for Intelligence Activities of the United States Government*, S. Rept. 99–307, 99th Cong., 2d sess., 1986, p. 5; Lowenthal, *U.S. Intelligence*, pp. 81–82.
60. Turner, *Secrecy and Democracy*, pp. 266–67.
61. Senior member of the IC Staff, confidential discussion with the author, 28 April 1987.
62. Scott D. Breckinridge, *The CIA and the U.S. Intelligence System* (Boulder, Colo.: Westview Press, 1986), pp. 44–45; Lowenthal, *U.S. Intelligence*, p. 82.
63. Breckinridge, *The CIA and the U.S. Intelligence System*, p. 46; Lowenthal, *U.S. Intelligence*, p. 83.
64. Flanagan, "The Coordination of National Intelligence," p. 160.
65. Church Committee, *Supplementary Detailed Staff Reports on Foreign and Military Intelligence*, 94th Cong., 2d sess., 1976, Book IV, pp. 11, 25; John Ranelagh, *The Agency: The Rise and Decline of the CIA* (New York: Simon & Schuster, 1986), pp. 166–67; Victoria S. Price, *The DCI's Role in Producing Strategic Intelligence Estimates* (Newport, R.I.: Naval War College, 1980), pp. 10–13.
66. Church Committee, *Supplementary Detailed Staff Reports*, pp. 11–12; Church Committee, *Foreign and Military Intelligence*, p. 104; Ray S. Cline, *The CIA: Reality vs. Myth* (Washington, D.C.: Acropolis Books, 1982), pp. 129–40.
67. Price, *The DCI's Role*, pp. 14–15; 86–87; Church Committee, *Supplementary Detailed Staff Reports*, pp. 18–20.
68. Church Committee, *Foreign and Military Intelligence*, pp. 111–12; Church Committee, *Supplementary Detailed Staff Reports*, pp. 45–50; Ranelagh, *The Agency*, p. 220; Laqueur, *A World of Secrets*, pp. 75–78.
69. Church Committee, *Foreign and Military Intelligence*, pp. 110–11, 113–14; Church Committee, *Supplementary Detailed Staff Reports*, pp. 60–63.
70. Price, *The DCI's Role*, pp. 19–26, 33–43, 60–62, 74, 76; Church Committee, *Supplementary Detailed Staff Reports*, pp. 55–60.
71. Price, *The DCI's Role*, p. 61.
72. Church Committee, *Supplementary Detailed Staff Reports*, p. 73.
73. Church Committee, *Foreign and Military Intelligence*, pp. 117, 119, 121.
74. Cline, *The CIA: Reality vs. Myth*, pp. 219, 225; Ranelagh, *The Agency*, pp. 413, 422–23, 447.

75. Price, *The DCI's Role*, pp. 63–65, 79–80, 88–89; Lawrence Freedman, *U.S. Intelligence and the Soviet Strategic Threat* (Boulder, Colo.: Westview Press, 1977), p. 124.

76. Quoted in Ranelagh, *The Agency*, p. 424.

77. Ibid., pp. 448, 526–30, 539–41. See also, Thomas Powers, *The Man Who Kept the Secrets* (New York: Alfred A. Knopf, 1979).

78. Henry Kissinger, *White House Years* (Boston: Little, Brown, 1979), pp. 36–37; Ray Cline, *The CIA Under Reagan, Bush and Casey* (Washington, D.C.: Acropolis Books, 1981), p. 240; Ranelagh, *The Agency*, pp. 450–51, 467, 484, 500–502; Church Committee, *Foreign and Military Intelligence*, pp. 122, 433.

79. However, Helms did delete a paragraph from NIE 11–8–69, at the request of Secretary of Defense Melvin Laird, before it went to the USIB (Price, *The DCI's Role*, pp. 66–67).

80. Ibid., pp. 82–83, 90–91.

81. Ibid., pp. 44, 67–68, 83; Ranelagh, *The Agency*, pp. 548–51.

82. Church Committee, *Foreign and Military Intelligence*, p. 123.

83. Quoted in Ranelagh, *The Agency*, pp. 586–87, 624.

84. Price, *The DCI's Role*, pp. 68–69, 84, 92–94. Colby states that Kissinger "never—and I repeat never—suggested what positions I should take or even asked what I would be saying before [an NSC] meeting" (Colby, *Honorable Men*, p. 375).

85. Cord Meyer, *Facing Reality: From World Federalism to the CIA* (New York: Harper & Row, 1980), pp. 225–26.

86. Richard K. Betts, "American Strategic Intelligence: Politics, Priorities, and Direction," in Robert L. Pfaltzgraff, Jr., Uri Ra'anan, and Warren Milberg, eds., *Intelligence Policy and National Security* (London: Macmillan Press, 1981), pp. 261–62; Turner, *Secrecy and Democracy*, p. 197; Ranelagh, *The Agency*, pp. 635–36.

87. Turner, *Secrecy and Democracy*, pp. 132–34; Zbigniew Brzezinski, *Power and Principle: Memoirs of the National Security Adviser, 1977–1981* (New York: Farrar, Straus & Giroux, 1983), pp. 64, 68, 72–73.

88. Woodward, *Veil*, p. 99; Price, *The DCI's Role*, pp. 47–50, 69–72, 86, 94–95. Former Turner aide George Thibault stated that Turner insisted "on *rigorous* analysis, requiring analysts to defend their conclusions. Some were not accustomed to this 'interference' " (Thibault, written communication to the author, 12 April 1987).

89. *Report: Iran-Contra Affair*, p. 20. Concerning Casey's role, see this report, and Woodward, *Veil*, pp. 466ff., 483ff.

90. John Prados, *Presidents' Secret Wars* (New York: Quill/William Morrow, 1986), p. 396; Woodward, *Veil*, pp. 206, 331.

91. Letter to editor by Barry Goldwater, *Washington Post*, 11 April 1984, p. A17; Harry Howe Ransom, "Intelligence and Partisan Politics," in Maurer, Tunstall, and Keagle, *Intelligence*; pp. 38–39.

92. *Report: Iran-Contra Affair*, pp. 375, 381–83; Woodward, *Veil*.

93. Quoted in "Shultz Says Lies and Clashes Were Rife over Iran Deal," *New York Times*, 24 July 1987, p. 1; Woodward, *Veil*, pp. 489, 497.

94. *Report: Iran-Contra Affair*, p. 18. See also, *Report of the President's Special Review Board* (Tower Commission Report) (Washington, D.C.: Government

Printing Office, 26 February 1987), p. V-6; Walter Pincus, "CIA Aides Considered Ghorbanifar a 'Crook'," *Washington Post*, 27 August 1987, p. A1.

95. ABA, *Oversight and Accountability*, p. 98. See also, Strobe Talbott, *Deadly Gambits* (New York: Alfred A. Knopf, 1984), p. 289; Allen E. Goodman, "Dateline Langley: Fixing the Intelligence Mess," *Foreign Policy* 57 (Winter 1984–1985): 171. The Goodman article prompted an unusually lengthy CIA letter to the editor, to which Goodman responded with additional information ("Letters," *Foreign Policy* 58 [Spring 1985]: 171–77).

96. HPSCI, *U.S. Intelligence Performance on Central America*, p. 20; Ranelagh, *The Agency*, pp. 692–93; Bob Woodward and Lou Cannon, "CIA Document Based on Lobby Techniques," *Washington Post*, 1 March 1986, p. A1.

97. John Horton, "The Real Intelligence Failure," *Foreign Service Journal* 62 (February 1985): 22–25; Robert M. Gates, "Is the CIA's Analysis Any Good?" *Washington Post*, 12 December 1984, p. A25; John Horton, "Why I Quit the CIA," *Washington Post*, 2 January 1985, p. A15; William Casey, "Mr. Casey Replies," *Washington Post*, 13 January 1985, p. B6; Goodman, "Dateline Langley," pp. 171–72. An account of the Horton episode, as well as of Horton's "right-wing zealot" predecessor as NIO for Latin America, is found in Woodward, *Veil*, pp. 137, 139, 255, 257–58, 341–44. The two congressional intelligence committees have played an important role in examining such allegations and in improving the quality of intelligence (see SSCI, *Report*, p. 29; ABA, *Oversight and Accountability*, pp. 27–28; Schmitt, "Oversight—What for and How Effective," pp. 137–39).

98. Woodward, *Veil*, p. 344.

99. See, for example, David Ottaway and Patrick Tyler, "DIA Alone in Optimism for Savimbi," *Washington Post*, 7 February 1986, p. A1; Woodward, *Veil*, pp. 124–29, 203, 437–38; *Washington Post*, 20 January 1987, pp. A1, A12.

100. Confidential discussion with the author, 28 April 1987.

101. Confidential discussion with the author, 27 April 1987.

102. Gates, "The CIA and American Foreign Policy," pp. 227–28.

103. "Shultz Says Lies and Clashes Were Rife," p. 1.

104. See May Thornton and Charles Babcock, "Webster Restored FBI's Image," *Washington Post*, 4 March 1987, p. A6; David Ottaway, "CIA Adopts Stricter Procedures," *Washington Post*, 30 September 1987, p. A1; Bob Woodward and Walter Pincus, "CIA's Webster Disciplines Seven Employees over Iran Affair," *Washington Post*, 18 December 1987, p. A12; Gates, "The CIA and American Foreign Policy," p. 229.

105. One of the best treatments of this subject is Flanagan, "The Coordination of National Intelligence," pp. 172–75. See also, Jack E. Thomas, "The Intelligence Community," in Gerald W. Hopple and Bruce W. Watson, eds., *The Military Intelligence Community* (Boulder, Colo.: Westview Press, 1986), pp. 8–10; Church Committee, *Foreign and Military Intelligence*, pp. 87–89.

106. Church Committee, *Foreign and Military Intelligence*, p. 89.

107. SSCI, *Report* (1985), pp. 45, 47.

108. E.O. 12036, Sec. 1–602, 43 *Federal Register* 3674 (1978).

109. Turner, *Secrecy and Democracy*, pp. 258–59.

110. E.O. 12333, Sec. 1(5)(n), 48 *Federal Register* 5994 (1981).

111. Flanagan, "The Coordination of National Intelligence," pp. 174–75.
112. Ibid., pp. 175–76; Church Committee, *Foreign and Military Intelligence*, pp. 83–86. Cf., Breckinridge, *The CIA and the U.S. Intelligence System*, pp. 56–57.
113. The KIQs also had other limitations; see Macy, "Issues on Intelligence Resource Management," pp. 53–54; Flanagan, "The Coordination of National Intelligence," p. 176; Church Committee, *Foreign and Military Intelligence*, p. 87. There are NFIB collection committees—the Committee on Imagery Requirements and Exploitation, the SIGINT Committee, and the Human Resources Committee—through which the DCI is supposed to address competing demands and see that community interests are furthered by the operation of the various collectors. These bodies play useful roles, but in each of them the DCI has encountered difficulties in acting as coordinator (Flanagan, "The Coordination of National Intelligence," pp. 177–79).
114. Turner, *Secrecy and Democracy*, pp. 260–62; Richelson, *The U.S. Intelligence Community*, p. 342; Flanagan, "The Coordination of National Intelligence," pp. 177–79. Former Turner aide George Thibault observes: "Fundamentally it's a turf struggle. If I own the satellite (usually DOD) it doesn't get used for your intelligence collection (usually national [intelligence])" (Thibault, written communication to the author, 12 April 1987).
115. Collectors are also sometimes inclined to collect what they know they can collect rather than what might *need* to be collected.
116. William J. Barnds, "Intelligence and Policymaking in an Institutional Context," in Murphy Commission, *Intelligence Functions and Analyses*, pp. 33–34; Turner, *Secrecy and Democracy*, pp. 262–65; Gates, "The CIA and American Foreign Policy," p. 226. For a proposal to create a central collection agency, see Goodman, "Dateline Langley," p. 176. This proposal is criticized in Breckinridge, *The CIA and the U.S. Intelligence System*, pp. 318–19.
117. Church Committee, *Foreign and Military Intelligence*, pp. 48–60. See also, Treverton, *Covert Action*, pp. 230–31, 233–35; Marchetti and Marks, *The CIA and the Cult of Intelligence*, pp. 327–28.
118. ABA, *Oversight and Accountability*, p. 105. See also, Kissinger, *White House Years*, p. 661.
119. *Report: Iran-Contra Affair*, pp. 17–18, 378–80. See also, Walter Pincus, "Reagan Sidestepped '82 Security Order," *Washington Post*, 12, December 1986, p. A1; Patrick Tyler and David Ottaway, "Casey Enforces 'Reagan Doctrine' with Reinvigorated Covert Action," *Washington Post*, 9 March 1986, p. A1.
120. *Report: Iran-Contra Affair*, pp. 423–26.
121. Church Committee, *Foreign and Military Intelligence*, p. 86, n. 44.
122. ABA, *Oversight and Accountability*, p. 53. See generally Steven Emerson, *Secret Warriors: Inside the Covert Military Operations of the Reagan Era* (New York: G. P. Putnam's Sons, 1988).
123. Turner, *Secrecy and Democracy*, pp. 188–89. See also, Church Committee, *Supplementary Detailed Staff Reports*, p. 94. William Colby was the first DCI who tried to compel the DDO to interact with other CIA units. He once brought twelve CIA country specialists together in the same room, only to

discover that most had never met one another. (Price, *The DCI's Role*, p. 46).

124. Turner, *Secrecy and Democracy*, pp. 274–75.

125. Gates, "The CIA and American Foreign Policy," p. 223. However, a senior DDI official told the author that, while DDI-DDO relations were a bit better, they were still "uneven." He added also that it was still career-enhancing for a DDI analyst to go to DDO, but not vice versa (confidential discussion with the author, 28 April 1987).

126. Church Committee *Supplementary Detailed Staff Reports*, p. 57; Flanagan, "The Coordination of National Intelligence," p. 184; Laqueur, *A World of Secrets*, p. 36.

127. Ranelagh, *The Agency*, p. 193.

128. See, for example, Price, *The DCI's Role*, p. 23.

129. See generally Flanagan, "The Coordination of National Intelligence," pp. 183–84. For a detailed description of the NIE process, see Bruce Berkowitz, "Intelligence in the Organizational Context: Coordination and Error in National Estimates," *Orbis* 29 (Fall 1985): 577–83; Prados, *The Soviet Estimate*, Freedman, *U.S. Intelligence and the Soviet Strategic Threat*.

130. Flanagan, "The Coordination of National Intelligence," pp. 184–85; Boatner, "The Evaluation of Intelligence," pp. 19–23.

131. Quoted in Church Committee, *Foreign and Military Intelligence*, p. 75.

132. Murphy Commission, *Report* (Washington, D.C.: Government Printing Office, 1975), p. 103.

133. Price, *The DCI's Role*, p. 57; Church Committee, *Foreign and Military Intelligence*, p. 75, n. 16.

134. Huizenga, "Comments on 'Intelligence and Policymaking in an Institutional Context'," p. 43.

135. Colby, *Honorable Men*, p. 353.

136. Flanagan, "The Coordination of National Intelligence," pp. 185–86.

137. Church Committee, *Foreign and Military Intelligence*, pp. 75, 77–78; Ranelagh, *The Agency*, pp. 493–99.

138. Huizenga, "Comments on 'Intelligence and Policymaking in an Institutional Context'," pp. 43–44; Barnds, "Intelligence and Policymaking in an Institutional Context," p. 38.

139. Flanagan, "The Coordination of National Intelligence," p. 186; Woodward, *Veil*, p. 257.

140. Testimony of Richard Lehman in HFAC, *The Role of Intelligence*, p. 134.

141. Ibid., pp. 106, 134; Flanagan, "The Coordination of National Intelligence," p. 187; Philip Taubman, "Casey and His CIA on the Rebound," *New York Times*, 16 January 1983, p. 21.

142. Cline, *The CIA: Reality vs. Myth*, pp. 303–304; HFAC, *The Role of Intelligence*, pp. 77, 135.

143. Flanagan, "The Coordination of National Intelligence," pp. 172, 188–89; Ranelagh, *The Agency*, p. 686; Gates, "The CIA and American Foreign Policy," p. 218; Charles Babcock, "Shultz Sees Lesson in Casey's Dual Roles," *Washington Post*, 26 July 1987, p. A16. At Casey's request, an SSCI staff member, who was a former respected CIA analyst described as "totally

credible" by those who knew him, rejoined the agency to advise the director on the estimates. He later returned to the committee (confidential interviews).

144. William W. Kaufmann, *A Reasonable Defense* (Washington, D.C.: The Brookings Institution, 1986), p. 108. To my knowledge, there is no book or even substantial scholarly article devoted entirely to DIA. This is a project that can and should be undertaken.

145. Church Committee, *Foreign and Military Intelligence*, pp. 26, 325, 349; U.S. Department of Defense, Blue Ribbon Defense Panel, *Report to the President and the Secretary of Defense on the Department of Defense* (hereafter cited as Fitzhugh Report) (Washington, D.C.: Government Printing Office, 1970), p. 45. In 1964, in 1965, and in subsequent years, DIA acquired several additional responsibilities. For a discussion of these functions and DIA's internal organizational structure, see Richelson, *The U.S. Intelligence Community*, pp. 35–41; J. Thompson Strong, "The Defense Intelligence Community," in Hopple and Watson, *The Military Intelligence Community*, pp. 17–22.

146. Fitzhugh Report, p. 45.

147. Ibid., p. 45; Lowenthal, *U.S. Intelligence*, p. 96; Church Committee, *Foreign and Military Intelligence*, p. 350.

148. Turner, *Secrecy and Democracy*, p. 251; James E. Stilwell, "DIA Deficiencies," *Washington Post* 19, January 1986, p. G6. Stilwell was former Deputy Chief of DIA's Office of Counterintelligence and Security. See also, testimony of former Secretary of Defense Harold Brown, U.S. Congress, House of Representatives, Committee on Armed Services, Investigations Subcommittee, *Hearings: Reorganization of the Department of Defense*, 99th Cong., 2d sess., 1986, p. 291; Bobby R. Inman, "The Military Perspective," in Thomas J. Hirschfeld, ed., *Intelligence and Arms Control* (Austin: University of Texas at Austin, Lyndon B. Johnson School of Public Affairs, 1987), pp. 53–54.

149. Fitzhugh Report, p. 45; Church Committee, *Foreign and Military Intelligence*, pp. 341, 463. The DIA director has acquired more leverage in fiscal matters since the Fitzhugh Report. He now manages the General Defense Intelligence Program (GDIP), a component of the NFIP budget. Yet even this authority is diluted substantially, as the GDIP *excludes* satellite, cryptologic, and counterintelligence programs. Nor does he have decisive authority over the TIARA budget (Strong, "The Defense Intelligence Community," pp. 17–19).

150. Paradoxically, at least in the past, DIA was limited in making threat assessments precisely because most of the resources for doing so were retained by the services (Fitzhugh Report, pp. 45–46; Church Committee, *Foreign and Military Intelligence*, p. 349).

151. See Giza, "The Problems of the Intelligence Consumer," p. 200; Patrick J. McGarvey, *CIA: The Myth and the Madness* (Baltimore, Md.: Penguin Books, 1972), ch. 7.

152. John M. Collins, *U.S. Defense Planning: A Critique* (Boulder, Colo.: Westview Press, 1982), pp. 128–29; Church Committee, *Foreign and Military Intelligence*, pp. 350–52, 464. One 1987 report states that DIA "has essentially become an Army and Air Force fiefdom, with the Navy sending those

people whose absence will least affect its operational needs. . . . According to one DIA analyst, Navy personnel are usually Lieutenant Commanders or below, females, or officers destined never again to hold an intelligence assignment." Henry S. Bienen, Conference Director, *Policy Memorandum No. 43: The United States Intelligence Community* (Princeton, N.J.: Center of International Studies, The Woodrow Wilson School of Public and International Affairs, Princeton University, 1987), p. 19. But cf., Lieutenant General Eugene Tighe, Jr., "The DIA Is as Good as the CIA," *Washington Post*, 22 February 1986, p. A23.

153. McGarvey, *The CIA: The Myth and the Madness*, p. 158; Church Committee, *Foreign and Military Intelligence*, p. 352; Turner, *Secrecy and Democracy*, p. 276; SSCI, *Report* (1985), p. 50.

154. See McGarvey, *The CIA: The Myth and the Madness*, p. 158. Although it depends importantly on what one does within the agency, as well as on the value a particular individual places on objective, independent analysis, my own informal discussions with intelligence officers from DIA and other intelligence agencies generally confirm this.

155. SSCI, *Report* (1985), p. 50.

156. Church Committee, *Foreign and Military Intelligence*, p. 352.

157. Major General Daniel O. Graham, "Estimating the Threat: A Soldier's Job," *Army* (April 1973): 14–16. See also, McGarvey, *The CIA: The Myth and the Madness*, pp. 154–56.

158. Graham, "Estimating the Threat," p. 16.

159. Church Committee, *Foreign and Military Intelligence*, p. 350 (and see n. 28); Turner, *Secrecy and Democracy*, p. 245.

160. Lowenthal, *U.S. Intelligence*, p. 97; Church Committee, *Foreign and Military Intelligence*, p. 351; Turner, *Secrecy and Democracy*, pp. 246–47, 276. See also, Woodward, *Veil*, p. 126.

161. Kaufmann, *A Reasonable Defense*, pp. 108–109. Admiral Turner states: It is difficult to overstate the . . . pressure the military hierarchy can impose. . . . [I]t can even pressure military intelligence specialists to abandon the code of . . . unbiased reporting in favor of the military one of loyal support of the commander's decision . . . [T]he budgetary process . . . virtually forces the military to use intelligence to overstate the threats. . . . If [it] does not exaggerate the threat, it is almost certain to have its budget cut (Turner, *Secrecy and Democracy*, pp. 247–48).

162. Church Committee, *Foreign and Military Intelligence*, p. 76; Kissinger, *White House Years*, pp. 1180–1181.

163. Turner, *Secrecy and Democracy*, p. 246.

164. See also, Gates, "The CIA and American Foreign Policy," p. 222.

165. Barnds, "Intelligence and Policymaking in an Institutional Context," p. 29.

166. Turner, *Secrecy and Democracy*, pp. 247, 276; Bienen, *Policy Memorandum No. 43*, p. 21.

167. U.S. Congress, House of Representatives, Select Committee on Intelligence (Pike Committee), *U.S. Intelligence Agencies and Activities: Costs and Fiscal Procedures*, 94th Cong., 1st sess., 1975, p. 2161.

168. See Richelson, *The U.S. Intelligence Community*, p. 37.

169. Kaufmann, *A Reasonable Defense*, pp. 108–109; Church Committee, *Foreign and Military Intelligence*, p. 465.

170. For a more detailed treatment of the arguments for and against a comprehensive statutory charter for the intelligence community, see SSCI, *National Intelligence Reorganization and Reform Act of 1978*, 1978. See also, Stansfield Turner and George Thibault, "Intelligence: The Right Rules," *Foreign Policy* 48 (Fall 1982): 137–38; Anne Karalekas, "Intelligence Oversight: Has Anything Changed?" *Washington Quarterly* 6 (Summer 1983): 23–25; ABA, *Oversight and Accountability*, p. 86; Church Committee, *Foreign and Military Intelligence*, pp. 426–27. Concerning intelligence-related legislation enacted between 1947 and 1984 and various domestic measures by the first Reagan administration in the intelligence/secrecy areas, see Clarke and Neveleff, "Secrecy, Foreign Intelligence, and Civil Liberties," pp. 493–513.

CHAPTER 6

Executive-Legislative Consultation

with Chris J. Brantley

"To study one branch of government in isolation from the others," says Louis Fisher, "is usually an exercise in make-believe."[1] Few significant actions of Congress and the executive branch are wholly independent. Initiatives by one trigger reactions by the other, whether of a conflictive or cooperative nature. The focus here is on a key factor in executive-legislative interactions: consultation. After delineating the issue, the chapter examines major impediments to effective consultation and assesses various proposals for change.[2]

The Issue of Consultation

At the most general level, the necessity for adequate consultation between the executive and legislative branches of government appears virtually self-evident. The American democratic system simply cannot effectively support major foreign and defense policies over the long term without an acceptable degree of consensus between Congress and the president, and for this to happen, some degree of consultation would seem essential. But there are conflicting views as to what, specifically, constitutes adequate consultation because judgments on this matter are influenced by preferences and choices in three overlapping areas:[3] substantive policy preferences, assumptions about executive and legislative functions and responsibilities, and definitions of consultation.

Substantive Policy Preferences

The adequacy of consultation often inheres in substantive policy preferences: consultative procedures are endorsed if they further one's policy preferences. If the president articulates and supports certain preferences, he (and congressmen sharing his preferences) may be inclined to consider as obstructionists those legislators with different policy stances—those who frequently then call for "better" consultation.

While consultation sometimes facilitates acceptable compromises between Congress and the president, it cannot always resolve fundamental policy differences. Some members of Congress, for instance, would have opposed President Reagan's Central American and Persian Gulf policies whatever the level of consultation. So consultation may help engender policy consensus, but it is not always a sufficient condition for it.

Assumptions About Executive and Legislative Functions/ Responsibilities

Expectations about executive-legislative relations affect assessments about consultation. What we believe influences what we would like to see. So if it is thought, especially in national security affairs, that the president initiates and Congress merely reacts and ratifies, the tendency is to grant the chief executive a broad mandate, institute relatively loose oversight of executive agencies, and be generally content with the level and quality of consultation that the president offers Congress. However, if Congress and the president are deemed equals with coordinate powers, there will very likely be a disposition toward restricting the executive branch's freedom of action, as well as vigorous oversight and insistence upon a degree of consultation that *Congress* finds sufficient.[4]

Most observers hold that the congressional resurgence of the 1970s importantly and permanently influenced executive-legislative relations, for better or for worse, by greatly enlarging Congress's foreign policy role. This view is reinforced by the growing linkage of domestic with foreign policy ("intermestic" policy), which has compelled changes in modes of executive-legislative interaction.[5] Even Henry Kissinger, perhaps grudgingly, conceded that the "struggle . . . over executive dominance in foreign affairs is over. The recognition that Congress is a coequal branch of government is the dominant fact of national politics today. . . . [F]oreign policy must be a shared enterprise."[6]

As Congress's foreign policy role grows, the importance of consultative exchanges increases correspondingly. Yet a common sentiment in Congress is that consultation between the two branches is seriously inadequate.[7] Instances of poor consultation or no consultation abound. The following are merely illustrative: the executive branch's continued avoidance of detailed consultation with Congress on even some major arms sales until the decision to sell is already made, despite various legally mandated reporting requirements; President Carter's 1978 announcement of the opening of diplomatic relations with the People's Republic of China, which took Congress by surprise; President Reagan's nonconsultation with Congress prior to his announced March 1983 decision concerning the Strategic Defense Initiative, which had profound defense, foreign policy, arms control, and budgetary implications; the Reagan administration's unilateral, revisionist reinterpretation of the ABM Treaty, which prompted Senator Sam Nunn and others to vigorously reassert the traditional interpretation and contributed to SDI funding cuts; and President Reagan's controversial 1987 decision, taken without a prior intelligence assessment of potential risks and without consulting Congress, to afford U.S. naval protection to reflagged Kuwaiti oil tankers in the Persian Gulf.[8]

Defining Consultation

Assessments of consultation are conditioned by perceptions of what it is and should be.

Preferred Definition in the Executive Branch. Presidents (and many in Congress) define *consultation*, in actual practice, simply as the exchange of various communications between the two branches. There is substantial difference of opinion, however, as to what should be the purpose of such communications. A typical presidential view was offered by President Reagan: "If there is something that we [the executive] feel that we'd have trouble with and, perhaps, have to find ourselves in a veto position, we see that they [Congress] are aware of that and what it is that puts us in that position . . . and then keep in constant touch."[9] The president here defines consultation narrowly as legislative strategy: the avoidance of unsettling surprises so as to facilitate Congress's receptiveness to his policy proposals. Congress, however, while recognizing unique presidential prerogatives in foreign affairs, usually believes that the purpose of interbranch communications should be to enhance joint participation in policymaking.

Presidential communications to Congress in a "consultative" context are of three sorts: notification, lobbying, and information gathering.

Notification. The principal method of executive communication is notification, through reports, briefings, and telephone calls, to inform congressmen of policy proposals or decisions already made—not to solicit active congressional participation in an ongoing decisionmaking process.[10] Since the executive branch controls the timing of notification and crucial informational resources, a congressional policy input can often be foreclosed, at least in the short run.

Lobbying. When substantial legislative opposition is anticipated, and when simple notification is not thought to be the most assured route to success, the executive branch must persuade or lobby Congress for support.[11] Here it is usually important for the executive branch to allow for policy alterations in order to mollify powerful legislators or, if opposition is formidable, to engage in bargaining for purposes of damage limitation while still preserving the central thrust of the president's position.[12]

The executive branch enjoys distinct advantages when lobbying Congress. The president's standing as chief diplomat and commander-in-chief affords him considerable leeway in presenting and framing the issues. This was evident, for example, in the final weeks of the debate over the sale of AWACS to Saudi Arabia in 1981. The Reagan administration shifted the focus of debate from the merits of the arms transfer itself to a test of the stature and integrity of the president in foreign policy, emphasizing the supposed harm that a legislative veto would cause to U.S. credibility and the impropriety of foreign influence in America's affairs that was inherent in the slogan (which did not originate in the executive branch), "Reagan or Begin."[13]

The executive branch is further aided by its frequent monopoly of vital informational and analytical resources. Moreover, legislators are often susceptible to presidential favors or services, flattery, and appeals to personal loyalty or the national interest. But enlisting support from wavering congressmen comes at a cost, whether in time and energy expended or in special favors. And all lobbying efforts may fail if the presidential request contravenes a legislator's principles or his constituents' interests.[14]

Information Gathering. Collecting information about congressional attitudes may constitute consultation, at least from the president's perspective. Executive branch congressional liaison staffs count prospective votes and test the water for receptiveness to policy initiatives; congressional allies are singled out for consultation to assist in planning joint strategy for steering the president's policy proposals through Congress; and the executive branch assesses the actions, concerns, and public statements of individual members.[15]

Congress also initiates communications of a consultative nature. Members use executive branch liaison staffs and key administration officials to express their views, request information, seek support, or circumvent bureaucratic barriers. While many congressional hearings are devoted primarily to oversight, they also provide a formal mechanism for communicating views to the executive branch. Indeed, augmented congressional research and analytical capabilities have made hearings an increasingly significant vehicle for addressing emerging issues, weighing options, and recommending courses of action.[16] Some of the most effective consultations, however, occur in private meetings, not in public hearings.

Congress's Preferred Definition. While the above usually constitutes interbranch consultation in practice, most members of Congress hold that effective consultation should be defined as the timely and active involvement of an appropriate spectrum of members in the joint making of significant defense and foreign policy decisions. This definition has four components: (1) spectrum or range of members consulted, (2) timing, (3) significance of the issue, and (4) (implicitly) the attitudes of involved parties.[17]

Spectrum of Members Consulted. Consultation may occur at four levels: congressional leadership, committees, subcommittees, or with informal networks of interested individuals or groups.[18]

A decision on where to consult is largely one of executive strategy: by determining what range of consultation is necessary for incorporating the concerns of a sufficient number of pertinent legislators, a policy might be designed that Congress will support.

There are advantages and disadvantages to consultation at each level. Consulting congressional leaders allows the executive branch to tap their political influence and intuition. But the leadership may lack the specialized knowledge and interests of individual members of committees. Accordingly, the frequent practice is to focus on the chairmen and ranking minority members of key authorizing committees, especially the House and Senate Armed Services Committees, the House Foreign Affairs Committee, and the Senate Foreign Relations Committee.[19] But this, too, generates difficulties, partly because of overlapping committee jurisdictions, a problem that is magnified by the proliferation of subcommittees, several of which may have an interest in a particular issue. Moreover, the executive branch often overestimates the power of authorizing committees. The executive branch confronts a dilemma: expanding the scope of consultation takes time and strains executive staff resources, yet restricting consultation to key committees may, among other things, alienate excluded legislators and overlook the concerns of potentially consequential members.

The executive branch, therefore, must often consult with other interested members, caucuses, and/or key congressional staffers. Consultations with interested legislators—particularly those thought to be most likely to organize opposition or introduce unwelcome floor amendments—are invariably designed to secure support, or at least to deflect opposition. Such individuals must be identified, and their interests determined. Close consultation with caucuses, however, is often avoided, particularly when their generally pronounced policy orientations, as well as those of the special interest groups to which they are often connected, run counter to executive policy preferences. But the influence and accessibility of congressional staffers make them targets of consultative efforts, although executive branch officials cannot presume that staffers can deliver the support of their congressmen and committees.[20]

Timing. Timing communication is critical. When to include Congress in decisionmaking depends upon the role Congress is expected to play. Three possibilities are consultation (1) when issues first emerge, (2) when policy options are considered, but before decisions are made, and (3) after the executive branch decision phase.

The executive branch usually communicates with Congress only after policy options are developed. While Congress recognizes a need to defer to the president on certain time- and security-sensitive matters, the general consensus on the Hill is that consultation should occur as early as feasible, but certainly as soon as possible after options have been formulated.[21]

Obstacles to consultation at the issue genesis stage are often formidable, especially when the subject concerns what Colonel Robert Lockwood, U.S. Army, calls "threat policy"—the process of identifying emerging threats to national security. Lockwood finds that consultation on threat policy issues has regularly proven difficult or unworkable, partly because of the problem of establishing timely contact with a diffuse Congress—many of whose members might legitimately demand a right of consultation—and also because Congress lacks "real-time" intelligence.[22] Even if such impediments are overcome, the desirability of congressional involvement at this stage is questionable. Executive branch information and analysis is likely to be incomplete, particularly when international events are changing daily or even hourly; congressional involvement at this point could hamper ongoing internal deliberations among executive branch actors.

The policy option stage is another matter. Approaching Congress after issues have been identified and alternative courses of action have been weighed preserves presidential leadership and bureaucratic discipline and is generally sufficient to establish the executive branch's good faith. Consultation at this still relatively early phase of the policy process, instead of after a decision is made, may facilitate consensus building by giving Congress a stake in the outcome. There is certainly broad-based congressional agreement in, for instance, the arms sales area, where timely consultation is required by the Arms Export Control Act, that contemplated transactions be discussed with legislators long before a potential recipient government concludes that it has received a commitment to sell from Washington.[23]

Significance of the Issue. For purposes of effective consultation, any issue or action requiring the support of Congress is significant. This clearly includes, among other things, appropriations, a wide range of legislation, treaties, presidential nominations, and major, sustained overseas commitments of the armed forces. Since the ideal goal of consultation is policy consensus—which goal is very often a practical necessity as well—the executive branch may be well advised to consult on any issue that arouses substantial congressional interest.

Attitudes. An essential element of effective consultation is a forthcoming attitude toward the other branch. Ideally, this is manifested by the executive branch when it solicits congressional views, candidly discusses policy options, and furnishes adequate and timely information. Conversely—again, ideally—congressional behavior should be such as to avoid creating understandable grounds for mistrust. At a minimum, effective consultation requires mutual recognition of the problems and responsibilities of the respective branches and an acknowledgement that each has a legitimate role in the foreign policy process.

Impediments to Effective Consultation

Seven broad factors may impede consultation: attitudes, conflicting political and institutional interests, lack of knowledge and understanding of the other branch, personalities, time pressures, structural problems, and interest groups.[24]

Attitudes

Throughout the national security bureaucracy, and certainly in the Department of State, a common sentiment is that Congress's role in defense and foreign policy should be minimal. Two former assistant secretaries of state for congressional relations—Frederick Dutton (1961–1964) and Marshall Wright (1973–1974)—respectively described State's attitude toward Congress as "enemy territory" and "fearful."[25] Patsy Mink, former member of Congress and Assistant Secretary of State for Oceans, International Environment, and Scientific Affairs in the Carter administration, states that the Foreign Service officers find Congress "amateurish, uninterested, unschooled, mildly xenophobic . . . [and believing] that State regularly plots to give away what rightfully belongs to the American people."[26]

Other widely held executive branch attitudes that hinder consultation include the following:

- Minimal consultation worked reasonably well in the past, and at any rate, Congress lacks the information, organization, and usually the responsibility to do what only professionals are capable of doing: formulating coherent, consistent national security policy.[27]
- The president is the most legitimate representative of the public; Congress reflects only the sum of its constituent parts. And despite legislation mandating consultation, such as the War Powers Resolution, there is no constitutional obligation to do so.[28]
- Politics should stop at the water's edge: foreign policy should be a game of follow-the-leader, or, ideally, follow-the-leaders ("bipartisanship"). Congress cannot lead since it is too parochial, as well as incapable of keeping secrets, excessively swayed by public opinion (members are obsessed with re-election), and prone to sacrifice national interests to the appeals of special interest groups.[29]
- The subculture attitudes of career personnel in the State Department, especially of the Foreign Service officers, encourage an "elitism" that makes cooperation with a "lesser" congressional partner difficult and dulls sensitivity to the importance of domestic politics.[30]

Rear Admiral John Poindexter, President Reagan's fourth National Security Assistant, misled Congress and excluded it from crucial policy matters. Explaining his circumvention of established congressional oversight procedures and mechanisms in the Iran-Contra affair, Poindexter stated, "I simply didn't want any outside interference."[31]

The sharp, immediate response this comment elicited from conservative and liberal legislators alike reveals some of the severe costs that result from such an openly hostile attitude. Poindexter's view, said Democratic Congressman Lee Hamilton, chairman of the House Iran-Contra investigating committee, "reflects an attitude which makes . . . our constitutional system of checks and balances unworkable. . . . You cannot gain and sustain the support of Congress . . . and the American people for significant foreign policy decisions when they are uninformed."[32] Two Republican legislators supportive of Reagan's general policy toward Nicaragua were equally critical. "The reason for not misleading the Congress is a very practical one," said Congressman Dick Cheney. "It's stupid. It's self-defeating. Because, while it may . . . allow you to prevail in the problem of the moment, eventually you destroy the president's credibility."[33] And Congressman Henry Hyde lectured Poindexter: "The problem with deceiving Congress is that your friends get deceived and they go out and talk to the media . . . and insist that what you have told us is true, and it can be very embarrassing. And it affects our credibility."[34]

Congress has its own sets of attitudes (only two of which are mentioned here) that can hamper cooperation. Many members defer to the executive branch because they believe that Congress lacks expertise, the Constitution gives the president primacy, Congress cannot speak with one voice, and/or Congress exceeded its proper foreign policy role in the 1970s and restoration of presidential prerogatives is therefore necessary.[35] Conversely, other members avoid consultation in order to prevent co-option by the executive branch and to preserve Congress's essential role as an independent body that must often be critical of executive policies.[36]

Conflicting Political and Institutional Interests

Negative attitudes toward consultation are reinforced by tensions between the two branches' institutional and political interests, processes, and behavioral patterns. Career enhancement and job security in Congress is rooted in constituent support. Legislators who neglect the political and economic interests of constituents risk their offices. The imperative of reelection—which, some assert, may take precedence over foreign policy substance or even national interest—instills at least three types of behaviors in congressmen: advertising one's name, claiming credit, and taking positions on those issues of particular concern to constituent interests.[37] The reelection imperative, combined with the importance and accessibility of the media, may encourage grandstanding, gratuitous promises, excessive attention to matters of minimal significance to national needs but of exceptional importance to special interests, and micromanagement of, for example, defense programs. Such behavior in congressmen is common when, for instance, the Pentagon proposes closing a military base, or makes decisions that affect other income-producing activities and jobs in a legislator's home state or district.[38]

Other distinctive features of policy processes may hinder effective consultation. While most congressmen are—and must be—"quick study generalists" who focus only sporadically on defense or foreign policy, the executive branch rewards expertise and discretion in the daily management of national security policy. Moreover, the legislative process emphasizes political compromise, open debate, access to information, and (often) lengthy deliberations.[39] In contrast, although political compromise is common in executive branch processes, compromise with Congress somehow appears inappropriate to executive officials when national security is at stake, especially when a presidential decision has already been made. Likewise, the notion of public, give-and-take debate with Congress is alien to executive officials who know the importance of confidentiality in the conduct of diplomacy; for these officials, *control* of information is considered necessary—both for security reasons and because information is a key to their power and influence.

Finally, while the executive branch has been somewhat more receptive to a congressional role in broad policy matters since the mid-1970s, it zealously guards its prerogative to design the tactics of policy. Legislation or congressional actions that jeopardize this tactical freedom are consistently criticized as unwarranted micromanagement.[40]

Lack of Understanding and Experience

Tension between the institutional interests of the two branches is sometimes heightened by a lack of experience with or understanding of the interests of the other branch. This problem is exacerbated in the executive branch by the continual turnover of personnel, especially political appointees. For example, four secretaries of state and eight assistant secretaries for congressional relations served between 1978 and 1983.[41] Similarly, career Foreign Service officers who rotate tours of duty every two or three years have little opportunity or incentive to acquire experience in legislative relations. On the congressional side, demands on members' time usually means that their staffs engage in much of the essential contact with the executive branch. Many (by no means all) staffers lack an understanding of the executive branch's milieu and practices. Also, some legislatively imposed restrictions in the foreign policy area suggest insensitivity to or unawareness of the real world of executive branch officials.[42]

Personality

The personalities of actors can, of course, be a decisive factor in the quality of consultation, starting with the president's personality, which affects the overall executive-legislative relationship. The president's standing with Congress and his ability to nurture congressional support through personal contacts, private briefings, and ceremonial gatherings set the parameters within which White House and departmental congressional liaison staffs work. A chief executive who gives this function skillful priority sends a powerful signal throughout government: that working interpersonal relationships are crucial to successful consultations.[43]

Sometimes the personality of one official can cloud executive-legislative relations. Henry Kissinger, already criticized for his condescending attitude toward Congress, lectured freshman Democratic congressmen in 1974 as if they were graduate students. Frank Moore, President Carter's personal assistant for congressional liaison, was considered disdainful of and unresponsive to Congress.[44] But there have been very successful personalities. Lawrence O'Brien built bridges between the two branches in the Kennedy and Johnson years. Likewise, the cooperative personal styles of Special Trade Representatives William Eberle, Robert Straus, and William Brock facilitated congressional support for foreign trade policies.[45]

Positive personal chemistry, while vital, is substantially a matter of chance. Even the most engaging president or secretary of state will not charm all 535 of the hearty individualists in Congress. But if the president emphasizes personal consultations, and if the executive branch provides incentives to build quality and continuity into liaison staffs, personal discord may be minimized.

Time Pressures

Time pressures impede effective consultation. Crises pose special problems, especially when consultation is mandated by legislation such as the War Powers Resolution. Fast-breaking events in a fluid situation, about which information is imperfect, combine with security concerns to make a president disinclined to consult fully with Congress. Even if he wishes to consult, his own policy options may not be formulated in time to elicit a reasoned congressional response; nor are there developed crisis consultation mechanisms for sharing information with legislators.[46]

The daily demands on legislators and executive officials also effect consultation. In addition to constituent services and reelection efforts, by 1984 the average senator served on eleven committees and subcommittees. The total number of committee and subcommittee meetings in the House rose from 3210 in the 84th Congress to 6179 in the 97th Congress. Moreover, Congress is in session longer than it was in the 1950s.[47] Legislators, then, have little time to think systematically about most issues or to function in a sustained, active process of policy codetermination.

Congressional activism and the proliferation of committees also burden the time of executive officials. The secretaries of state and defense commonly spend 25 percent or more of their time preparing for and testifying before Congress, often delivering identical testimony to different committees. This detracts from their principal responsibilities and engenders resentment toward the consultative process.[48]

Structural Problems

Consultation is complicated by the structural diffusion of decisionmaking authority in both branches. The executive branch is hesitant to consult Congress until there is internal consensus on the direction of policy, and even then, achieving consensus among several executive branch actors is often so arduous—and when obtained, tenuous—that policymakers are reluctant to expose it to congressional scrutiny. When the executive branch does elect to consult, internal differences are generally not divulged and certain policy options are deemphasized.[49]

The dispersion of decisionmaking authority within the executive branch creates many opportunities for confusing or misleading Congress. State Department communications to Congress may be seriously defective if State has been excluded from say, a White House–Defense Department decision. Moreover, breakdowns in intra–executive branch communications and coordination can result in miscommunication to Capitol Hill. The dispersion of executive liaison offices and the frequently inadequate coordination among them also contribute to the problem, one that is often further exacerbated by insufficient numbers of foreign policy specialists on liaison staffs and a tendency for these staffs to develop special relationships with "their" congressional committees. These special relationships encourage "end runs" around administration policy in pursuit of parochial, departmental interests.[50]

The lack of hierarchical authority in Congress makes the diffusion of power even more pronounced in the legislative branch. This condition was intensified after the structural and procedural reforms of the 1970s, which, inter alia, made seniority less decisive in committee assignments, limited the powers of committee chairmen, and reduced committee control over subcommittees while dispersing power among individual members at the expense of party leadership and committee chairmen. As a result, the executive branch must grope to ascertain the will of Congress and to know where and with whom to consult. There is no longer any assurance that the perceptions of a few key legislators will reflect a congressional consensus. The executive branch's dilemma, then, is to limit lines of communication to a manageable scale without excluding vital congressional actors.[51]

More than 100 committees and subcommittees regularly address bills on some aspect of national security policy. The prospect of consulting such an array of entities (many with overlapping jurisdictiions)—much less individual members and their staffs— has a chilling effect on executive branch attitudes.[52] In 1987, for example, Secretary of Defense Caspar Weinberger had to appeal to the Speaker of the House to settle a heated jurisdictional dispute between the House Armed Services Committee and a subcommittee of the House Energy and Commerce Committee over which unit had the right to receive a Pentagon report.[53]

Consultation is further complicated by the increasingly blurred jurisdiction between authorizing and appropriating committees. Authorizing committees are constraining appropriations, while appropriating committees are including substantive, additional legislative provisions in appropriations bills. In 1984, for instance, appropriations committees appropriated $3 billion in defense programs that were not authorized by prior legislation. Hence authorizing and appropriating procedures are becoming competitive, rather than complementary.[54] In addition to impeding effective consultation and engendering turf fights among committees and subcommittees, Congress's structural fragmentation and the blurring of jurisdictional authority make coherent, well-integrated legislation difficult or impossible and contribute to sparse committee attendance.[55]

Interest Groups

The reluctance of the executive branch to consult with a legislature that plays an active role in foreign policy is partly attributable to the role of special interest lobbies in Congress and to the supposed inclination of some legislators to compromise the national interest in return for the political and financial support of such groups. But these lobbies also often provide useful advocative information to Congress and are sometimes indirect channels of communication between the two branches.

It appears, on balance, that when an influential interest group seeks to steer foreign policy in a direction opposed by the executive branch, early and forthcoming executive-legislative consultation is advisable. The executive branch can thereby seek to offset the political benefits of supporting that group with political promises (or threats) of its own. Early consultation also gives Congress a broader range of information on the issues. This may dilute the influence of a single powerful lobby and, additionally, may permit groups that are less well organized to contribute to the debate.[56]

Proposals for Reform

However formidable the impediments, sound foreign policy requires a working consultative framework that accommodates the inevitable interbranch differences. Three areas deserve particular attention: congressional access to timely and accurate information; attitudinal changes that indicate a willingness to cooperate and to recognize the other branch's concerns; and better organization for managing consultation.

Strengthening Congressional Information Sources and Assessment

Information is the currency of decisionmakers. Although Congress acquires information from many sources, it is substantially dependent on the executive branch for much current defense and foreign policy information and assessment. And some of the information that inundates Congress is ill suited to effective decisionmaking.[57] What is required for responsible congressional deliberations is full, accurate, timely information, as well as assessment and analytical capabilities to process and filter out unnecessary information. Toward these ends, several measures have been proposed to augment access to executive information sources, develop independent sources, facilitate crisis consultation, and strengthen information filtering and assessment resources.

Informal Briefings. Regular informal briefings of members (including bipartisan groups of congressional leaders) by senior administration officials might reduce reliance on time-consuming hearings, provide an opportunity for candid discussion of policy options, and afford a forum for crisis consultation. But legislators are sometimes dissatisfied with such informal sessions, either because of the executive's lack of candor or because the sessions are used to garner political support for administration policies. These meetings will have restricted value for Congress unless the quality of information imparted by administration officials improves. Consideration might be given to occasionally shifting the focus from a one-way to a two-way discussion—which might be even more productive if the State Department provided members with a weekly, written "foreign policy bulletin" on significant international developments and U.S. policy responses.[58]

Tightening Reporting Mechanisms. By 1984 Congress had required the president to submit annually 225 foreign policy and national security reports, in addition to the 65 and 460 reports issued by the Departments of State and Defense, respectively.[59] Such reports serve a variety of useful functions, including: supplying otherwise inaccessible information, such as details of executive agreements; providing a public record and focus for national debate; and sometimes avoiding divisive conflict by the timely submission of information on potentially controversial issues.[60]

But some required reports are used ineffectively by Congress, and the sheer number required burdens the executive branch. These problems have prompted congressional committees to conduct several comprehensive reviews of reporting requirements.

The Goldwater-Nichols Department of Defense Reorganization Act of 1986 sought to reduce the number of defense reports required by Congress from the president and the Defense Department by about two-thirds. There is a need to eliminate obsolete and duplicative reports in other areas. Consideration should also be given on a case-by-case basis to lengthening the reporting period in order to reduce the burden on the executive branch. Some observers have also recommended that Congress hold more oversight hearings devoted to considering issues raised in the reports.[61]

Annual Report by the President or Secretary of State. Some have suggested that an annual "state of the world" report by the president or secretary of state, similar to one issued by the first Nixon administration, could be a useful basis for congressional debate on the overall objectives and assumptions of U.S. foreign policy.[62] But the utility of such an exercise is questionable: it would consume considerable executive branch time and effort (the last report issued by the Nixon administration was 743 pages long); unless someone with unique authority directs its drafting, an annual report is likely to consist of uninformative generalizations (when National Security Assistant Henry Kissinger directed the report's preparation, it received some attention, but when this responsibility passed to Secretary of State William Rogers, it went unread); and if, as is probable, an annual report does not assess alternative policy options, Congress may see it as a self-serving exercise.[63]

Access to Classified Information. Congress's ability to address national security issues effectively may be impaired by limitations on its access to security-sensitive information. This was an acute problem prior to the mid-1970s. But President Ford and, especially, President Carter were reasonably forthcoming with classified information, and passage of the Intelligence Oversight Act of 1980 (P.L. 96-450) gave Congress a statutory right to be fully and currently informed of all intelligence activities. Therefore, until the Reagan administration, most members of Congress and key committees were generally content with the quantity and quality of classified information received.[64]

This changed. About the Iran-Contra affair and at least one

other Reagan administration covert action, Congress was uninformed, not informed in a clear and timely manner, and/or knowingly misled by senior officials like NSA Poindexter and DCI William Casey. In some instances, the Intelligence Oversight Act and other legislation were either violated or, at the very least, interpreted by administration officials in a dubious fashion. The Iran-Contra committees made twenty-seven recommendations in 1987 for upgrading congressional and executive oversight of covert actions. Bills were introduced to institute some of these recommendations.[65]

Information is often classified for reasons of administrative convenience or to avoid political embarrassment, and some presidents (like President Reagan) sharply expanded the amount of information classified—to the real or perceived detriment of Congress. But Congress has traditionally deferred to the president's practice of establishing the national security classification system by executive order. The Murphy Commission (1975) recommended creation of a statutory classification system explicitly designating the types of information subject to classification. Bills have been introduced to this effect, but none has ever been enacted into law.[66]

New Links to the National Security Council. In 1979 Senator Edward Zorinsky introduced legislation to make the appointment of the President's Assistant for National Security Affairs subject to Senate confirmation. Senator Zorinsky's proposal, which never became law, had two objectives: to subject the NSA[67] to congressional oversight, and to eliminate a gap that sometimes exists between what the secretary of state tells Congress and what the NSC, in fact, decides. Implicit in the proposal was the assumption that the NSA would have to testify before Congress. In hearings on the bill, the Carter administration, former NSA Brent Scowcroft, and all other witnesses spoke in opposition. Witnesses agreed that, among other things, such a law would jeopardize the NSA's role as facilitator and coordinator of national security policy, restrict the president's necessary flexibility in formulating policy, and increase tension between the NSA and the secretary of state.[68] This was also the position of President Reagan's Tower Commission, despite its finding that NSA John Poindexter and other NSC staffers had improperly participated in the covert sale of arms to Iran and diversion of funds to the Nicaraguan Contras. Likewise, the Iran-Contra committees rejected the Senate confirmation option, although they did recommend legislation "requiring that the President report to Congress periodically on the organization, size, function, and procedures of the NSC staff."[69]

It appears that substantive policy communications to Congress from the NSA will, and should, continue to be informal and at the president's discretion. The example of NSA Frank Carlucci (1987) might serve as a useful model. Carlucci fostered extensive personal contacts with legislators, a practice that was well received in Congress.[70]

A Question Hour. It has been suggested that the British parliamentary system offers a device that could improve executive-legislation consultation—a "question hour" in which Cabinet officers and/or the president appear before the full Congress (or alternate their appearances between the two chambers) to engage in a question-and-answer exchange on foreign policy. But whatever benefits might accrue from such a practice seem clearly outweighed by the drawbacks: it is unlikely to be a productive source of new information; the time expenditure would be substantial; and it would invite partisan attacks on policy and grandstanding in full view of the media. The need for such a procedure in the British Parliament, where members are heavily dependent on the question hour for foreign policy information, is far greater than it is for the U.S. Congress, and several congressional committees might view a question hour as threatening their competence and integrity.[71]

Congressional Travel Abroad. Congressional travel abroad retains its negative public image ("junket"), sometimes strains embassy resources, confers rather mixed benefits on members who serve as advisers at international conferences, and occasionally embarrasses the administration. Still, there is wide agreement in Congress that foreign travel is beneficial. It exposes members to foreign policy problems, provides a conduit for information flow to Congress (through reports filed by returning members), and enhances Congress's ability to pinpoint areas of concern to the executive branch.[72]

Congressional Crisis Information Center. Although Congress's role in crisis consultation is ill defined, members are vocal in demanding full and timely information on evolving crises. Yet even when the executive branch is well disposed toward this demand (which is infrequent), it is difficult to disseminate useful, discriminately selected information to a widely dispersed Congress in a timely fashion. One solution would be to create a congressional crisis information center.

A central problem is defining such a center's exact role. One proposal has it staffed with former executive branch officials, placed as a congressional support agency, answerable to the congressional leadership, and performing the following functions:

Communicate with the staffs of executive branch crisis centers; receive selected and critical messages which the executive branch believes should be brought to the attention of Congress; seek and receive crisis information from a range of nonexecutive branch sources; compile chronologies of events to aid decision-making and to facilitate the later evaluation of the crisis management experience; draft and discuss policy options for the Congress, as well as for the executive branch; prepare the congressional leadership for meetings with executive branch crisis managers; draft and circulate situation reports to the general congressional leadership; and alert the congressional leadership to breaking crises which may require their attention.[73]

This is a formidable mission. Under the best of circumstances, it is likely to cause unease in the executive branch, especially if the center conducts crisis *analyses*. It may be advisable, then, for such a center (which probably should be directed by the congressional leadership—the president's historically preferred contact group) to serve exclusively as a focal point and facilitator of interbranch crisis communications. The center's analytical functions, if any, should be modest and directed solely at serving Congress's needs.

There is a danger that a crisis center might become just another organizational layer, one that actually slows communications, sparks controversy, and itself attempts to influence policy. And what would the center's staff do between crises to justify their existence? Because of these concerns, consideration might be given to having the congressional leadership's own staffs act as an ad hoc crisis committee. That is, add a function, not a structure.

Strengthening Assessment. Since the mid-1970s, Congress has greatly expanded its institutional capability to assess, evaluate, and monitor the constant flow of information on national security policy. Staff resources have increased and support agencies—the Congressional Research Service, the General Accounting Office, the Congressional Budget Office, and the Office of Technology Assessment—provide objective, balanced information and analyses. Excepting crisis assessment, support agencies now meet most of Congress's internal analytical needs.[74]

Alton Frye of the Council on Foreign Relations has proposed creating a congressional "foreign policy auditor" to monitor the analytic output of the NSC, the intelligence community, and other executive bodies.[75] But most presidents would surely oppose or otherwise thwart such "meddling" in executive branch affairs.

Affecting Attitudes and Building Confidence

A competitive tension between the two branches is rooted in the Constitution. But negative attitudes toward consultation and cooperation are often exacerbated by misunderstandings, communication breakdowns, and a lack of empathy for the concerns of the other branch. Several measures might be explored with an eye toward building an acceptable level of mutual confidence.

A Congressional Code of Conduct. Congress could take various steps to build executive confidence that, collectively, might constitute an informal code of conduct. Some practices, like safeguarding classified information (on which Congress's record since 1976 is better than the executive's), would be obvious elements in such a code. Others, such as the executive branch's insistent call for a halt to "overly intrusive" legislation in areas like human rights and nuclear nonproliferation, are unlikely to be included as long as policy differences between the branches exist—which will be for a very long time indeed.

Congress is largely known for the quality of laws that it passes, yet the frequent attachment of nongermane amendments to legislation in the Senate—which is often done to outflank executive (and sometimes legislative) opposition—discredits the legislative process and creates tension with the executive branch. Since the president is unlikely to veto annual defense or foreign affairs authorization or appropriations bills, they become convenient vehicles for forcing through often ill-considered, uncoordinated legislative proposals—many only remotely germane to the primary legislation—that the president cannot avoid signing into law, except at his political peril. This occurs because the leadership lets it occur. Stricter enforcement of rules prohibiting nongermane amendments to appropriations bills would help prevent the use of continuing resolutions and government by deadlock. The Senate might similarly consider adopting the recurrent proposal under which a two-thirds majority of those senators present and voting would be required to overturn a nongermane ruling from the chair.[76]

The Senate should also exercise more discretion in confirming presidential nominees. There are instances when the confirmation process rightly evolves into a public and contentious debate, and senators will at times seek to extract policy promises from nominees. But a price is often paid in executive branch confidence. This was certainly so when a single legislator, Senator Jesse Helms, repeatedly held up the confirmation of numerous Reagan administration nominees. Because of the costs to executive-legislative relations and the expenditure of senators' time, the Senate might consider either reducing the number of foreign affairs nominations required by law (currently averaging 1400 annually) or limiting the number of full committee confirmation hearings.[77]

Finally, Congress can reduce the workload of both branches by enforcing existing rules limiting the number of committee assignments a member can hold and reducing the number of subcommittees. This would also improve committee attendance and consolidate overlapping subcommittee jurisdictions.[78]

Policy Directives. Secretary of State Cyrus Vance's 1978 directive to his department is often cited as a turning point in State's relations with Congress during the Carter administration. That directive could serve as a useful model for other administrations and department heads. It authorized and encouraged consultation, designated classes of information to be provided, set forth specific guidelines for withholding limited types of information and for creating review procedures to evaluate questionable material, and specified the officials responsible for consultative duties.[79]

An Undersecretary for Congressional Relations. The assistant secretary of state for congressional relations might be upgraded to an under secretary on the assumption that this would symbolize

State's commitment to consultation, provide a more prestigious State Department route to Congress, and enhance those intra-departmental forces favoring closer consultative ties to Congress.[80] While this measure might succeed if the new under secretary had the full confidence of the secretary, it is not very promising. An official's actual authority and staff resources matter more than his title, and it is questionable whether this new under secretary would retain effective control over the Bureau of Congressional Relations. Indeed, State Department under secretaries typically do not have direct bureau responsibilities. Moreover, State's regional and functional bureaus have long resisted efforts to centralize liaison activities. Finally, for liaison purposes, a secretary can just as effectively place confidence in an assistant secretary as in an under secretary.[81]

Appointing Members of Congress to the Executive Branch. A perennial proposal for improving mutual understanding is to appoint legislators to executive branch positions. The proposal takes various forms, each designed to tap the perceived benefits of a parliamentary system of government. One noteworthy variation calls for House and Senate leaders from the president's party to sit as members of the executive cabinet, in pursuit of a more collegial decisionmaking process.[82]

There are numerous specific problems with this proposal, but the chief concern should be for the constitutional system of checks and balances. In addition to requiring a constitutional amendment (Article I, Section 6, of the Constitution prohibits members of Congress from serving as "officers" of the United States), the real prospect is raised that these two-hatted legislators serving in the executive branch would be impaired from functioning either as effective "checks and balances" of the executive or as loyal administration officials. These problems can, of course, be circumvented if the president appoints former legislators to executive posts. Secretaries of State John Foster Dulles, Christian Herter, and Edmund Muskie, Secretary of Defense Melvin Laird, White House Chief of Staff Howard Baker, and Trade Representative William Brock are among the many in this category.

Personnel Exchanges and Training. Stereotypes that color each branch's perceptions of the other can be partly dispelled through sustained programs of personnel exchange and effective training.

Some mid-level career officers in the Departments of State and Defense are assigned to Congress for one year under established programs. These programs, which might usefully be expanded, have been highly praised for improving basic attitudes and establishing working relationships that continue for many years.[83] Misunderstandings might be reduced further by greater participation in various training programs and workshops currently available to executive and legislative officials through, for instance, the Foreign Service Institute, State's congressional seminar program, the Congressional Research Service, and university foreign affairs centers.[84]

Organizational Reforms

Major structural changes commonly evoke formidable resistance and, by themselves, rarely resolve the central issues of executive-legislative consultation. Nevertheless, some recommendations for organizational alterations may merit attention.

Improving Intra–Executive Branch Coordination. The quality of executive-legislative consultative processes is substantially dependent on a subject too vast to be addressed here: the overall effectiveness of executive branch coordination and integration of the many strands of national security policy. At the very least, however, the creation of a vigorous legislative liaison/strategy function within the White House, like President Reagan's Legislative Strategy Group, seems important for coordinating the liaison efforts of executive departments and for sustaining priority attention to consultation. Within the State and Defense Departments there may also be a need to clarify liaison responsibilities among various offices.[85]

Reforming the Budget Process. No serious reform of the congressional budget process is easy because it alters existing power/authority arrangements among members and committees and, on occasion, between Congress and the executive branch. An acute sensitivity to the need for equity is therefore mandatory in any proposed redistribution of authority.

The present congressional budget process complicates the executive branch's consultative task by requiring liaison at three levels of review: budget committees, authorizing committees, and appropriations committees. Eliminating one level—perhaps by consolidating the authorization and appropriations functions into a new "program" committee—would simplify the process. It would also give Congress much needed time for considering budgetary and other matters. But this sensible proposal has a decisive shortcoming—its political infeasibility. "Committee consolidation" is a euphemism for taking power from some committees and giving it to others. Legislators who stand to lose will resist.[86]

Two changes in the defense sector may be advisable. There is recurrent congressional interest in establishing a biennial budget for the Defense Department (which has obvious implications for the entire federal budget). In the first year of a new Congress, the administration would submit a two-year authorization and appropriation proposal that would be debated, amended, and approved by Congress. In the second year, committees would concentrate on reviewing, evaluating, and overseeing existing programs, with authorizing committees addressing broad defense policy questions and appropriations committees paying particular attention to efficient program management. This procedurally (if not politically) simple step could ease the burden on both branches, ensure more attention being given to budgetary and oversight issues, bring greater stability to the defense planning process, and permit more reflection on long-term security terms.[87]

In compliance with a provision of the Defense Authorization Act of 1986, the Pentagon submitted a two-year budget to Congress in 1987. In that year, the armed services committees were generally receptive. Indeed, the National Defense Authorization Act for FY 1988 and 1989 authorized 60 percent of the budget request for the second year. But the appropriations committees continued to insist upon annual appropriations. Consequently, by 1988 the proposal for a biennial defense budget appeared to be dead or rapidly dying.

If a biennial budget is impossible to achieve, Congress might consider shifting from annual reviews of major weapons programs to a process whereby funds for such programs are authorized and appropriated only when the development cycle reaches a major decision milestone. The process would resemble the Pentagon's internal procedure and would work much like authorizations for new ships do now. Specifically:

Congress [would] authorize and appropriate multi-year funds for each major weapons system at four milestone decision points: (1) initial development, (2) full-scale development, (3) initial production, and (4) full production. As a weapon neared each milestone, the administration would request sufficient funds in the next year's budget to pay for the complete upcoming segment of the weapon's development or production, even though the funds would actually be obligated and expended over a several year period.[88]

Proponents believe this reform could bring greater program stability, more effective long-term policy, and better program management by conforming the congressional process more closely to the Pentagon's and by moving Congress away from its current tendency to review some decisions several times each year. But Professor James Lindsay argues tellingly that milestone authorizations will not cure micromanagement because the appropriations committees will continue to appropriate funds annually. And if only these committees make decisions on a yearly basis, their influence over the defense budget will grow at the expense of the authorizations committees. Hence, the milestone process is unlikely to be applied to much of the defense budget.[89]

New Consultative Bodies.   Some have suggested that Congress consider new institutional arrangements to facilitate consultation: new permanent committees, ad hoc committees, or joint executive-legislative commissions. But there is little congressional support for various proposals to create ad hoc consultative committees or a new national security committee.[90] In 1987 the House Foreign Affairs Committee and Senator Richard Lugar, former chairman of the Senate Foreign Relations Committee, did propose creation of an executive-legislative consultative group that would hold informal but regular meetings on major foreign policy initiatives. President Reagan, however, had no interest in the proposal.[91]

Nor is there enthusiasm in either branch for joint executive-legislative commissions. The output of these commissions cannot be controlled. Therefore, their recommendations generally receive scant attention and are seldom implemented. A joint commission might serve a useful role, but only if three conditions are met: it addresses issues ripe for decision, membership is balanced and bipartisan, and its findings reflect a politically sustainable compromise between both branches and both political parties.[92]

Strengthening the Congressional System. The task of consultation would be eased if the traditional focus of the executive branch on the congressional leadership is reinforced. This is easier said than done. The congressional reforms of the 1970s reduced the leaders' influence. Still, given the requisite will to use them, the leadership retains various tools to encourage support for its initiatives, including the power to schedule debate on legislation and the authority to appoint members of the key budget and rules committees.[93]

The jurisdictional scope of the two committees on foreign affairs has expanded somewhat since the 1970s. They might be further strengthened to enable them to serve as focal points for foreign policy consultations. But several factors probably preclude this: other committees will continue to deal with some foreign policy issues; the supposed liberal orientation of the foreign affairs committees may prevent them from being able to ensure general congressional support for their positions; and these committees may lack the political base to prevail in Congress since they are often not linked as closely as other committees to powerful domestic interests.[94]

Perhaps the most promising option is the increased use of joint hearings among committees and subcommittees with overlapping jurisdictions. Joint hearings between House and Senate committees are rare, but such hearings within one chamber are now a more common occurrence. Joint hearings do raise certain procedural questions and might at times threaten a committee's traditional turf, but they do save time for both legislators and those executive officials called to testify. They also afford committees an opportunity to share expertise and staff resources.[95]

Conclusion

In one sense, this subject has no readily identifiable conclusion. The broad parameters for interplay and discourse between Congress and the president are substantially set by the Constitution. There will always be contrasting views about the adequacy of executive-legislative consultations on various defense and foreign policy matters.

However, it seems clear that mere after-the-fact notification to Congress of significant executive decisions is an increasingly unacceptable form of "consultation." Congress generally insists upon full, timely and accurate information flow. Of course, this congressional standard for "acceptable consultation" will not invariably create harmony between the branches. But without something reasonably close to it, the kind of broad-based policy consensus that must accompany any successful, long-term foreign policy is unlikely to be developed and sustained. When the president consults actively with Congress, he is moving toward securing the foundations of the nation's foreign policy.

There is room for enhancing the quality of the consultative process. Some proposals for improving consultations are neither desirable nor doable, and others are attractive yet unworkable; but some are both positive and feasible. There is no single "answer." However, the national interest, by anyone's definition, requires constant sensitivity and attention to this issue. Former Senator Charles McC. Mathias, Jr., went to the heart of the matter: "[W]e're losing track of a very essential word in the whole federal system, which is coordinate: the separate, equal, *coordinate* branches of government. . . . There's a lack of that spirit of coordination that is really the heart of the whole constitutional scheme."[96]

Notes

1. Louis Fisher, *The Politics of Shared Power: Congress and the Executive*, 2d ed. (Washington, D.C.: Congressional Quarterly Press, 1987), p. ix.
2. In 1985 my research assistant, Chris Brantley (now an attorney in Washington, D.C.), completed a lengthy draft on selected aspects of executive-legislative consultation in defense and foreign policy. I prepared a second, condensed draft that we presented jointly as a paper at the 1986 International Studies Association Convention. The paper was then reviewed by several scholars and government officials, twice revised, and published in James P. Piffner, ed., *The Presidency in Transition* (New York: Center for the Study of the Presidency, 1988). With some revisions, additions, and clarifications, this chapter is substantially the same as the above piece and is reprinted here in altered form by permission of the Center for the Study of the Presidency.
3. Cf., Morris S. Ogul, *Congress Oversees the Bureaucracy* (Pittsburgh, Pa.: University of Pittsburgh Press, 1976), pp. 5–9.
4. Another assumption affects attitudes toward consultation: the erroneous belief that Congress is a *bureaucracy* that manages operations and formulates policies. Those of this view invariably find Congress inept. Consultation with such an allegedly irresponsible actor is thought to be, at best, hazardous. For a crisp detailing of distinctions between Congress and a classic bureaucracy, see Stanley J. Heginbotham, "Congress and Defense Policy

Making: Toward Realistic Expectations in a System of Countervailing Parochialisms," in Robert L. Pfaltzgraff, Jr. and Uri Ra'anan, eds., *National Security Policy: The Decision-making Process* (Hamden, Ct.: Archon Books, 1984), pp. 251–55.

5. Thomas M. Franck and Edward Weisband, *Foreign Policy by Congress* (New York: Oxford University Press, 1979), pp. 6–8; Bayless Manning, "The Congress, the Executive and Intermestic Affairs: Three Proposals," *Foreign Affairs* 55 (January 1977): 306–324. But see John Rourke, *Congress and the President in U.S. Foreign Policymaking* (Boulder, Colo.: Westview Press, 1983), p. 290.

6. Henry Kissinger, address to the American Society of Newspaper Editors, 17 April 1975, reprinted in *Department of State Bulletin*, 5 May 1975. See also, Ronald Reagan, interview with Paul Duke in *Public Papers of the Presidents of the United States—1982* (Washington, D.C.: Government Printing Office, 1983), p. 949.

7. U.S. Congress, House of Representatives, Committee on International Relations, Special Subcommittee on Investigations, *Report: Congress and Foreign Policy*, Committee Print, 94th Cong., 2d sess., 1977, p. 2; U.S. Congress, House of Representatives, Committee on Foreign Affairs (hereafter cited as HFAC), *Strengthening Executive-Legislative Consultation on Foreign Policy* (hereafter cited as *Strengthening Executive-Legislative Consultation*), Congress and Foreign Policy Series No. 8 (Washington, D.C.: Government Printing Office, 1983), p. 14. The Congress and Foreign Policy Series was prepared for the committee by the Congressional Research Service (CRS).

8. Paul B. Stares, *The Militarization of Space: U.S. Policy, 1945–84* (Ithaca, N.Y.: Cornell University Press, 1985), p. 225; HFAC, *Executive-Legislative Consultation on United States Arms Sales*, Congress and Foreign Policy Series No. 7 (Washington, D.C.: Government Printing Office, 1982), p. 3; Richard Haas, *Congressional Power: Implications for American Security Policy*, Adelphi Paper 153 (London: International Institute for Strategic Studies, 1979), pp. 25–26; HFAC, *Executive-Legislative Consultations on China Policy, 1978–79*, Congress and Foreign Policy Series No. 1 (Washington, D.C.: Government Printing Office, 1980),; Dusko Doder, "Nunn: No Basis for Shift on ABM Treaty," *Washington Post*, 14 March 1987, p. A1; David Ottaway and David Hoffman, "Reagan Plan Lacks Bipartisan Support," *Washington Post*, 5 July 1987, p. A1.

9. Reagan, *Public Papers of the Presidents* (1982), p. 949.

10. HFAC, *Strengthening Executive-Legislative Consultations*, p. 14; Robert E. Hunter and Wayne L. Berman, eds., *Making the Government Work: Legislative-Executive Reform* (Washington, D.C.: Center for Strategic and International Studies, Georgetown University, 1985), p. 7.

11. See U.S. Congress, Senate, Committee on Foreign Relations, *Congress, Information and Foreign Affairs*, 95th Cong., 2d sess. (Washington, D.C.: Government Printing Office 1978), p. 97; HFAC, *Strengthening Executive-Legislative Consultation*, p. 17; John F. Manley, "Presidential Power and White House Lobbying," *Political Science Quarterly* 93 (Summer 1978): 255–75.

12. HFAC, *Strengthening Executive-Legislative Consultation*, pp. 17–18; HFAC, *Executive-Legislative Consultation on United States Arms Sales*, pp. 3, 36–39.

13. Richard F. Grimmett, "Arms Sales to Saudi Arabia: AWACs and the F-15 Enhancements," in HFAC, *Congress and Foreign Policy—1981*, Committee Print, 97th Cong., 2d sess., 1982, pp. 24–48; HFAC, *Executive-Legislative Consultation on United States Arms Sales*, pp. 33–35.
14. See John Hart, "Congressional Reactions to White House Lobbying," *Presidential Studies Quarterly* 11 (Winter 1981): 86–88; Fisher, *The Politics of Shared Powers*, p. 61.
15. HFAC, *Strengthening Executive-Legislative Consultation*, pp. 16–17.
16. House Committee on International Relations, *Report: Congress and Foreign Policy*, p. 25; HFAC, *Strengthening Executive-Legislative Consultation*, pp. 60–63; Hart, "Congressional Reactions to White House Lobbying," pp. 83–86; HFAC, *Executive-Legislative Consultation on Foreign Policy: Strengthening the Legislative Side* (hereafter cited as *Strengthening the Legislative Side*), Congress and Foreign Policy Series No. 5 (Washington, D.C.: Government Printing Office, 1982), pp. 37–73.
17. HFAC, *Strengthening Executive-Legislative Consultation*, pp. 1, 18–19.
18. HFAC, *Strengthening the Legislative Side*, pp. 16–25.
19. Ibid., pp. 17–22; House Committee on International Relations, *Report: Congress and Foreign Policy*, p. 7.
20. HFAC, *Executive-Legislative Consultation on Foreign Policy: Strengthening Executive Branch Procedures* (hereafter cited as *Strengthening Executive Branch Procedures*), Congress and Foreign Policy Series No. 2 (Washington, D.C: Government Printing Office, 1981), pp. 24–25, 52–53; HFAC, Subcommittees on International Security, Arms Control and Scientific Affairs and on Western Hemispheric Affairs, *Hearings: U.S. Military Actions in Grenada: Implications for U.S. Policy in the Eastern Caribbean*, 98th Cong., 1st sess., 1983, pp. 4, 32 (concerning the Congressional Black Caucus); HFAC, *Strengthening the Legislative Side*, pp. 23–26.
21. HFAC, *Strengthening Executive Branch Procedures*, pp. 2, 46–51; HFAC, *Strengthening Executive-Legislative Consultation*, pp. 18–19; House Committee on International Relations, *Report: Congress and Foreign Policy*, p, 24.
22. Robert Lockwood, "Conceptualizing the National Security Policy Process: A Framework for the Analysis of Executive-Legislative Relations," in Duncan L. Clarke, ed., *Public Policy and Political Institutions: United States Defense and Foreign Policy—Policy Coordination and Integration* (Greenwich, Ct.: JAI Press, 1985), pp. 46–47.
23. Hunter and Berman, *Making the Government Work*, p. 20; HFAC, *Strengthening Executive Branch Procedures*, pp. 49–50; HFAC, *Strengthening Executive-Legislative Consultation*, pp. 19–20; HFAC, *Executive-Legislative Consultation on United States Arms Sales*, p. 37.
24. HFAC, *Strengthening Executive-Legislative Consultation*, pp. 3–5. See also, Joseph T. Kendrick, "The Consultation Process: The Legislative-Executive Relationship in the Formulation of Foreign Policy" (Ph.D. dissertation, George Washington University, 1979), chs. 7–8.
25. U.S. Congress, House of Representatives, Committee on International Relations, Special Subcommittee on Investigations, *Hearings: Congress and Foreign Policy*, 94th Cong., 2d sess., 1976, pp. 139, 142.
26. Patsy T. Mink, "Institutional Perspective: Misunderstandings, Myths, and

Misperceptions: How Congress and the State Department See Each Other," in Thomas M. Franck, ed., *The Tethered Presidency: Congressional Restraints on Executive Power* (New York: New York University Press, 1981), p. 65.

27. Haas, *Congressional Power*, p. 30; HFAC, *Strengthening Executive-Legislative Consultation*, p. 40; House Committee on International Relations, *Hearings: Congress and Foreign Policy*, pp. 138–41, 180–82.

28. Mink, "Institutional Perspective," p. 68.

29. Ibid., pp. 73–74; William I. Bacchus, *Staffing for Foreign Affairs* (Princeton, N.J.: Princeton University Press, 1983), p. 30.

30. I. M. Destler, *Presidents, Bureaucrats and Foreign Policy* (Princeton, N.J.: Princeton University Press, 1972), pp. 70–71, 162–64; Leslie H. Gelb, "Why Not the State Department?" in Charles W. Kegley, Jr. and Eugene R. Wittkopf, eds., *Perspectives on American Foreign Policy* (New York: St. Martin's Press, 1983), p. 284; Bacchus, *Staffing for Foreign Affairs*, pp. 57, 100, 103.

31. U.S. Congress, *Report of the Congressional Committees Investigating the Iran-Contra Affair* (hereafter cited as *Report: Iran-Contra Affair*), H. Rept. 100–433, 100th Cong., 1st sess., 1987, p. 387.

32. "Closing Statement by Rep. Hamilton," *Washington Post*, 22 July 1987, p. A8.

33. *Report: Iran-Contra Affair*, p. 392.

34. Quoted in Haynes Johnson, "Admiral's Goal: 'No Interference'," *Washington Post*, 18 July 1987, p. A1.

35. House Committee on International Relations, *Report: Congress and Foreign Policy*, pp. 18–19; Les Aspin, "Why Doesn't Congress Do Something?" *Foreign Policy* 15 (Summer 1974): 73; HFAC, *Strengthening the Legislative Side*, pp. 8–10; I.M. Destler, "Executive-Congressional Conflict in Foreign Policy: Explaining It, Coping with It," in Laurence C. Dodd and Bruce I. Oppenheimer, eds., *Congress Reconsidered* (Washington, D.C.: Congressional Quarterly Press, 1981), pp. 296–316.

36. HFAC, *Strengthening the Legislative Side*, p. 10; HFAC, *Strengthening Executive-Legislative Consultation*, pp. 40–42; House Committee on International Relations, *Hearings: Congress and Foreign Policy*, p. 3; Franck and Weisband, *Foreign Policy by Congress*, pp. 132–34.

37. David R. Mayhew, *Congress: The Electoral Connection* (New Haven, Ct.: Yale University Press, 1974), pp. 49–65.

38. Lockwood, "Conceptualizing the National Security Policy Process," pp. 408, 478; Richard Stubbing, *The Defense Game* (New York: Harper & Row, 1986), pp. 88–105. Other factors contribute to congressional micromanagement of defense programs, including an annual budget review process and the existence of standing subcommittees with specific substantive jurisdiction. Statutory restrictions on defense programs increased 233 percent between 1970 and 1985. During this period, the length of the Defense Authorization Act increased from 9 to 169 pages (U.S. Congress, Senate, Committee on Armed Services (hereafter cited as SASC), *Defense Organization: The Need for Change*, Staff Report, S. Prt. 99–86, 99th Cong., 1st sess., 1985, pp. 591–93).

39. Stanley J. Heginbotham, "Dateline Washington: The Rules of the Game," *Foreign Policy* 53 (Winter 1983–84): 158–60.

40. Destler, "Executive-Congressional Conflict in Foreign Policy," pp. 302–303;

testimony of Zbigniew Brzezinski, U.S. Congress, Senate, Committee on Governmental Affairs, *Hearings: Relationship Between Congress and the Executive in the Formulation and Implementation of Foreign Policy* (hereafter cited as *Relationship Between Congress and the Executive*), 98th Cong., 2d sess., 1984, Part I, p. 68. Louis Fisher remarks, "No better formula for legislative impotence has ever been devised than to allocate 'broad policy questions' to Congress and assign 'administrative details' to the executive"; and " '[f]lexibility' is often a code word used by executive officials who want to be left alone" (Louis Fisher, *The Politics of Shared Power: Congress and the Executive* [Washington, D.C.: Congressional Quarterly Press, 1981], pp. 74, 104).

41. HFAC, *Strengthening Executive-Legislative Consultation*, pp. 4, 43–44.
42. Statement of Amos Jordon, Senate Committee on Governmental Affairs, *Relationship Between Congress and the Executive*, p. 109; Franck and Weisband, *Foreign Policy by Congress*, pp. 100–103; Zbigniew Brzezinski, *Power and Principle: Memoirs of the National Security Adviser, 1977–1981* (New York: Farrar, Straus & Giroux, 1983), p. 126.
43. Manley, "Presidential Power and White House Lobbying," p. 270; William F. Mullen, "Perceptions of Carter's Legislative Successes and Failures: Views from the Hill and the Liaison Staff," *Presidential Studies Quarterly* 12 (Fall 1982): 532.
44. Edward Feigenbaum, "Staffing, Organization and Decisionmaking in the Ford and Carter White Houses," *Presidential Studies Quarterly* 10 (Summer 1980): 376; R. Gordon Hoxie, "Staffing the Ford and Carter Presidencies," *Presidential Studies Quarterly* 10 (Summer 1980): 378–401; HFAC, *Strengthening Executive-Legislative Consultation*, pp. 44–55; U.S. Congress, HFAC, *Congressional-Executive Relations and the Turkish Arms Embargo*, Congress and Foreign Policy Series No. 3 (Washington, D.C.: Government Printing Office, 1981), pp. 19, 29.
45. Manley, "Presidential Power and White House Lobbying," p. 274; I.M. Destler, *Making Foreign Economic Policy* (Washington, D.C.: The Brookings Institution, 1980); Raymond Ahern, "Congress and Foreign Trade Policy," in U.S. Congress, HFAC, *Congress and Foreign Affairs—1979*, Committee Print, 96th Cong., 2d sess., 1980, p. 135.
46. U.S. Congress, HFAC, *The War Powers Resolution: A Special Study*, Committee Print, 97th Cong., 1st sess., 1982; Ellen C. Collier, *The War Powers Resolution: A Decade of Experience*, Report No. 84–44F (Washington, D.C.: CRS, 6 February 1984); U.S. Congress, HFAC, *Executive-Legislative Consultation on Foreign Policy: Strengthening Foreign Policy Information Sources for Congress* (hereafter cited as *Strengthening Foreign Policy Information Sources*), Congress and Foreign Policy Series No. 4 (Washington, D.C.: Government Printing Office, 1982), p. 1; Senate Committee on Governmental Affairs, *Relationship Between Congress and the Executive*, p. 8.
47. Norman J. Ornstein, Thomas E. Mann, Michael J. Malkin, Allen Schick, and John F. Bibby, *Vital Statistics on Congress, 1984–1985* (Washington, D.C.: American Enterprise Institute, 1984), pp. 111, 143–46. There is also evidence that the corresponding enlargement of congressional staffs may have actually

increased demands on legislators' time (see Destler, "Executive-Congressional Conflict in Foreign Policy," pp. 304–305; Haas, *Congressional Power*, p. 10).

48. See Warren Christopher, "Ceasefire Between the Branches: A Compact in Foreign Affairs," *Foreign Affairs* 60 (Summer 1983): 1000.

49. See HFAC, *Executive-Legislative Consultation on China Policy, 1978–79*, p. 38; House Committee on International Relations *Report: Congress and Foreign Policy*, p. 12.

50. HFAC, *Strengthening Executive-Legislative Consultation*, p. 46; HFAC, *Strengthening Executive Branch Procedures*, pp. 17–25; Franck and Weisband, *Foreign Policy by Congress*, pp. 284–85; Hunter and Berman, *Making the Government Work*, p. 16. See also, HFAC, *Executive-Legislative Consultation on China Policy, 1978–79*, p. 25.

51. HFAC, *Strengthening Executive-Legislative Consultation*, p. 46; Franck and Weisband, *Foreign Policy by Congress*, pp. 210–26; Thomas E. Cavanagh, "The Dispersion of Authority in the House of Representatives," *Political Science Quarterly* 97 (Winter 1982–83): 623–37; Leroy N. Rieselbach, *Congressional Reform* (Washington, D.C.: Congressional Quarterly Press, 1986).

52. Cavanagh, "The Dispersion of Authority," p. 630; House Committee on International Relations, *Report: Congress and Foreign Policy*. p. 20; HFAC, *Strengthening the Legislative Side*, pp. 18–21. However, Louis Fisher notes that "earlier presidents complained that the *centralization* of power in Congress made it impossible to get bills past uncooperative committee chairmen. Legislative decentralization can be an opportunity, not an obstacle, because it opens up lines of communication" (Fisher, *The Politics of Shared Power* [1987], p. 61).

53. Molly Moore, "Defense Oversight: War of the Watchdogs," *Washington Post*, 12 October 1987, p. A17.

54. SASC, *Defense Organization*, pp. 578, 582.

55. Haas, *Congressional Power*, p. 7; Cavanagh, "The Dispersion of Authority," pp. 630–31.

56. J. William Fulbright, "The Legislator as Educator," *Foreign Affairs* 57 (Spring 1979): 727; HFAC, *Strengthening Executive-Legislative Consultation*, pp. 5, 47–48; HFAC, *Strengthening Foreign Policy Information Sources*, pp. 2, 38–58; Charles McC. Mathias, Jr., "Ethnic Groups and Foreign Policy," *Foreign Affairs* 59 (Summer 1981): 975–96. Views differ about the weight to be accorded interest groups within the constellation of factors that generally affect major issues. Interest group influence may be overestimated or underestimated. Executive officials acknowledged retrospectively their own overestimation of the "China Lobby" when they expressed regret for their failure to give Congress prior notice of President Carter's normalization of relations with China (HFAC, *Executive-Legislative Consultations on China Policy, 1978–79*, p. 24). Those who are members of, or who identify normatively with, *successful ethnic* lobbies often (not always) *publicly* downplay their impact. Theodore Couloumbis and Sallie Hicks, for instance, largely discount the influence of Greek-American constituencies on congressional measures related to Turkey's invasion of Cyprus and the subsequent U.S. arms embargo (Sallie M. Hicks and

Theodore A. Couloumbis, "The 'Greek Lobby': Illusion or Reality?" in Abdul Aziz Said, ed., *Ethnicity and U.S. Foreign Policy* [New York: Praeger, 1977], pp. 83–115; Professor Couloumbis worked closely with the "Greek Lobby"; Sallie Hicks was his graduate student). Likewise, Edward Glick and Steven Spiegel, who find the unique U.S.-Israel relationship highly advantageous to both nations, deemphasize the role of the American Israel Public Affairs Committee (AIPAC) in U.S. policy toward Israel. Conversely, Paul Findley and Edward Tivnan, who find many aspects of this relationship inimical to U.S. interests, stress AIPAC's influence (Edward Bernard Glick, *The Triangular Connection: America, Israel and American Jews* [Winchester, Mass.: Allen & Unwin, 1982], pp. 95–106; Steven Spiegel, *The Other Arab-Israel Conflict: Making America's Middle East Policy, from Truman to Reagan* [Chicago: University of Chicago Press, 1985], pp. 388–89; Edward Tivnan, *The Lobby: Jewish Political Power and American Foreign Policy* [New York: Simon & Schuster, 1987]; Paul Findley, *They Dare to Speak Out: People and Institutions Confront Israel's Lobby* [Westport, Ct.: Lawrence Hill, 1985]).

57. HFAC, *Strengthening Foreign Policy Information Sources*, p. 17. For a historical accounting of Congress's informational dependency on the executive and its implications, see U.S. Congress, Senate, Committee on Foreign Relations, *Congress, Information and Foreign Affairs*, 95th Cong., 2d sess., 1978. A senior Pentagon congressional liaison official said, "It is incredible the way we can mold what we wish to say [to Congress] to serve our own purposes" (confidential interview with the author, 14 April 1986).

58. House Committee on International Relations, *Report: Congress and Foreign Policy*, pp. 8–10; HFAC, *Strengthening Executive-Legislative Consultation*, pp. 62–63, 144; Senate Committee on Governmental Affairs, *Relationship Between Congress and the Executive*, pp. 13, 101.

59. U.S. Congress, House of Representatives, Committee on Administration, *Reports to Be Made to Congress: Communications from the Clerk*, 98th Cong., 2d sess., 1984.

60. Ellen C. Collier, "Foreign Policy Reporting Requirements," *Washington Quarterly* 11 (Winter 1988): 75–84. The utility of the latter "function" is illustrated by a provision of the Trade Act of 1974 stipulating that Congress receive at least ninety days' notice prior to the conclusion of trade agreements negotiated at the Tokyo Round of the Multilateral Trade Negotiations. Congress, given this opportunity to voice its concerns, then committed itself to vote implementing legislation, without amendment, within ninety days of submission. This "fast track" procedure contributed significantly to the easy passage of the Trade Act of 1979 (Trade Act of 1974, 88 *Statutes at Large*, 19 U.S.C. Secs. 2111, 2112, 2191 (1978); Chris Brantley, "The Trade Act of 1974: A Case Study of Executive-Legislative Relations" (The American University, Washington, D.C., 1985) (mimeo); Robert C. Cassidy, Jr., "Negotiating About Negotiation: The Geneva Multilateral Trade Talks," in Franck, *The Tethered Presidency*, pp. 278–80).

61. HFAC, *Strengthening the Legislative Side*, pp. 48–50; Senate Committee on Governmental Affairs, *Relationship Between Congress and the Executive*, p. 79; House Committee on International Relations, *Report: Congress and Foreign Policy*, p. 6; Goldwater-Nichols Department of Defense Reorganization Act

of 1986, 100 *Statutes at Large* Sec. 1066; *Congressional Record—House*, 12 September 1986, p. H6858.

62. House Committee on International Relations, *Report: Congress and Foreign Policy*, p. 14.

63. HFAC, *Strengthening the Legislative Side*, p. 55.

64. *Report: Iran-Contra Affair*, p. 378; Duncan L. Clarke and Edward L. Neveleff, "Secrecy, Foreign Intelligence, and Civil Liberties: Has the Pendulum Swung Too Far?" *Political Science Quarterly* 99 (Fall 1984): 495; House Committee on International Relations, *Hearings: Congress and Foreign Policy*, p. 303. One troublesome issue is internal to Congress—the frequent difficulty experienced by legislators who are not on one of the two intelligence committees in gaining access to classified information held by these committees (see U.S. Congress, House of Representatives, Permanent Select Committee on Intelligence, *Adverse Report: Resolution of Inquiry with Respect to United States Military Involvement in Hostilities in Central America*, H. Rept. 98–742, 98th Cong., 2d sess., 1984; U.S. Congress, House of Representatives, *Rules of Procedure for the Permanent Select Committee on Intelligence* [Washington, D.C.: Government Printing Office, 1985]; U.S. Congress, Senate, *Rules of Procedure for the Select Committee on Intelligence* [Washington, D.C.: Government Printing Office, 1981]).

65. *Report: Iran-Contra Affair*, pp. 375, 378–82, 423–27; *Report of the President's Special Review Board* (hereafter cited as Tower Commission Report) (Washington, D.C.: Government Printing Office, 26 February 1987), p. IV-7; Bob Woodward, *Veil: The Secret Wars of the CIA, 1981–1987* (New York: Simon & Schuster, 1987).

66. Clarke and Neveleff, "Secrecy, Foreign Intelligence, and Civil Liberties," pp. 506–508; Commission on the Organization of Government for the Conduct of Foreign Policy (Murphy Commission), *Report* (Washington, D.C.: Government Printing Office, 1975), pp. 201–202.

67. See Chapter 1, note 2.

68. Zbigniew Brzezinski has offered a variant of the Zorinsky proposal; see Brzezinski, *Power and Principle*, pp. 536–37; Zbigniew Brzezinski, "NSC's Midlife Crisis," *Foreign Policy* 69 (Winter 1987–88): 94–95. See also, U.S. Congress, Senate, Committee on Foreign Relations, *Hearings: The National Security Adviser: Role and Accountability*, 96th Cong., 2d sess., 1980, especially pp. 128–29; House Committee on International Relations, *Hearings: Congress and Foreign Policy*, pp. 49, 64, 53, 83, 110, 113.

69. Tower Commission Report, p. V-5; *Report: Iran-Contra Affair*, p. 425.

70. Lou Cannon and David Ottaway, "Carlucci, Aide in Four Administrations," *Washington Post*, 3 November 1987, p. A16.

71. House Committee on International Relations, *Report: Congress and Foreign Policy*, p. 10; Lee Hamilton and Michael Van Dusen, "Making the Separation of Powers Work," *Foreign Affairs* 57 (Fall 1978): 37–38; HFAC, *Strengthening Foreign Policy Information Sources*, pp. 2, 68, 70.

72. HFAC, *Strengthening Executive-Legislative Consultation*, p. 64; House Committee on International Relations, *Report: Congress and Foreign Policy*, pp. 13–14.

73. HFAC, *Strengthening Foreign Policy Information Sources*, pp. 106–107.

74. Ibid., p. 28. But see Destler, "Executive-Congressional Conflict in Foreign Policy," p. 314.
75. Statement of Alton Frye, House Committee on International Relations, *Hearings: Congress and Foreign Policy*, pp. 17–20, 26–27.
76. Hunter and Berman, *Making the Government Work*, pp. 27–28; SASC, *Defense Organization*, pp. 588–89, 610. A larger issue that will not soon be solved is the explosive increase in the number of proposed *floor* amendments to authorization bills in the House and Senate. They receive little or no legislative scrutiny (since most skirt the committee process) and are often poorly coordinated with the executive branch (James M. Lindsay, "Congress and the Defense Budget," *Washington Quarterly* 11 [Winter 1988]: 60).
77. U.S. Congress, Senate, Committee on Foreign Relations, *The Senate's Role in Foreign Affairs Appointments*, 97th Cong., 2d sess., 1982, pp. 1–3.
78. Hunter and Berman, *Making the Government Work*, p. 28.
79. HFAC, *Strengthening Executive Branch Procedures*, pp. 42–43, 73–76.
80. House Committee on International Relations, *Report: Congress and Foreign Policy*, pp. 11, 103, 133.
81. I. M. Destler, "State: A Department or 'Something More'?" in Clarke, *Public Policy and Political Institutions*, pp. 98–99; HFAC, *Strengthening Executive Branch Procedures*, pp. 23–24, 60.
82. Stephen Hess, *Organizing the Presidency* (Washington, D.C.: The Brookings Institution, 1976), p. 209. See also, James L. Sundquist, *Constitutional Reform and Effective Government* (Washington, D.C.: The Brookings Institution, 1986), pp. 168–74.
83. HFAC, *Strengthening Executive Branch Procedures*, p. 45. But congressional staff are not afforded a similar opportunity to serve in the executive branch.
84. Ibid., pp. 2, 43–45; Heginbotham, "Dateline Washington," p. 171.
85. Hunter and Berman, *Making the Government Work*, pp. 15–16; HFAC, *Strengthening Executive Branch Procedures*, p. 3.
86. Hunter and Berman, *Making the Government Work*, p. 9; SASC, *Defense Organization*, pp. 603–604.
87. On the benefits as well as the possible disadvantages of a biennial defense budget, see "Report of the Working Group on the Congressional Defense Budget Process," in Barry M. Blechman and William J. Lynn, eds., *Toward a More Effective Defense: Report of the Defense Organization Project* (Cambridge, Mass.: Ballinger, 1985), pp. 109–110; SASC, *Defense Organization*, pp. 594–95, 602–603; Center for Strategic and International Studies, *U.S. Defense Acquisition: A Process in Trouble* (Washington, D.C.: Center for Strategic and International Studies, Georgetown University, 1987), pp. 83–84; President's Blue Ribbon Commission on Defense Management (hereafter cited as Packard Commission), *A Quest for Excellence* (Washington, D.C.: Government Printing Office, June 1986), pp. 25–26. The Packard Commission, which strongly endorsed a biennial defense budget, asserted: "Today, there is no rational system whereby the Executive Branch and the Congress reach coherent and enduring agreement on national military strategy, the forces to carry it out, and the funding that should be provided" (p. xvii).
88. "Report of the Working Group on the Congressional Defense Budget Project," p. 110.

89. Ibid., pp. 110–11; Packard Commission, *A Quest for Excellence*, pp. 26–27; SASC, *Defense Organization*, pp. 599, 607–608; Lindsay, "Congress and the Defense Budget," p. 70. In 1987, the armed services committees agreed to five-year milestone authorizations for four major weapons programs. But the appropriations committees refused to go along, insisting instead on annual appropriations for these and other programs.

90. For summaries of the many problems with these and similar proposals, see Hamilton and Van Dusen, "Making the Separation of Powers Work," p. 36; Destler, "Executive-Legislative Conflict in Foreign Policy," p. 312; HFAC, *Strengthening the Legislative Side*, pp. 28–31; HFAC, *Strengthening Executive-Legislative Consultation*, p. 69.

91. Ottaway and Hoffman, "Reagan Plan Lacks Bipartisan Support," p. Al.

92. HFAC, *Strengthening the Legislative Side*, pp. 31–32; Hunter and Berman, *Making the Government Work*, pp. 19–20.

93. Richard E. Cohen, *Congressional Leadership: Seeking a New Role* (Beverly Hills, Calif.: Sage, 1980), pp. 58, 76, 78; Destler, "Executive-Congressional Conflict in Foreign Policy," p. 312.

94. House Committee on International Relations, *Report: Congress and Foreign Policy*, p. 4; HFAC, *Strengthening the Legislative Side*, pp. 19–20.

95. HFAC, *Strengthening Executive-Legislative Consultation*, pp. 140–41; HFAC, *Strengthening the Legislative Side*, pp. 3, 34.

96. Charles McC. Mathias, Jr., "Reflections on a System Spinning out of Control," *Washington Post*, 11 December, 1986, p. A21.

INDEX

About the Author

Duncan L. Clarke is professor of international relations and co-ordinator of the U.S. foreign policy field at the School of International Service, American University. He was a Ford Foundation arms control fellow and professor of foreign affairs at the National War College (1979–1981). Clarke's books include *Politics of Arms Control: The Role and Effectiveness of the U.S. Arms Control and Disarmament Agency, Decisionmaking for Arms Limitation*, and *Public Policy and Political Institutions: United States Defense and Foreign Policy—Policy Coordination and Integration*. His articles have appeared in *Foreign Policy, Political Science Quarterly, Middle East Journal, Presidential Studies Quarterly*, and elsewhere.